WAGING WAR WITHOUT WARRIORS?

IISS Studies in International Security
Mats Berdal, Series Editor

WAGING WAR WITHOUT WARRIORS?

The Changing Culture of Military Conflict

CHRISTOPHER COKER

LYNNE
RIENNER
PUBLISHERS

BOULDER
LONDON

Published in the United States of America in 2002 by
Lynne Rienner Publishers, Inc.
1800 30th Street, Boulder, Colorado 80301
www.rienner.com

and in the United Kingdom by
Lynne Rienner Publishers, Inc.
3 Henrietta Street, Covent Garden, London WC2E 8LU

Library of Congress Cataloging-in-Publication Data
Coker, Christopher.
 Waging war without warriors? : the changing culture of military conflict / Christopher Coker.
  p. cm.
 Includes bibliographical references and index.
 ISBN 1-58826-105-0 (alk. paper) — ISBN 1-58826-130-1 (pbk. : alk. paper)
 1. War. 2. Military art and science—History—21st century. 3. World politics—21st
century. I. Title.

U21.2.C6424 2002
355.02—dc21
                                                              2002069820

British Cataloguing in Publication Data
A Cataloguing in Publication record for this book
is available from the British Library.

Printed and bound in the United States of America

The paper used in this publication meets the requirements
of the American National Standard for Permanence of
Paper for Printed Library Materials Z39.48-1984.

 5 4 3 2 1

In memory of Philip Windsor

Contents

1

The Warrior's Dishonor

The attack on the World Trade Center on September 11, 2001, has been treated by many analysts as "Year Zero," the moment when everything changed. We should know enough from history to recognize that little changes overnight. In plying their trade, historians and political scientists try to identify historic turning points and date them precisely, but history is more modest. Its essential dates remain secret for some time.

Whether the attack was a turning point, only future historians can judge. In this book, I am interested in another question: the extent to which the West no longer understands war as it once did. President George W. Bush was quick to call the war on terrorism "the first war of the twenty-first century," but if it was a war on the West's part, it was a war without warriors. Once the air campaign against the Taliban began, it was also a war against warriors, whose chief distinguishing feature was the tenacity of their faith.

LIKE FALLING CHERRY BLOSSOMS: THE SAMURAI SUICIDE BOMBERS

One of the most shocking elements of the World Trade Center attack was how a small group of fundamentalists, armed with their faith in Islam, were prepared not only to hazard their lives but also to seek out their own death. It was ironic that several politicians should have called the attack "the Pearl Harbor of the twenty-first century," for the Americans first came across suicide bombers in the war with Japan. Then the bombers were crashing not into buildings in New York but the decks of U.S. warships in the great and bloody campaigns of Iwo Jima and Okinawa. But the Americans had first come across the phenomenon in the summer of 1944. It was then that they had stumbled upon the *tokkotai*, the "special forces" that flew suicide missions against U.S. shipping. Better known as kamikaze pilots, the Japanese drew inspiration from the kamikaze (divine wind), the typhoon that had destroyed the Mongol invasion fleet in the thirteenth century. Seven centuries later, faced with another invasion and given the desperate situation in which the high command found both itself and the country, it was inevitable that the Japanese would engage in desperate measures.

The pilots who volunteered for kamikaze missions did so from a sense of duty. Like the Muslim pilots on September 11, they had a lot of time to think about their decision, for almost no one was sent off immediately after volunteering. In some cases, the pilots waited weeks or even months before their assignment came, a fact that makes their commitment all the more remarkable. Before their mission, they would don a white head scarf (*hachimaki*) with the rising sun emblazoned on the center. Sometimes, they also wore a ceremonial waist sash (*senninbari*), called a "1,000-stitch belt" because 1,000 women in Japan had sewn one stitch each in order to show the widespread national support for their actions. Often they composed death poems, traditional for samurai warriors prior to suicide. Many of those poems displayed a specifically Japanese characteristic: the poetic contemplation of nature at the moment of death. Thus in 1945, a twenty-two-year-old pilot wrote:

> If only we might fall
> Like cherry blossoms in the Spring—
> So pure and radiant

So close are the Japanese to nature that they have a word for the season of cherry blossom viewing—*hanami*. Though during World War II, only the U.S. sailors on their ships viewed the fall, and what they saw was, for them, a completely senseless loss of life that did some local damage but not enough to materially change the outcome of the war.

With their rigidly instrumental attitude toward war, the Americans thought the Japanese were mad. In June 1944, the Americans commissioned a noted anthropologist, Ruth Benedict, to explain the kamikaze phenomenon. The central conclusion she reached in her study, *The Chrysanthemum and the Sword,* was that in war, as in peace, the Japanese had "acted in character." Unlike the West, Japan had a shame rather than a guilt culture, with all its humanistic implications for freedom and moral autonomy.[1] For guilt is experienced in the face of abstractions such as the moral law, which is part, or becomes part, of the subjects themselves. The moral law is internalized. People feel guilty about their behavior toward others. Their attention turns to the victim. Shame, by contrast, is more narcissistic. It involves a strong sense of being at a disadvantage. This sense of powerlessness is doubled when it involves the outside world.

Benedict's analysis has not weathered well. Few anthropologists today would endorse her conclusions. But what of the Japanese, the object of her study? What did they make of the U.S. way of warfare? Largely they too saw their U.S. adversaries in an unflattering light. True, with their technological superiority—their B29 bombers, flamethrowers, and nuclear bombs—they were instrumentally formidable. But they seemed to lack the warrior's spirit. They did not fight to the death, even though the motto of the U.S. Marines was "Death before dishonor." In the early months of the war, they often seemed demoralized.

Even as the war came to an end, the Japanese were horrified rather than impressed with the ruthlessness the Americans showed because it was largely manifest in "disengaged" conflict: airpower. In March 1945, the U.S. Air Force "torched" Tokyo in a raid that claimed 120,000 lives. In *The World as Representation and Will* (1819), Arthur Schopenhauer speaks of music as "pure will." The Japanese were fascinated and horrified at the same time that the United States, a country that had wholly lost (or appeared to have lost) the sense of war as representation, had wholly preserved the idea of war as "will."

Whether we are living through a major turning-point in our lives, the September 11 attack reintroduced Americans to a different way of warfare. Once again, they found themselves living in a different time zone from their enemies, as they had in 1945. Both have a totally different understanding of war and the role of the warrior. Both worlds are remote, psychologically and emotionally. The trouble is that they intersect from time to time through war or acts of terrorism.

Expressive War

Contemporary history, it has been said, begins when those factors that are important in our own lives first began to take shape in our imagination. With the benefit of hindsight, we can glimpse an intimation of the events of September 11 in a remarkable novel by Joseph Conrad that was published in 1906. Central to the story of *The Secret Agent* is a plot to blow up the Greenwich Observatory. Conrad was inspired to write the novel by a real event, an incident in Greenwich Park in 1894 in which a bomb exploded, killing the anarchist sympathizer who was carrying it.

The novel was dedicated to H. G. Wells, "the historian of the future," and the dedication was nothing if not ironic. Although Conrad was a genuine admirer of Wells and his work, he set out to challenge the heady optimism Wells had shown in his "London" novels, *Love and Mr. Lewisham* (1900) and *Kipps* (1905). Conrad's book is set in London, but it is a metropolis at war with itself. For London, the center of the world in the early twentieth century, harbors an anarchist cell whose members are intent on the destruction of the bourgeois way of life. This was territory Conrad had explored before, notably in *Heart of Darkness* (1902), especially in the person of Mr. Kurtz, who "lies at the bottom of a precipice in which the sun never shines." Conrad did not analyze the nihilism of the nineteenth century in the manner of Friedrich Nietzsche, but he knew the feel of it more consciously and keenly than his British contemporaries.

And in *The Secret Agent,* he captured its spirit in the person of Mr. Vladimir, the shadowy puppet master who uses the anarchists for his own cynical ends. He is a true nihilist in spirit. In conversation with the double agent Verloc, Vladimir waxes lyrical. What is needed, he muses, is a set of outrages that must be sufficiently startling to astonish the bourgeoisie. What act of terror would disconcert them the most? Not an attempt on a crowned head or a president—that would be mere sensationalism; not a bomb in a church, which might be construed wrongly as a crime against organized religion; and not blowing up a restaurant and the people eating in it, for that might be dismissed as a social crime, the act of a hungry man. Not an attack on the National Gallery, for no one in England would miss it. But what of an attack on reason? Pity it was impossible to blow up pure mathematics. The next best thing was zero longitude, a very unreal concept, but one that was essential to the commerce and communications of a world centered on London. Such an outrage, Vladimir concludes, would be an act of "gratuitous blasphemy" against the modern age.[2]

Blasphemy is the vernacular of the weak. It is expressive, not instrumental, for it is not intended to change the world. To be blasphemous in a secular or irreligious age, an act of terror must be aimed at the civic religion of the hour. In this case, the act was designed to strike at the heart of the heady confidence of Edwardian England in progress. As a "gratuitous" or "meaningless" act, it challenged the country's invincible faith in the future.

One reason for the consternation about anarchism at the time was its expressive nature. Unlike acts of war, acts of terror did not seem to be aimed at any rational end or involve any concrete purpose: they appeared to be random. And the anarchists employed a new weapon not used by governments: not gunpowder but dynamite. It was a relatively new invention, a compound of nitroglycerine but much more powerful than its forerunner. Dynamite was from this time to become every anarchist's preferred weapon. The fear of being blown up haunted popular culture.

When people use expressive violence for such ends, much depends on the perspective of those involved, including perpetrators and victims, witnesses and bystanders. This kind of violence is intended not to make people more frightened or fearful but *anxious*. Sigmund Freud tells us that all three are social constructs and that they vary from culture to culture and even from era to era. In his 1920 study, *Beyond the Pleasure Principle,* he distinguished between the three according to the relationship between the subject and the danger. Thus fright refers to the state we fall into when we are suddenly confronted by a dangerous situation for which we are unprepared. Fear presupposes a definite object of which one is afraid and perhaps has been for some time. Anxiety, however, refers to a state characterized by expecting and preparing for a danger that is pervasive but unknown and largely unknowable. Freud stressed the fact that common usage tended to employ each term interchangeably. It was an error he wanted to correct.[3]

The Secret Agent addresses the *anxiety* that all "senseless" acts inspire in the complacent and sensible. Edwardian society was not frightened or fearful of anarchism. It was anxious about it. Today the terrorist targets our anxiety in the risk societies we have become. For we too find violence meaningless and irrational. Terrorists play on our uncertainties and anxieties; our anxiety about the side effects of our own technological advances, and in the case of September 11, our anxieties about the underside of globalization. "For the foreseeable future," the U.S. defense secretary William Cohen claimed in 1998, "there are few who will have the power to match us militarily . . . but they will be dedicated to exploiting the weakness of our very strength."[4] The more globalized we are, the more vulnerable we apparently become. As we introduce more sophisticated technology, new risks proliferate at an exponential rate. The information technologies of today facilitate international crime and assist terrorism. And it is now a commonplace idea that the risks we face are more catastrophic than those of the past because they are global.

The World Trade Center attack, therefore, threw into relief a dialectical relationship between two worlds, the postmodern and the modern. The gap between them makes it possible for one to use *expressive* violence against the other as never before because of the symbolic impact of violent acts in a globalized world. Symbolism involves the meaning the use of violence has both for the victim (anxiety and humiliation, both of which were involved on September 11) and for the offender (status, prestige, and reputation in his own group, in this case the Islamic world). I do not mean to say, of course, that we are dealing only with "symbolic" violence. Far from it. The anarchists and fundamentalists differ in this respect: one wanted to terrify, and the other wants to kill—and to kill as many people as possible. What I do mean is that the effective use of violence in a globalized age depends increasingly on its symbolic form.[5]

The problem is that we so want to understand violence primarily in utilitarian, rational terms, in terms of means and ends, that the question of what violence "signifies," "says," or "expresses" seems, at best, to be of secondary importance. Yet there was a time when the West saw violence in expressive terms. Take the European duel and the honor code, which was a historically developed cultural construction. What was at stake in these tests of strength was symbolic: identity, pride, and meaning and the group membership implied in them. What was deployed and sacrificed for them was described by the German sociologist Georg Simmel at the time Conrad was writing: "To maintain honour is so much a duty that one derives from it the most terrible sacrifices—not only self-inflicted ones but also sacrifices imposed on others."[6] But now, of course, Europeans have got out of the dueling business, and it is a mark of our civility that we have also turned our back on expressive forms of war. In instrumentalizing war as much as it has, the West has reached a point at which it no longer understands the expressive element. Instead, it tends to dismiss it as "cowardly," "irrational," or "barbaric." To call violence by these names reflects a very Western bias for the technical and tends to divorce cases of violence from their social context. However repugnant acts of terrorism may be, the one thing they are not is "senseless."

The Existential Warrior

But what the warrior *is,* is no less important than what he or she does. Expressive violence is not only aimed at an enemy but also affirms a way of life. We find this in all cultures, though it is especially commended, for example, in *The Bhagavad Gita,* where it is exemplified best by the great archer Arjuna, who is instructed by Krishna to be unconcerned for consequences. A disinterested participation in battle is the path to follow if release is sought from karma. Violence is not only instrumental; it is also the moral essence of the warrior. For true warriors, war-making is not so much what they do but what they *are.*

In that sense, the true warrior is a *moral agent.* This sense of agency was clearly expressed in nineteenth-century Western literature too, though it usually took a secular form. One of the texts in which it is expressed most forcefully is Nietzsche's *Genealogy of Morals,* in which we read: "unconcerned, mocking, violent—thus wisdom wants *us,* she is a woman, and always loves only a warrior." What sort of warrior is unconcerned? One for whom the means is an end and for whom war is fought for its own sake. Whom does the warrior mock? Clearly those still locked in the world of goals and purposes, those who fight for causes rather than for war's own sake. For the true warrior, violence is existential. There is, Nietzsche tells us in the first essay, "no being behind doing . . . the 'doer' is merely a fiction added to the deed."[7]

Indeed, back at the beginning of the twentieth century, the world Conrad understood so well, war was as much a means of realizing one's humanity as it was a means of achieving the objectives of the state. "You say that it is the good cause that hallows every war," Nietzsche writes. "I tell you that it is the good war that hallows every cause." "Of course our cause sanctifies battle," echoes that great twentieth-century warrior Ernst Junger (a man decorated with the Iron Cross in both world wars), "but how much more does battle itself sanctify the cause?"[8]

Yet by the mid–twentieth century, the existential dimension of war was dying in all advanced industrial countries, and for an example we need look no further than Japan, the land of the kamikazes. The author Mishima Yukio (who was often called "the last samurai") achieved notoriety in 1970 by an ill-conceived coup attempt that ended with him taking his own life. From early youth, he had been fascinated by the textbook of Bushido (the samurai honor code), *The Hagakure* (1716), which taught the importance of self-sacrifice. In a commentary on the work written a few years before his death, Mishima made an impassioned plea for a return to the warrior values of the past. His concluding words formed a cri de coeur for his own end, as well as that of the samurai tradition:

> We tend to suffer from the illusion that we are capable of dying for a belief or theory. What *Hagakure* is insisting is that even a merciless death, a futile death that knows neither flower nor fruit has dignity as the death of a human being. If we value so highly the dignity of life how can we not also value the dignity of death?[9]

For the samurai warrior, death had meaning. So too did honor, courage, and loyalty, all of which gave life meaning too. But by 1970 when Mishima staged his revolt, the warrior tradition was dead. His revolt and subsequent suicide (the samurai act of *seppuku*) were quickly forgotten. His call to arms found no resonance with the youth to whom it had been directed.

The existential dimension of war, however, survived in the non-Western world. In the 1950s, there was even an attempt to make war itself existential, one associated largely though not exclusively with Franz Fanon, a psychologist from Martinique who played an active part in the Algerian revolution. Fanon was an intellectual as well as a psychologist, but his writings had enormous appeal. His most famous patron, the French philosopher Jean-Paul Sartre, claimed that "in him the Third World finds itself and speaks to itself through his voice."[10] Yet it was a measure of the extent to which Western ideas still predominated that Fanon was a devotee of Sartre's own philosophy of existentialism, a philosophy once described by Paul Tillich as "a movement of rebellion against the dehumanization of man."[11] Fanon later went on to produce an existential philosophy that praised the national liberation freedom fighter in quasi-Nietzschean terms as a warrior who finds in war an expression of his or her own humanity in the face of the inhumanity of life.

Fanon took as his own starting point the belief that Africans were the victims of a situational neurosis, a socially constructed but very real situation of inferiority that they had internalized. As a psychologist who had looked after patients in Algeria and the West Indies, he traced the social origin of that neurosis to the attitude of white colonial society toward their blackness. Violence was the only way of authentic self-affirmation. That is why one should not be surprised when they employed "inhuman means"; it was the way that "less-than-men" won their humanity in the eyes of their oppressors. The violence they employed was not the resurrection of savage instincts. Through violence, a warrior "comes to know himself in that he himself creates his self." Fanon added that to kill a white man was not only to destroy an oppressor but also the man he oppressed at the same time. "Make no mistake about it," Sartre added, "by this mad fury, by this bitterness and spleen, by their ever present desire to kill us . . . they have become men."[12]

Although some writers now urge us to treat Fanon's writings as ironic, they were deeply felt. He saw violence as cathartic, an existential experience by which individuals liberated themselves from their colonial status and recognized their humanity at the same time. His work scandalized many because it struck a blow against Western humanism. The European had become "human" by denying humanity to others, by treating the colonized as little better than animals, or subhuman. The category "human" was therefore empty of universal meaning because it was a European invention. A less apocalyptic view, which is still widely held, is that when humanists talk of the Rights of Man, they are referring to "universal" (i.e., Western) values that are themselves "inhumane" because they deny both the local culture and the identity that alone made life humane.

Of course, the difference between Fanon's generation and that of Osama bin Laden today is pronounced. Fanon was born in the colonial world; he was shaped by a European sensibility. Whatever his critique of the West, his writings were part of the Western intellectual tradition, and Western ideas, especially Marxism, were their chief point of reference.

Today's Islamic fighters are not party to a Western philosophical discourse. They have no interest in strategies of authentication or existential realization and no interest in Marxist theories of emancipation. But, in one respect, their actions echo Fanon's ideas—the act of terror not only had an expressive meaning for the hijackers but an *existential* meaning as well. Even suicide can be life affirming.

Western societies find this alienating, for we no longer allow citizens to find war life affirming or to affirm their own humanity through violent acts. And we have shown little or no interest in the stylization of violence, the meaning and shift of meaning for the people who resort to it, as if the interest itself is somehow inappropriate. The Western understanding of war, therefore, is somewhat ambiguous: we pretend to know what it is, but we find it difficult to understand our enemies, so great is the psychological chasm between us.

The Bourgeois Versus the Barbarian

The response to the events of September 11 also revealed a third dialectic at play, what Pierre Hassner has called the dialectic between the bourgeois and the barbarian.[13] For whenever Westerners see warriors in Africa or the Middle East, they tend to see barbarians. Traveling around the world from 1993 to 1997 and seeking the identity of "postmodern warriors," Michael Ignatieff found them in the paramilitaries, guerrillas, and warlords—in "the barefoot boys with Kalishnikovs, the paramilitaries in wraparound sunglasses, the turbaned zealots of the Taliban who checked their prayer mats next to their guns."[14] Barbara Ehrenreich too saw a new kind of war, more barbaric than the old, often fought by "ill clad bands more resembling gangs than armies."[15]

Sometimes, of course, Westerners rely on the barbarians, as in the war in Afghanistan (beginning in 2001). For the Northern Alliance was no more than a bunch of warlords, most of whom had supported themselves for years from the sale of heroin. Barbarous or not, we have to cultivate them to do the fighting for us. The problem is not that they are in many cases "savage," but that they always have been. The Afghan warriors the British fought and professed to admire in their own way were totally divorced from the Christian evangelical ethic that sustained the Victorians in their own idea of their civilizing mission. Not much has changed in the intervening years; but we have. We find all warriors and warlords criminal in their intent.

As former U.S. senator Gary Hart wrote a few days after the World Trade Center attack, "September 11 was the date on which the nature of warfare changed: the distinction between war and crime was eliminated."[16] He was writing, of course, about a clear act of terrorism, but some military analysts have been making the same claim for some time on a much wider canvas. The U.S. journalist Robert Kaplan speaks of "reprimitivized man" and regrets the reemergence of warrior societies because he takes their reemergence to be evidence of regression into a premodern condition.[17] Emerging patterns of violence, Martin van Creveld predicts, "will have more in common with the struggles of primitive tribes than with large-scale conventional war."[18] Their way of fighting has no rules or moral conventions worth studying. Indeed, they engage in operations that defy the classic Western understanding of logic or ethics. According to Ralph Peters, an influential U.S. military analyst, "When we face warriors we face men who have acquired a taste for killing, who do not behave rationally according to our definition of rationality, who are capable of atrocities that challenge the descriptive powers of language."[19] Our enemies in the future will be "not soldiers . . . but warriors—erratic primitives with shifting allegiances, habituated to violence with no stake in civic order." In the end, he writes, "there is only rage."[20]

What are they raging against? Like all "barbarians," they are raging against the norms of civilized life. Let us return to Conrad's novel. What it tells us is that many people who resort to force wish to assert themselves against the centrifugal forces that appear to dispossess people of their history and warriors of their profession. Our own age, Jean-Francois Lyotard tells us, has difficulty taking its own master narratives for granted. What is the postmodern age but one that shows "incredulity towards grand narratives" and prefers the fragment or detail to the whole or the master text? We deconstruct texts; the fragment is the symbol of our condition and our authenticity. But, of course, we subscribe to a historical narrative, globalization, just as Edwardian England subscribed to the master text of modernity. Both are alienating for many. What makes globalization even more unsettling is that it threatens to change not the political configuration of the world so much as the very texture of history. For history is now made—or so the critics of globalization contend—not by the actors or agents of modernity—peoples or nation-states—so much as the global market.

And the market has a center, if only in our collective imagination. Today it is New York, the center of world trade. The buildings that bore that name, the buildings that burned and then collapsed, stood not just on an island along the edge of North America but in the homeland of the global imagination representing power and boundless possibility. But at the turn of the twentieth century, the time Conrad was writing, the future was to be glimpsed in London, the great metropolis with Greenwich at its heart through which ran the line of longitude, the nerve end of the world's communications. Early-twentieth-century writers like Wells and Conrad glimpsed a city that was the storm center of politics, fragile and pregnant with violence and social conflict. But in place of the confusion and chaos of the Victorian city, at least, the Edwardian city seemed to have a meaning; it seemed to have its own semiotic. The novelists embarked on a quest for London's urban legibility, and they found it in the fact that it was the center of the world.

In *The Secret Agent,* the attack on Greenwich is an attack on the heart of the world and its wholeness. The novel ends with a chilling portrayal of the incorruptible fundamentalist, the anarchist professor walking the city's streets: "He walked frail, insignificant, shabby, miserable—and terrible in the simplicity of his idea, calling madness and despair to the regeneration of the world." Walking the streets with a lethal bomb in his pocket, primed to blow up any challengers and himself into fragments, he is what Frank Kermode calls "a booby trapped Lyotard," who would blow up, if he could, the master narrative of the world (progress) and London (its chosen center).[21]

What is fragmentary today is the barbarian's wish to assert local history or make it on his or her own terms. In Don DeLillo's postmodern version of *The Secret Agent,* his much acclaimed novel *Mao 2,* the center of terrorist activity is no longer the West, the breeding ground of nineteenth-century nihilism, but the Third World, the focal point of Islamic fundamentalism. As a terrorist says to his American hostage: "Terror makes the new future possible. We live in history as never before."[22]

The West must expect more attempts to assert the local over the global. We fight, of course, for purely instrumental ends, for the "interests of wider humanity," as British prime minister Tony Blair told an audience in Chicago in 1999, twenty-two days into the Kosovo War. They fight for themselves; for them, the existential is the local, the assertion of their own values. As we face the "barbarians" in the future, we should be careful to respect them for their skills, if not their intentions. Dismissing warriors (and yes, even *some* terrorists) as criminals tends to be dangerous, however. For many have the courage of their convictions, however misplaced and alien to our own. We do need to understand them. We put ourselves in a better position to respond to them and to fight them in the future by taking their true measure. Making the enemy smaller than he is blinds us to the danger he presents and gives him the advantage that comes from being underestimated.

Nietzsche's Warning

Because contemporary history may be said to begin when the issues that preoccupy us today were first discussed or brought to light, I began this chapter with Joseph Conrad's classic novel. It is an astonishing commentary on two worlds with two very different understandings of the use of violence. But there was another writer of the time who first perceived the death of the existential element in war. Nietzsche stands at the threshold of the postmodern age as he did his own. His problems are our problems, which is why his voice is so contemporary. His concerns are our concerns or should be. And what concerns many military analysts today is that in making war instrumental as much as it has, the West has lost touch with war's true nature.

Unlike many other philosophers, Nietzsche had firsthand experience of military life, when in 1867 he was drafted into the Fourth Regiment of Field Artillery. A photograph of the period shows him in the uniform of an artilleryman, gripping a long cavalry sword in his right hand. A few years later, he learned the news that France had declared war on Prussia. As excited by the nationalism of the hour as his countrymen, he chose to waive his Swiss citizenship and volunteer for military service as a medical orderly. His service at the front, however, was brief. For three days and nights, he traveled in a cattle truck with the war wounded, an experience that seems to have permanently damaged his health. He caught diphtheria and was discharged after only four months' service. He was never quite the same man again. Perhaps it was his personal experience that convinced him that only warriors or professional soldiers, men with a calling to arms, should be expected to experience the horrors of war firsthand.

But what depressed him most was the utilitarian ethic that he saw at work in mass military service, for he subscribed to the idea that the true warrior is a man who goes to war not for the utilitarian purpose of serving the state, but to serve himself. Certainly, he had no truck with evaluating war by standards external to itself. The warrior describes himself as "good" because he judges his actions as good. By those actions, he distances himself from others: "It was out of this pathos of distance that [men] first seized the right to create values and to coin names for them: what had they to do with utility?"[23]

Of course, what Nietzsche admired most was aristocratic *self*-assertion. He disliked the fact that nationalism made it possible for the first time for every citizen to be a warrior. From birth, every citizen was expected to serve in the ranks and to lay down his life for his country. To be born a European after 1870 was to be born a soldier. We do not need to share or sympathize with his skepticism of mass democracy to appreciate his perspicacity. Nietzsche was concerned that as the nineteenth century drew to a close, the existential nature of war (the extent to which it allowed the warrior to assert himself) was being gradually eroded by the rise of nationalism, populism, and democratic values. War could become almost entirely instrumental. He also feared that in the conflicts to come, nation would be set against nation. Respect for the enemy would give way to unbridled hatred. Only an aristocratic class could respect its enemies. A democratic soldier-citizenry would not. Only warriors who recognized duties to their peers (including their enemies) could experience war as an intersubjective experience. Soldier-citizens, by contrast, would despise their enemies as thugs, criminals, enemies of the cause and demand their unconditional surrender at the cost of engaging in interminable wars of attrition.

Surely Nietzsche was vindicated by what happened in the first half of the twentieth century, and he is still contemporaneous. Although the West is out of the game of great wars between industrial nations, many of the factors he identified—the attempt to criminalize warriors different from ourselves and to reduce war to a policing action—have been realized today. We think of our enemies as criminal or mafiosi figures and deny them the title of warriors, a title they claim themselves. We assume that "war," as we once understood it, has become a criminal activity involving bandits, thugs, and terrorists. We tell ourselves that the nature of war has changed; that the distinction between crime and war has been eliminated. As such, we are imperfectly placed to recognize that it is we, perhaps—not others—who have lost touch with war's true nature.

Since there is no turning back, we can only go forward—by changing the nature of war itself, by continuing *to emphasize the technological over the human*. How we intend to do this—and why—is the subject of this book. And if we seek to understand the way we will practice war in the future, we must start, as did Nietzsche, with its origins. Like a true genealogist, we must go back to the Greeks.

2

The Origins of the
Western Way of Warfare

We must overcome even the Greeks.
—Nietzsche, *The Gay Science*

The nineteenth century had an unrequited love affair with the ancient Greeks. They were considered to be the fathers of Western civilization. The Western literary canon begins with them. And at the heart of the canon stands Homer, whose great poem *The Iliad* shaped the Western imagination and has influenced its ideal of heroic war ever since. At 16,000 words long, it is by far the longest epic poem of the ancient world and is more sophisticated in its imagery and use of language than any other. Its unsurpassed grammatical complexity makes it still the founding "master narrative" of Western history, which tells the story of the first conflict between East and West. The Athenians centuries later made this connection themselves: thus in the great *stoa poikile* on the agora (or marketplace of the city), a painting of the battle of Marathon was flanked by a scene from the Trojan War.

NIETZSCHE, HOMER, AND THE GREEKS

Typical nineteenth-century educated Europeans tended to see ancient Greece as a mirror image of their own society. "We are all Greeks," the poet Percy Shelley wrote in 1822, "our laws, our literature, our religion, our arts had their roots in Greece." It was natural for them to see the Greeks as nineteenth-century liberals. The Victorians, Bernard Knox writes, appropriated the Greeks and imagined them as contemporaries whose writings could be used as weapons in their own ideological wars.[1]

15

The trouble with the mid-Victorian generation was that they made light of the profound differences between their own world and that of the ancients—the gods and the blood guilt, the sacrifices and slaves (although on the last count they were nearer to the Greeks than we are). But the Victorians recognized something that we often do not in twenty-first-century anthropological study of Greek culture. If the Greeks were a tribal society, they were *our* tribe. They demonstrably forged a past that made possible the European creation of modernity. They are the source of the way we still think about life and the world.

Nietzsche too was of the same persuasion, but he was unusual among his contemporaries in insisting on seeing the Greeks in a less flattering light. In an unpublished fragment, "Homer's Contest" (one of *Five Prefaces to Five Unwritten Books,* which was written in 1872, at the outset of his productive life), he insisted that the Greeks were "the most humane men of ancient times," by which he meant they were the most humanistic. But he was also one of the first modern writers to recognize they shared "a trait for cruelty," one that he found time and again in Greek literature. The whole Greek world, he wrote, exulted over the combat scenes of *The Iliad.* Indeed, Homer did little to disguise the brutality and horror of war.[2] There are plenty of references in the poem to the ground littered with corpses, to the axles of chariots spattered with the blood of those who had fallen beneath the wheels, and to the earth dyed with the blood of the fallen (the anonymous dead, such is the extent of the carnage). It is true that Homer did gloss over three of the universal realities of war: casualties from friendly fire, the suffering of the wounded, and the suffering of civilians, particularly women. But if there are few, if any, invocations of mass death save for a reference in Book 1 to the fact that "[the funeral] pyres burned day and night," the Greek audience, unlike ours, was doubtless aware of the undercurrents in Homer's story.

But that is what Nietzsche claimed to find most admirable about the Greeks—their lack of self-doubt. Unlike ourselves—us moderns—they were not given to self-reflection or psychological or excessive self-consciousness. "The Greeks were superficial out of profundity," Nietzsche famously declared. Living on the surface, they experienced life to the full. Even the carnage of war (and they were at war with each other most of the time) was considered of no great moment. For the more the Greeks saw themselves as frightening, the more they found themselves interesting. Their conviction that they were destined for greatness was expressed in artistic images not only of beauty but of strength, courage, and heroic combat. Their sculptors found it necessary to give form again and again to war and combat in innumerable repetitions, those "distended human bodies, their sinews tense with hatred or the arrogance of triumph."[3] Behind the art(istry), the Greeks unveiled a life united by strife, in which combat was salvation and victory over others the supreme affirmation of life.

In stating his opinions so provocatively, Nietzsche broke with convention by refusing to claim that the Greeks were more "humane" than other ancient people because they had risen above nature or the instinctive. As a philologist, he interrogated them with greater honesty than most of his professional colleagues because he found their humanity best illustrated in the way they understood and dramatized conflict. For the Greeks, conflict or the contest *was* life. Not that the Greeks glorified war—in fact, quite the reverse. Homer's characters call it "baneful," "bloody," "cruel," and "destructive," but they accepted that it was inevitable; it was part of the human condition. In making the most of war, they made it into a contest and thus transformed it into a *humanistic* endeavor.

In other words, their lust for battle and for contest was not only instrumental in nature; it was also expressive of their humanity. The tragic poets, like Homer, managed to transfigure the suffering and give it a disquieting beauty: the triumph of human beings over adversity. One of the few Greek writers to dispute the Homeric insight that conflict is the essential human condition was Plato, who tried to banish the poets from his ideal republic to prevent them from encouraging people not to live in harmony with society or themselves. All of Plato, suggested the ancient critic Longinus, was a contest with Homer but he lost the fight. In matters of war Homer, not Plato, became central in the Greek literary imagination and in time the Western as well.[4] With his dactylic hexameters (each of the six metrical feet per line contained one long syllable followed by two short ones), Homer even offered a kind of Morse code of human life.

WAR AND AGON

The agonistic element is also the danger in every development;
it overstimulates the creative impulse.
—Nietzsche, *We Philologists*

One must be careful when reading any Nietzsche, of course, to distinguish his general diagnosis of history from his general philosophy. From the early days of his youth, he regretted the absence of heroism in contemporary life. As a young man, he was overwhelmed by Shelley's *Prometheus*

Unbound (1820). From the early *Untimely Meditations* (1873–1876) to the final work, *Ecce Homo* (published posthumously in 1908), one finds the all-embracing idea that struggle is the expression of one's humanity. Throughout his work, one finds the need for courage. From the beginning, he asked his readers to have the courage to "become" themselves. The self is not a static but a dynamic expression of the will to power. War offers the chance to become something higher, to experience oneself at the highest level. Indeed, it is often only in the presence of death that one asks the important question—or what Socrates tells us is the most important question of all—How should we live?

But when Nietzsche declared that "strife is the perpetual food of the soul," he was not only advancing his own beliefs, he was also—and more importantly—paraphrasing Heraclitus, the most famous of the pre-Socratics, who claimed, "war is the father of all things." Nietzsche was one of the first nineteenth-century philosophers to rediscover a philosopher whose work had survived only in fragments. Not only did he write about the Greeks, but, Robert Calasso added, from time to time he wrote as a Greek. Some of the entries in his notebooks could be fragments by Heraclitus or his contemporaries.[5]

Heraclitus, Nietzsche wrote in another work from the same period of his life, had conceived of life as a struggle between opposites. It was a conception "drawn from the purest fount of Hellenism . . . the idea of a contest . . . translated out of the . . . artistic *agonistics,* out of the struggle of the political parties and the cities, into the most general principle, so that the machinery of the universe is regulated by it."[6]

Agon is an untranslatable word normally rendered "struggle," though the English descendant *agony* captures its overtones more successfully. Every Greek man knew of the agon in his life from its absence in other cultures with which his countrymen were in direct contact; witness Herodotus on Egypt (2:91) or Lucian's *Anacharsis.*[7] It is this problematizing of the human condition that makes the Western understanding of life humanistic, for it is only through conflict that we can achieve a subjective understanding of ourselves. It is for that reason, Jean-Pierre Vernant writes, that Heraclitus can be considered the father of Western humanism. For like us, the Greeks recognized "under the different names of *Polemos, Eris, Neikos* the same force of competition which Hesiod places at the roots of the world and Heraclitus celebrates as father and king of the universe."[8] Nothing, Nietzsche added, distinguished the Greek world from his own so much as *Eris* (discord). For the Greeks, the contest was everything: "The greater and more sublime a Greek is the brighter the flame of ambition that flares out of him."

It is important, nonetheless, to recognize that when Heraclitus claims that conflict is the father of everything, he does not mean it literally, only that beneath the harmony of the universe, there is flux. Everything is a battleground of conflicting opposites. His philosophy is in keeping with the Western tradition, which is dialectical. Conflict is dialectical, for it also produces unity. Just as night and day are one, so are life and death. Another example he produces is more subtle: "it is disease that makes health sweet and good," by which he means it is disease that gives health its significance. The same might be said of war and peace. As Bernard Knox writes, war was the most concentrated expression of those *competitive* values that the Greeks so valued in their dramatic festivals and in their athletic contests, both of which were taken to be reflections of life.[9]

The Greeks believed that war forced combatants to challenge every first principle and every inner belief or conviction. Thus Heraclitus insisted that Homer was wrong when Homer said, "Would that conflict might vanish from among the gods and men . . . for there would be no attainment without high and low notes . . . the high and low notes at the opposite ends of the musical scale." For himself, Heraclitus accepted conflict not as an evil but as an intrinsic part of nature. He discovered no injunction to live in harmony, either with nature or with ourselves. Instead, there is an inner demand of history that we ask only one question, the question posed by Nietzsche toward the end of his life: "What can yet be made of Man?"

GREEK HUMANISM

To speak of the Western way of warfare as humanistic is not to judge it as more "humane" because of its human interest. War for the Greeks became inhumane when it belittled humanity, when it denied a human possibility. Plato pointed out that one can fail at being a human being, which is the greatest failure of all. To act inhumanely is to be less than human and to harm others for no reason is to make them less than human, to prevent them too from realizing their full humanity.

It was not their "humanity" in terms of their actions toward others or themselves but their idea of the indispensability of man that differentiates the Greeks at their most scientific or skeptical from other societies of the ancient world. The Czech philosopher Jan Patocka claims that Western culture is based on the Greek interest in human motivation.[10] What is telling is the fact that the great Greek writers did not write any major manuals or even treatises on war, a fact that distinguishes them from the Chinese in the same era. If we wish to understand the Greek way of warfare, we have to turn to their historians, to Herodotus, Thucydides, and Xenophon, who make up for the lack of insight in the surviving military writings of the time by their understanding of human behavior.

Aristotle characterized history as the story of human affairs. In that sense, the historians are philosophers as well as phenomenologists of war. Thomas Hobbes understood the historian very well when he translated Thucydides' phrase "human nature being what it is" as "the condition of humanity." The meaning of life became a search for truth. Human beings were no longer marginal. They were essential to history. The way to make meaning was to question the human condition, and that is where philosophy played a vital role.

In problematizing life, the Greeks challenged every first principle and belief and subjected themselves to inner strife and turmoil. What we find in the great tragedies is a refusal to present human beings who are in harmony with their world and are reluctant to live in a world that could instruct us how to be in harmony with it. In the plays of Sophocles, human action becomes a subject of reflection and debate. For Vernant, the tragedies should be read not only for their literary merit but for their historical significance as part of an evolutionary step on the development of "autonomous human action."[11] The great tragedians asked the question, What scope is there for human ambition? Such questions were to become increasingly important by the time of Socrates, when the religious concepts of shame and necessity had given way to guilt. When necessity is removed from the picture, the only thing that holds back human action is not God or providence but the knowledge that there are limits to what human beings, even the most gifted, can aspire.

Thus in Thucydides' account of the war with Sparta, we find the classic tragic problem of hubris (or arrogance) punished. As one of the leading Athenian soldiers remarked during the war, they had been "seized by a mad passion to possess that which is out of reach." They were the victims not so much of their ambition as their very nature. In a classic description of his own countrymen, Thucydides himself described them as "daring beyond their power, bold beyond their judgement." In that respect, the Greeks pioneered a way of war that was dangerous, at least as a tragic poet would have grasped the term.

For the essence of danger in tragedy is irony. The hero is usually unaware that he has undone himself. In the case of Athens, the very restlessness, ingenuity, and rationalism that had given it the intellectual leadership of the Greek world had also led to its eventual fall. The Athenians fell victim to their own tragic flaws. "To describe their character," Thucydides wrote, "one might truly say that they were born into the world to take no rest themselves and to give none to others." That restlessness led them to rethink war, to reengineer its first principles and reinvent its rules—in ways that worked against Persia but failed against Sparta, their former allies. No wonder that after witnessing the fall of the city, Plato chose to condemn Athenian thinking for its "originality."[12]

THE GREEK WAY OF WARFARE

In a word, war for the Greeks revealed the ways in which reason could be used to extend the scope of human ambition. Julia Kristeva traces back to the Greeks the Western concern with "the idea and practice of subjective freedom."[13] At the hands of Western generals (the most creative), societies (the most ruthless), and strategists (the most interesting), war became something special. I use that word in the threefold meaning of G. W. F. Hegel's famous pun *Aufgehohen*—it was preserved, transcended, and raised to a higher level. *Higher* does not mean more humane or more virtuous, and it certainly does not mean more rational—though we tend still to attribute these features to something called the Western "mentality."

We might also claim that for the Greeks war provided a test of their "vitality" as a people. And we must not allow our contemporary antiwar attitudes to color the use of the word. The fact that the West's vitality owes much to success in war is reason enough to study it. Vitality, of course, is difficult to define. It does not refer to stability or harmony or equity or justice or liberty or prosperity or security—or peace. Such values may be the product of vitality, but they do not define it. Its essence is instead captured by such concepts as innovation, dynamism, effectiveness, performance, efficiency, capability, élan, morale, or spirit (many of them words that we apply to warfare). In a value sense, vitality is neutral. It may be exercised for good or bad purposes. The fact that we may abhor war and claim to see through the pieties and cruelties of those who have practiced it in the past must not blind us to the restless energy of an Alexander or the ambition of a Caesar.

So in claiming that the Western way of war is humanistic, I am making two claims that stem from what has gone before. First, I am claiming that the instrumental dimension of war has always been more pronounced in Western thinking because of the social institutions it was the first to invent: from the city-state to the nation-state of the late nineteenth century, Second, the *existential* dimension of the Western way of warfare has differed from the non-Western in its humanism: the importance it places on human agency; the need for one to experience war subjectively; and, through an intersubjective relationship with one's enemies, the chance to obey the chief injunction of Western philosophy: to know oneself.

Instrumental War

One of the most important books of recent years is G. E. Lloyd's *Demystifying Mentalities* (1990), which challenges all the theories that suggest different cultures have distinct cultural mentalities, such as Viviane Levy-Bruhl's belief in a "primitive mentality" or James Frazier's notion of magic, religious, and scientific mentalities as a series of progressive stages through which higher civilizations have to ascend to realize their potential. In discussing the significant differences between Chinese and Western scientific endeavors, Lloyd is much more interested in discovering what questions they were trying to answer and identifying the different problems they were trying to address.

In Lloyd's own work, he finds the explanation for differences of approach not in mentalities, but in styles of enquiry and their polemical purpose. The Greek love of abstract thinking can be traced directly to their passion for political innovation. The Greeks may have inherited the city-state structure and their passion for founding colonies (as well as their language) from the Phoenicians, but they pioneered the art of constitution making. They took a tabula rasa and imposed a design. Cleisthenes' reforms of 508 B.C.E., from which historians date the rise of Athens, are based on abstract principles that were all the more impressive because he imposed them on an old tribal system. Attica was divided into three regions (city, coast, and inland); each of its ten designated tribes had representative *demes* (villages). Using geometry to design the political system reflects a social interest in mathematical thinking, including the geometry of the cosmos associated with the philosopher Anaximander in the mid–sixth century.[14]

Lloyd accepts that other societies were also mathematically advanced. The Indians, for example, developed geometrical methods in the context of building altars, in the course of which they showed themselves highly skilled in handling problems of squares, rectangles, and right-angled triangles. But there is no clear evidence in works such as the *Sulbasutra* (500–100 B.C.E.) of a clear and explicit concept of proof. The Indians failed to distinguish between approximations and exact results, not because they were less clever than the Greeks but because they were interested in practical questions, not procedures of proof. Thus, although the Greeks did not invent mathematics, they were the first people to raise second order questions and to engage in the analysis of its status as a science, its methods, and its foundations, especially the notion of exact proof.

What Lloyd offers readers is a difference between cultures not on the basis of mentalities (one culture being more rational than another or more interested in abstract thinking) but on the basis of cognitive operations. For what purpose were the Greeks and Indians using reason? To argue in a law court requires a high concept of proof and takes one into the realm of jurisprudence. To build an altar requires different considerations and different sums.[15]

And no ancient society was as argumentative as Athens. In his funeral speech to commemorate those who had died in the war with Sparta, Pericles remarked that the Athenians were especially renowned for one *capability* (not innate ability), the opportunity they were given to speak and debate before the political assembly and juries. "We Athenians . . . do not think that there is an incompatibility between words and deeds; the worst thing is to rush into action before the consequences have been properly debated." In a comedy of the time by the playwright Aristophanes, a student guides a simple farmer around his school.

> *Student:* And here we have a map of the world. This is Athens.
> *Strepsiades:* Come off it! I don't believe you. Where are the juries?

As a simple but astute farmer, Strepsiades is interested in sending his sons to school for one reason only—he wants them to be able to fight their corner in the bankruptcy courts. Whatever their social station, argument is what all Athenians valued most.[16]

Indeed, it would seem that the polis, or city-state, emerged from argument, in this case from the warrior cultures of Mycenaean Greece and from the procedures of military life we find in *The Iliad*, such as funeral games, the distribution of booty, and, above all, the warrior assemblies in which the great debates between Achilles and Agamemnon are conducted. As Achilles' old tutor Phoenix remarks, a hero is one who is brought up to be a speaker of words as well as a doer of deeds. In the Mycenaean period, warriors' ability to sway the opinion of their fellows in arms counted for as much as their bravery in battle; both gave them special status. Later, when the age of individual combat as depicted in Homer's description of the Trojan War gave way to infantry battles in which soldiers fought shoulder to shoulder with their comrades, warrior privileges were gradually extended to the citizens of the city.[17]

We can discern another change from the days of Homer. Not every character in *The Iliad* supports war. One who does not, indeed, one who is vociferous in his opposition to it, Theristes, is the only nonaristocratic Achaean who is allowed to speak in the assembly. His voice heralds the

democratic voice of Athens three centuries later. What happened was that
the rise of hoplite warfare democratized warfare—it involved everyone,
not only the aristocracy. The phalanx introduced the peasant to political
society, and the growth of the navy brought in the previous "untouchables,
the *thetes*," the poorest people of all, the impecunious artisans and paid
laborers, the lowest of Solon's classification of Athenians. When the
Theristeses of the fifth century B.C.E. voted to go to war, they were influenced by populist leaders such as Cleon, a former tanner, and
Hyperboreus, a former lamp seller. By the time of Demosthenes in the following century, they had the decisive voice.

Why did this process happen only in Greece? We still do not know for
certain, but we do know it happened between the seventh and sixth centuries B.C.E. with the hoplite reform, which was itself a product of new
mental structures: the construction of a system of rational thought that dramatically broke with the old religion and produced the transition from
myth to reason. Both were not a "miracle" that happened independent of
social change. Both the conceptual framework and mental techniques
favoring the emergence of rational thought developed in social life. In the
law courts, oaths were devalued, and witnesses were heard only if they
produced proof. The speeches now made were intended to put forward
arguments to sway juries and judges alike. Through speech, people were
effective in the assembly and were able to influence and dominate others.
Warriors too had to be capable of winning over and influencing not only
their peers but those who served under them or those they served. In
Thucydides, we find nothing but dialogue over contending principles:
rational decision and chance, speech and fact, law and nature, and peace
and war. All illustrate the idea, Pierre Vidal Naquet writes, that "history
takes the form of . . . a gigantic political argument."[18]

The value of speech. Speech is what gave the Greeks power over others in
the assembly or law courts, and it evolved as society evolved, structuring
society in ways that benefited philosophy but, interestingly, not science.
The Sophists' reflections on *techne,* the means of extending one's power
and perfecting one's tools, led neither to technological thinking nor to a
philosophy of technology. They led instead to rhetoric and fostered dialectic and logic. And, in particular, they fostered an entirely new concept of
war.

As a supremely philosophical people, the Greeks thought of war in
highly conceptual terms, considering, for example, the importance of
decisiveness in battle. These concepts and the theories based on them constituted an art of war. Conceptual thinking relies on observing the world

closely as well as making comparisons, both of which were introduced
into the Greek worldview by mathematics, science, and logic. The Greeks
rationally systematized all three and turned them into academic disciplines
for the first time. They also humanized them, for they made all practical
action humanly comprehensible, and that included the discipline of war.
Of course, as a premodern people, they were still superstitious. They sacrificed to the gods before battle. Alexander the Great carried with him
what he thought was the shield of Achilles (in India, it saved his life). But
they recognized that success or failure in the field was a matter of human
ingenuity and, above all, will. Once human possibilities could be tapped,
battle could become decisive—everything could be hazarded in one throw
of the dice.

Other peoples in the ancient world tended to avoid risking everything
in one day's fighting. Even the Assyrians, the most feared ancient people,
avoided war when they could and whenever possible got others to do the
fighting for them. And when they did commit forces to battle, they hus-
banded their resources. They were more keenly aware than others of the
risk of incurring too many casualties that would weaken their army, the
bulwark of their power. The Persians, despite deploying the largest army
in the ancient world after the Romans (more than 200,000 men), preferred
to outmaneuver their enemies rather than outfight them. That is why at
Marathon (490 B.C.E.), the Persian commander Mardonius was surprised
that the Greeks had sought to decide the outcome of war in the space of a
single afternoon.

In the account Herodotus left us, he was said to have told his king:

> These Greeks are wont to wage war against one another in the most fool-
> ish way through sheer perversity and foolishness. For no sooner is war
> proclaimed than they search out the smoothest and fairest plain that is to
> be found in all the land and there they assemble and fight: whence it
> comes to pass that even the conquerors depart with great loss. I say noth-
> ing of the conquered, for they are destroyed altogether. Now surely, as
> they are all of one speech they ought to interchange heralds and mes-
> sengers and make up their differences by any means other than battles;
> or, at the worst, if they must fight one another, they ought to post them-
> selves as strongly as possible and so try their quarrels.[19]

Herodotus thought that the spirit of the Greek soldiers was the defining
factor in the defeat of the Persians: they had more of it. They fought not
as soldiers but as men possessed. And they did so because they were largely fighting for themselves. Their strength was that of men whose loyalty
to the city was freely chosen.

The typical hoplite was an independent subsistence farmer, a man who owned enough land to support himself and his family (about 10 acres in all). In their wars with Persia, the Greeks made infantry the determining factor in their campaigns. With it, they introduced a novel notion— that property owners on foot, not horsemen alone, win wars. That is why property owners are better soldiers and tend to show more zeal in battle. As the historian Victor Hanson contends, they build, live on, and pass on land to their children. They do not readily give it up or yield ground to the enemy.[20] Aristotle agrees. In the *Nicomachean Ethics,* he tells us that professional soldiers may have many virtues that citizen-soldiers lack—but they are better at killing than dying. They often prove cowards when the danger becomes too great, and they find themselves at a disadvantage in numbers and equipment. "They are the first to run away while citizens stand their ground and die fighting," he concludes, because they are ashamed to run away. Courage in such cases transcends knowledge, experience, and training. It springs from motivation, duty, patriotism, and, above all, belief in a cause.[21]

As a concept, the idea of a decisive engagement is a vivid illustration of a general rule: that in war it is neither in the personal conduct of soldiers nor the technical superiority of an army that the most significant advantage is to be found. It lies in ideas about war that reflect the social context in which they are formulated. The polis was the crucible in which the Greek way of war was conceived and brought to life—hence the preference for citizen militias and civilian participation in decisionmaking.

Greek city-state. What made the city-states unique—and strong—is the fact that every citizen voted to go to war. As Pericles told his fellow citizens in his famous funeral oration, democracy gave every man a stake in the success of the city, and the same could be said of success in the field. Not to participate in the life of the community was a betrayal of a sacred duty: "We alone call the man who does not participate not a private man but a useless one."[22]

For the fifth-century Athenian, war was more instrumental than it was for the other empires they knew or had engaged in battle, such as the Persian, in large part because they took the decision to go to war themselves. And to discover why, we need only look to the discussion of the origin of war in Plato's *Republic,* in particular the discussion between Socrates and Glaucon:

> *Socrates:* When we have got hold of enough people to satisfy our many varied needs, we have assembled quite a large number of partners and

helpers together to live in one place; we give the resultant settlement the name of a state?

Glaucon: Yes, I agree.

Socrates: And in the community all mutual exchanges are made on the assumption that the parties to them stand to gain?

Glaucon: Certainly.

Socrates: Come then, let us make an imaginary sketch of the origin of the state. It originates, as we have seen from our needs. . . . [When our needs expand] we have to enlarge our state again . . . [for] the territory which was formerly enough to support us will now be too small.

Glaucon: That is understandable.

Socrates: If we are to have enough for pasture and plough we shall have to cut a slice off our neighbors' territory. And if they too are no longer confining themselves to necessities and have embarked on the pursuit of unlimited material possessions, they will want a slice of ours too.

Glaucon: The consequence is inevitable.

Socrates: And that will lead to war, Glaucon, will it not?

Glaucon: It will.

Socrates: For the moment, . . . we are not concerned with the effects of war, good or evil; let us go on to note merely that we have found its origin to be the same as that of most evil, individual and social.[23]

The instrumental nature of war is spelled out more compellingly in Plato's text than anywhere else because the Greek conception of the state was more sophisticated than that of other people. When Socrates tells Glaucon that the origin of war is to be found in "acquisitiveness," he is merely stating a general principle common to Greek writing at the time. "All wars are made for the sake of getting money," we read in another of Plato's works, the *Phaedo*. War, Aristotle tells us, is "a form of acquisitive activity."[24] In this case, the more prosperous the community (the more acquisitive, the more it needs material possessions), the more aggressive it will become. War is not, therefore, a matter of blood vendetta, revenge, or honor, as it is for a tribe or clan; it is a collective interest embodied in the state.

Aristotle saw the state as an association of clans, villages, and households sharing in a common life. The pursuit of luxury is not an amoral end (anymore than is war) because it makes the good life possible and social life complete. Wealth is a means to an end, as is slavery, which makes possible leisure. And we should not forget that the principal objective of war in this period was the acquisition of slaves. In the Greek and Roman worlds, freedom was defined primarily as freedom from work, which released time for political activity. It was beyond work that the realm of freedom commenced.

In short, the individual is dependent on the state for the fullness of life. Aristotle goes further and argues that there can be no individualism outside the state (or society). Human beings are by nature political animals. Their true nature (or humanity) lies in citizenship. And just as an end of their personal development is citizenship, so the end of their actions must be the "political good." In that sense, citizens' agency as human beings is determined by their instrumentality to the state. Both their desires and good are instrumental: they depend on the common good.

But the Greeks went even further in seeing war in instrumental terms. They believed war was progressive (that it could be used for ever more ambitious ends), an idea we find dramatically embodied in Thucydides' discussion of naval power. What Thucydides gives us is a history of military progress, tracing the history of naval power from myth (the fleet of Minos) to the Trojan War (which saw the Greeks project their power into Asia) to the triremes of Themistocles, which triumphed over the Persians at Salamis (480 B.C.E.) and gave Athens mastery of the seas.[25]

The Greeks extended their understanding of the instrumentality of war by treating it as a *technical* problem that could be solved by better tactics (larger armies) or technology (more destructive weapons). They had the advantage over other societies in the way they *thought* about war or the way in which they reasoned it out. Resources, Thucydides shows, were not as important as the use of them. Money was less important than what it was spent on. Technology alone was less critical than how it was applied. Thucydides' discussion of naval power is in the tradition of Protagoras, who talked about the human conquest of nature, and the Hippocratic texts, which talked of disease from the point of view of the doctor looking for a successful treatment. War too could be made more efficient and effective; it could maximize the power of a state and enhance the self-esteem of its citizens. Efficiency (or *arête*) could be taught by challenging traditions and reforming the *nomos* (state law or collective tradition). Such a hope was understandable in people who had witnessed the unexpected result of the Persian wars and the meteoric rise of Periclean Athens. What was this belief, if not the first manifestation of a new idea: progress?

In applying that idea to the problem of war, the Greeks also became the first people to invent the concept of long-term strategic analysis, a fact that can best be seen by looking at the strategic conundrum that faced

Athens at the beginning of the Peloponnesian War. At the outset of the conflict, Josiah Ober writes, Pericles had to decide how a sea power could defeat a land power if the latter (in this case, Sparta) was inaccessible by attack from the sea. The answer was to change the rules. When the Spartans invaded Attica, the Athenians remained within the walls of their city. Their empire provided revenues to continue the war; their merchantmen resupplied the city with grain from sources as far afield as Egypt and southern Russia. As a result, they were able to checkmate the Spartans. It was a revolutionary strategy. For it was one matter to evacuate Athens in the face of the Persian barbarians and quite another to evacuate the countryside, abandon farmland, and refuse every challenge from one's fellow Greeks. It was revolutionary because it contravened all the previous rules of Greek warfare.

As Ober contends, instead of worrying about the tactical problem of how to win a particular battle, Pericles was able to think through the interplay of military, financial, political, and psychological forces that constitutes "grand strategy." And doing that required something new: an inherent acceptance of the fact that at some point and at some time, strategies become outdated. As the Athenian state became more complex, it was able to rely more on naval power. As Pericles remarks, "The future belongs not to a land power but a naval power." And Thucydides tells us why—naval powers are wealthier and can project power anywhere, giving them a distinct advantage in war. They also tend to be more ruthless because they are democratic and can rely on national cohesion. While the Spartans pillaged Attica, the Athenians remained secure behind their city walls and secure also in the knowledge that no one was safe from their ships plying the sea lanes and landing troops on the coast.[26]

In the end, of course, the strategy was too ingenious by far. Its concept was probably sound, though this is still disputed by historians, but the execution was much less so, particularly once Pericles died. Athens lost the war and with it the power to defend Greece when the next invader arrived in the person of Philip of Macedon. The final result notwithstanding, the Greeks pioneered a novel way of thinking about war and its consequences, one that was to give even more advanced state structures like the Roman republic a critical instrumental advantage in the way they prosecuted it.

The Existential Warrior

Like the instrumental, the existential experience of war is found in every culture.

In Japan, for example, the samurai tradition enjoined warriors to be true to themselves. The seventeenth-century philosopher-samurai Yamaga Soko wrote that the warrior's chief business "consists in reflecting on his own station in life, on discharging loyal service to his master, if he has one; in deepening his fidelity in association with friends, and in . . . devoting himself to duty above all." In other words, the samurai derived their sense of self-worth not only from an instrumental obligation (to serve the political ambitions of a master); they owed their chief obligation to their own calling.[27]

The reason that warriors have fought war so enthusiastically is that it has offered them an existential experience found in no other walk of life. For war generates those supreme moments of danger and intensity of emotion that enliven the spirit. Even Carl von Clausewitz tells us as much in an early passage in *On War,* when he accompanies an imaginary young man to his first battle:

> Let us accompany a novice on the battlefield. As we approach, the rumble of guns grows louder and alternates with the whirr of cannonballs which begin to attract his attention. Shots begin to strike all around us . . . here cannonballs and bursting shells are frequent and life begins to seem more serious than the young man had imagined. Suddenly someone you know is wounded . . . you yourself are not as steady and collected as you were. . . . The air is filled with hissing bullets that sound like a sharp crack if they pass close to one's head. For a final shock, the sight of men being killed and mutilated moves our pounding hearts to awe and pity.
> The novice cannot pass through these layers of increasing intensity of danger without sensing that here ideas are governed by other factors, that the light of reason is refracted in a manner quite different from that which is normal in academic speculation.[28]

The key sentence in this account is "the light of reason is refracted." Reason is an instrumental idea of war, or war as the reason of state. But war is often so intense that reason can be refracted through the prism of experience. It teaches us—and it is a severe teacher—a great deal about ourselves. We may fail the test and be paralyzed by fear, or we may rise above it and find in ourselves hidden depths and inner reserves of strength. War is, in that sense, the ultimate existential experience and often makes peace seem impoverishing. "Once you have lain in her arms you can admit no other mistress," wrote one British veteran of World War I.[29] Such sentiments were not atypical of the literature of that war, though they tend to be obscured by the antiwar writing of the war poets, who succeeded in defining the struggle for the rest of us ever since.

Finally, war is existential because it involves another dimension as well: the ambiguous relationship between the warrior and the adversary. This intersubjective realm is ambiguous because the enemy is to be killed but not dishonored. There is no point in humiliating an enemy, for the warrior lives in the same world of death and in the imagination of the other. Warriors form a guild, sometimes even a fraternity; to be esteemed by others is to know greater self-esteem as well.

Both aspects of existential warfare are humanistic, and in the existential dimension of war they added their own stamp to the Western way of warfare. If Nietzsche was correct, however, to put more emphasis on the existential dimension than most of his contemporaries, he was wrong to imagine that it was Homer's Greece that embodied the ideal. The breakthrough society was fifth-century Athens. Traditionally, the heroic community depicted by Homer and extolled by Nietzsche saw courage as a virtue of a class or the leader of a clan committed to the preservation and well-being of the community. There was little humanism here, for there was no question of asking, Who am I? Such questions were never addressed in the Mycenaean age because one's identity was indistinguishable from what one did. Within this social framework, the word *virtue* (*arête*) described any quality that enabled one to discharge one's role. In a world without social mobility, courage was the virtue of a class, not a person.

By the fifth century, by comparison, it was clear that no Athenian could live like Achilles or Agamemnon, a problem that taxed Plato in particular. That did not mean that the heroic societies had been mistaken about war's social dimension. But rather the social structure had changed dramatically since Homer's day with the rise of the city-state. War too had changed its shape: it no longer denoted excellence in performance of a well-defined social role but now signified a quality that was applicable to human life in general. The good was now the corporate good. That explains why in *The Republic,* Plato contended that the true warrior lives in accordance with his true nature: the warrior's nature was to fight, but in fighting or showing courage he makes corporate life possible for everyone else.[30]

Nietzsche himself admired the Platonic ideal of war in which the instrumental and existential were conjoined. He recognized that the Greeks more than any other people had *humanized* the existential dimension of war—and in so doing had created a unique style of warfare that was inherently humanistic in respect of the three elements we must now discuss.

Agency

> *Homer is anthropomorphic. Achilles is not like Zeus,*
> *but Zeus to a degree is like Achilles.*
> —Harold Bloom, *Ruin the Sacred Truths*

"Surely, that philosopher's invention, so bold and so fateful which was then first devised for Europe, the invention of 'free will' . . . was designed above all to furnish a right to the idea that the interests of the gods, in man, in human virtue, *could never be exhausted.*" So Nietzsche writes in *On the Genealogy of Morals* (1887). In the Bible, by comparison, human achievement is constantly downplayed, even though the victories of the Hebrews clearly owed much to human ingenuity against their much more powerful neighbors. Through their philosophical rationalism, the Greeks took God out of the equation altogether and put human will (not providence) at the center of history. The Jews, like the Greeks, were unique in the ancient world but in a different way. It was not long before the prophets ceased to take refuge in the old cultic observances that projected God back into their own folklore. Instead, they forced the people to look history in the face and to accept the fact that a history including catastrophes as terrifying as the exodus to Babylon represented a dialogue with the Almighty. The difference by then was that God was no longer a tribal deity but the universal God, the orchestrator of all successes and defeats in war. Even the Assyrians and Babylonians who visited destruction upon the people of Israel did so because God wished it. Through them, he punished the sins or obduracy of his own chosen people.

What is intriguing about the Greeks, by comparison, is that human agency is very much to the fore. It was (as it was not for the Hebrew warriors) a central part of the soldier's sense of self. In this way, the Greeks were distinguished from other cultures such as the Hebrew, for whom God was still a warrior, a man of war who fought on their behalf or on occasion in their place. The great classics of the Greek canon posit warriors as moral agents who are on their own. In *The Iliad,* the last major description we have of the pre-hoplite way of warfare, the gods still play a role, for the woes of the Greeks are caused by their quarrels (the gods are represented as heartless and highly capricious, even though Zeus is always protesting how much he loves humanity). By the time we get to Thucydides' account of the war between Athens and Sparta, we are in a

completely different world. Kenneth Dover writes of Thucydides' generation "edging the divine out of the history of human affairs."[31]

Even if Plato criticized Homer for attributing the Trojan War to the
gods, not men, if we read *The Iliad* closely, we find that the gods are clearly mortals—magnified several times but often in an ironic vein.
Invariably, their actions are mean and without imagination and as a result
enhance the stature of mortal heroes like Achilles, as well as the dignity of
the other warriors. For the gods, Jonathan Shay writes, symbolize a power
that is unaccountable, beyond the understanding of the ordinary soldier.
They are what a later generation would call "rear echelon authorities." For
there are always two enemies the soldier confronts in battle: the enemy
who is out to kill him and the "rear echelon" officers who place him in a
position to get killed.[32]

What distinguishes Achilles from Apollo is that however reprehensi-
ble Achilles' behavior—his pettiness, arrogance, and vindictiveness—
however unheroic his actions at times, he is at least prepared to lead from
the front, to hazard all in battle, including his life. The gods, by contrast,
act behind the scenes. They are "above" the battle in both senses of the
word. They waste lives, show a heartless disregard for casualties, and res-
olutely prevent every attempt by both parties to reach a compromise
peace. They are always thwarting human attempts to bring the war to an
end. Treating the gods metaphorically enabled the Greeks to show another face of humanism. It is ourselves and only ourselves of whom we
should be afraid.

Ultimately, what is interesting about the Greeks is that unlike all other
ancient peoples, they were fascinated not by the gods but by the heroes
who were considered to have lived in, not outside, human history. In other
cultures, myths are concerned with relationships between culture and
nature. Greek myths, by contrast, are interested in testing the limits of
human agency, the limits in which excellence can be won.[33] In *The Iliad*
we find that *arête* (or excellence) is won chiefly in battle. The battlefield
is the place where warriors discover themselves and are discovered by
others through the fame of their deeds. That is why we find Agamemnon
"driving eagerly towards the fighting where men will win glory."[34]

Such resolve was expected of them and was what they expected of
themselves. In his great speech to Glaucus on the theme of noblesse oblige
(nobility obligates), the hero Sarpedon begins by saying that as warriors,
it is their duty to fight in the front rank and then goes on to explain why.
"If by avoiding death we could make ourselves immortal; then I should
not fight; but we must die someday, so let us go to win glory ourselves, or
to serve the glory of others."[35] It is not unreflective or self-conscious hero-

ism that drives the Greek warrior but a response to the predicament of being human. Their own mortality forces human beings to live in the memory of others by virtuous deeds.

For Nietzsche, writing more than 2,000 years later, *The Iliad* was expressive of war as an act of will, the will to power that makes one into an agent of one's own destiny. The act is important, not its utility. In *On the Genealogy of Morals,* he cites the example of Pericles and his famous funeral oration, in which he told the Athenians: "Our daring has forced a path to every land and sea, erecting timeless memorials to itself everywhere for good *and ill*." Nietzsche himself italicizes the last two words, for what he finds commendable about the Greeks is their refusal to assess everything only in instrumental or utilitarian terms. Essentially, he claims, they were unconcerned for their own safety and comfort. In typical fashion, he shocks his readers by writing of the Athenians' "shocking . . . delight in all destruction."[36] By that he means they delighted in their power to force others to submit to them—for what is human agency if not celebration of the will to power? In the end, of course, this tendency proved to be their undoing because it made them hated (they were amazed to hear the great cheer that went up in the whole Greek world when the Spartans finally occupied the city and tore down Pericles' famous wooden walls).

Subjectivity. The great Athenian victory over the Persians at Salamis, Herodotus tells us, transformed the Athenians into "seafaring men," but it did more. It was fought at sea, an element that was considered to be the preserve of the Persians and their Phoenician subjects. It was fought against vastly superior odds and in defiance of the usual rules of engagement and was for that reason the first really decisive battle of the world. The Athenians were not cleverer than the Persians, and they were certainly not braver, but they were forced to come up with something original simply to survive as an independent people. In the event, they astonished everyone, including their fellow Greeks.

The battle, a contemporary historian writes, owes its importance to one factor above all: "It was a triumph of the Athenians over themselves."[37] The hoplites who fought so bravely in the face of apparently hopeless odds were men of rank used to fighting on land. At Salamis, they had to be retooled—to be trained as oarsmen, even though that meant sitting next to the poorest citizens. And instead of fighting the enemy man to man, which their honor code required, they had to face backward and exert all their strength to move the ships forward. Rarely has more been asked of a social class, but then, whether rich or poor, the Athenians saw all citizens as equal.

In that sense, the Greeks were the first people to transform war into a "democratic" experience and may be said to have invented what is often called "the democratic form of warfare." Plato, a great antidemocrat, complained that their victory at Salamis had made them "worse as a people." He was especially dismissive of the special praise bestowed on aristocrats like Cimon (the leader of the aristocratic faction in the city) and his friends in the cavalry, who on the eve of Salamis had abandoned their bridles and offered themselves for naval service. He had little good to say of this socially demeaning aspect of their volunteerism. In *The Laws,* the Athenian stranger has nothing but contempt for the *nautikos ochlos,* the "sailor rabble" that crewed Athens' triremes, remarking tartly that although the city's land battles had won it moral virtue, those fought at sea had precisely the opposite effect.[38]

It is this subjective dimension of war that proved so decisive, and it owed everything to the concept of citizenship. The Greek word for city is *polis* and the word for citizen *polites* (literally, defender of the citadel), and the word *agora* (place of assembly) is derived from the word *ageirein* (to collect together). In both cases, we find a new concept in history: the security of the civic order, like the safety of the soldier in a phalanx, is dependent on the responsibility of each citizen to the other. That responsibility *was* civic life, and it was immortalized in the deeds of those who contributed to the city's glory or survival. The discipline of the phalanx represented the reconciliation of individual desire with the public good. And the way in which the Greeks pursued victory and the zeal with which they fought in battle were reflections of pride. Thus the polis was sacramental, not secular in nature. As Epictetus asserts (*Fragments* 77), "Cities are made good habitations by the sentiments of those who live in them, not by wood and stone."[39]

It is this concept, first formulated in the Greek world and especially in the Athens of the fifth century, that helps unlock the Greek idea of war. The polis is the place of human life, and those who live outside it, Aristotle tells us, are not men (i.e., they are not individuals). Man is a *zoon politikon* (a political animal), and whatever immortality he can win can be won only through service to the city. Cities rise and fall, of course, but individuals remain in the collective memory. What we find in this claim is a defining "Western idea": that individuals actualize themselves through society as soldiers actualize themselves in battle.

We find this even in Homer, especially the description of Hector's death. Hector is punished in the end because he acts alone. He rejects the advice of Polydamus, who interprets an omen as a signal to retreat, and refuses to retreat after killing Patroclus. In putting his own bloodlust first, he loses contact with that social order that defined and generated his hero-ism. He has individuated himself outside the community, and his fate is to reject his parents' advice and to face Achilles alone. He has shamed him-self in that, in a moment of madness, he has ceased to be the hero who is responsive and responsible to his own city. He is exonerated posthumous-ly only because, as Homer makes clear, in this moment of madness, he acts out of character.

The discipline of the Greek infantry owed everything to the fact that Athens was a covenanting community, not a contractual one. Contracts are limited, often personal, and enforced by law or the threat of punishment. Covenants are open-ended, voluntary, and enforced by conscience and moral law. Athens was a community whose political identity was defined as the responsibility each citizen owed to the other. As Hegel writes, "only in the state does man have a rational existence," an enigmatic remark that can be taken to mean that "the basis of the state is the power of reason actualizing itself as will." The polis was the fundamental medium for the exercise of the will. Freedom is in essence social, and the Greek political genius lay in obeying laws of their own making. This is what Hegel means when he also writes enigmatically, "the will obeys itself and being itself is free."[40]

Only the free *man,* or citizen, was expected to fight for the city (even though there is some evidence that in its moment of crisis, Athens did ask slaves to row the triremes at Salamis). That is why no one in the Greek world ever questioned the necessity of war, though they often questioned its morality. For it was not separate from political life: it *was* political life, the supreme act of citizenship. The army was the popular assembly in arms or the city out campaigning. Indeed, in the absence of war, we may well ask whether there would have been a Greek civilization at all, for it was through conflict with each other that city-states were brought togeth-er in a community united by language, religion, customs, and forms of social life. In their own consciousness, at least, the regulation of war delin-eated them from those beyond their world: the barbarians.

Hegel mentioned that Salamis was symbolically significant for anoth-er fact: the battle intersected with the lives of the three great tragedians—Aeschylus fought in it, Sophocles danced at the festival to celebrate the victory, and Euripides is rumored to have been born on the same day. Tragedy also served the purpose of allowing the Greeks to interrogate themselves and discover what made them different from others. It enabled them to engage in great debates about the origins and sources and author-ity of law (*Antigone*), about the best political constitution (*Suppliants*), and about the contrasting virtues of persuasion and violence for a state. All this symbolized the influence upon drama exercised by argumentation in the *word-driven* culture that Athens had become. The great playwrights went so far as to raise disturbing questions about the values of the dominant ideology of Athens: Greek-ness and even Athenian-ness. They even subjected to critical exploration the very values such as democracy that licensed tragic questioning. Tragedy offers the extraordinary spectacle of a developing city putting its own developing language and structures of argument at risk.

Intersubjectivity. What is interesting about the Greeks is that they asked not only the first-order question (What makes us human?) but also a second-order question (What makes us Greek?). The "founder" of Western philosophy, Thales of Miletus, famously remarked that he was grateful to destiny for three things: for making him a man, not a beast; for being born male, not female; and for being a Greek, not a barbarian.[41] The Greeks were inveterate cataloguers in their study of the science of man, and they made war the master text by which ontologically they knew themselves better. They were the first people to treat war as a text that defined their humanity in terms of social categories: freedom distinguished the free man from the slave; manliness distinguished the male from the female; citizenship distinguished the citizen from the noncitizen. All three constituted the *humanity* of the Greeks, which enabled them to distance themselves from the barbarians.

But in distancing themselves, they also needed to earn the "other's" respect. War involved a dialogue with the adversary on the intersubjective plane. Nietzsche believed that Homer had shown that to be humanistic, a warrior must honor the enemy. No one is more ruthless in war than Achilles, but no one is more aware that his enemies deserve respect. As he tells Priam: "Here I sit by Troy, far from home, causing grief to you and to your children."[42] The object of war is to defeat the enemy, not humiliate him. Achilles may not have much self-consciousness compared with others, but even he sees his own actions in the light of the fact that warriors on all sides must die. Death puts the slayer and slain on the same level; thus Achilles can call Lyacon a "friend" as he kills him.

Looking back at Nietzsche's work as a whole, we can find all three features of humanism in his essay "On War and Warriors," in the most difficult and poetic of his books *Thus Spake Zarathustra* (1883–1892). "I see many soldiers: would that I saw many warriors," Zarathustra laments, looking at the citizens of his own day—those conscripted to go to the slaughter. For what is the warrior, if not an agent in his own life? Life is a struggle, and in that struggle, "you should have eyes that always seek an enemy—*your* enemy." The warrior's enemy must not be his nation's or community's but his own.

Likewise on the second feature, subjectivity, if life is a struggle, then war is a microcosm of life: "You say that it is the good cause that hallows every war? I tell you that it is the good war that hallows every cause." That is why the warrior ultimately fights for himself and through his valor wins out for his community. In hazarding all, including his life, he does so for his own ends, not for those of others. The moment of death must be freely chosen. We find this in Zarathustra's final injunction: "thus live your life of obedience and war. What matters long life? What warrior wants to be spared?"

And third, war is an intersubjective experience that demands that the warrior respect the adversary. "You may have only enemies whom you can hate not enemies you despise. You must be proud of your enemy: then the successes of your enemy are your success also."[43] Some of the greatest defeats make the best themes of lyric poetry. To be defeated is no disgrace. But to be humiliated is to be defeated by an enemy whose deeds can never be celebrated in poetry.

SYSTEMATIZING THE WESTERN WAY OF WARFARE

We define Western civilization as the unique fusion of Greek and Roman culture. The Greek way of warfare survived the decline of Greece itself because it was adopted—and adapted—by the Romans. In the process, it became "Western." Initially, of course, the Greeks saw the Romans as barbarians. "The barbarians are on the run," was the account of the first phase of the battle of Cynoscephalae (197 B.C.E.) brought from the front to the Macedonian king Philip V. When he encountered the Romans again, he was so impressed by them that he conceded that they could no longer be considered barbarous.[44] What made him change his mind was his admiration for their military qualities. Pyrrhus too is reported to have been impressed by the quality of Roman troops, not just by their fighting power and staying power in the field but above all by their organization and discipline. In time, they were adopted into the family of "civilized men." Two centuries later, Plutarch was rebuking the Greeks for their submissiveness to Rome. By then, Western civilization as we know it had been forged.

The Greek way of war was important for it was absorbed (as were many other factors of Greek culture) by the Romans. And what made the Roman experience decisive was that they introduced system into Greek warfare—they *systematized* it. In so doing, they made the Western way of warfare much more instrumental than the Greek and the warrior more of an instrument of the state.

First, although other armies in the past had boasted elite units like the Persian elite, and the Immortals and other societies had been devastatingly successful in war (Assyrians, Hittites), nothing matched the bureaucratic ethos of the Roman legion. At the height of Roman power, the legion gave the state a decisive advantage. The Romans normally fought in close order in waves of thin lines, avoiding the use of the "heavy battalions" such as the phalanx. The advantage of the Roman tactical system was that all available manpower could be brought into direct action along the line. When fighting untrained troops, they could not be defeated, and they were the only force in the ancient world to inflict heavy casualties on trained soldiers, even when they did suffer defeat.

By necessity, as the frontiers of its empire expanded, war became a profession rather than a civic duty. Rigorous training developed skill with weapons. Physical fitness was demanded of every soldier. Every legion was given a silver or gold eagle for its standard, which promoted a unique esprit de corps. The system functioned smoothly because of intense drilling and the use of a semiprofessional officer corps (the centurions). As the Jewish historian Josephus records, "The Romans are sure of victory . . . for their exercises are battles without bloodshed and their battles bloody exercises."[45] This was the reality of drill, which allowed the army to maneuver in close proximity to the enemy with little loss of life on its own side. A legionary could expect to serve an entire career in the ranks with minimal risk of death or serious injury.

Second, the Romans shared the Greek passion for ruthlessness. The Romans were systematic in their application of force. In eight years campaigning in Gaul, Caesar killed more than a million people in battle or retributive massacres and enslaved an equal number. In human and economic terms, his conquests were unmatched in their scale of destruction until the twentieth century. They were also ruthless in siege warfare. Josephus's description of the siege of Jerusalem in the first century C.E., with its scenes of assault and counterassault, constant artillery barrages, and endless and senseless killing, personifies, in Josiah Ober's words, "the long, complex, ugly western tradition of war . . . as a technological problem."[46]

Third, unlike Greek commanders such as Themistocles, Pyrrhus, and, of course, Alexander himself, the Romans rarely produced great generals. But then, they had no need to. Nothing could defeat a well-drilled Roman legion. The Romans could never be defeated because they never gave up (Roman warfare usually evokes the metaphor of a machine, Greek warfare a duel). The principal reason was that they drew on their own citizenry even more than the Greeks. The Roman republic was in the enviable position of being able to lose battle after battle and still field armies every year.

The man who tells us this in detail is the Greek historian Polybius, writing at the end of the first century B.C.E. Polybius accompanied his patron Scipio Aemilianus to Carthage in 146 B.C.E.. He was present when the city fell in the third and last of the Punic Wars. When Polybius reviewed the reasons for Rome's success, he concluded that its decisive advantage was its citizen army. The Roman, Polybius wrote, "had the courage to face the enemies of his country without relying on the inferior arts of the mercenary soldier." By contrast, the Carthaginians depended "on the courage of mercenaries to safeguard their prospects of freedom [whereas] the Romans rely on the bravery of their own citizens."[47]

There is no doubting the fact that Polybius's message has colored our thinking ever since. That is why, often quite unfairly, mercenaries have had such a bad press in the Western world. Indeed, it is probably fair to say that the intellectual case against them is more damning in our own culture than any other. But that said, Polybius was undoubtedly right to see that Roman superiority rested in its legionaries. Even after defeats such as Cannae (216 B.C.E.—the worst defeat suffered by Roman arms in the republican era), the state could always put another army into the field. In one account, 28 percent of the population of seventeen-year-old recruits served for sixteen years. Another estimate suggests that more than half of Roman citizens in the early second century B.C.E. served for a minimum of seven years, which, if true, would be the highest call-up of any society in history, including the twentieth century's industrialized states.[48] The Roman citizen was trained for war and war on an ever increasing scale. As Livy tells us, the Temple of Janus, whose doors were closed symbolically whenever there was peace, only closed them twice in the history of the republic.

The Romans, Livy also tells us, never lost their fascination for Carthage because they recognized they had come so close to defeat. They were amazed that a non-Roman way of war should have proved so successful. Carthage did not field citizen armies. It fielded separate mercenary armies, some tied by alliance to the city and others to a particular general. At the battle of Zama (202 B.C.E.), Hannibal's last campaign, the Carthaginian side consisted of three separate armies trained by three separate generals. But it was still the best system the Romans had ever faced, and it proved surprisingly durable. In the seventeen years the Romans fought Hannibal, his troops never mutinied once (unlike Alexander the Great's army, which threw in its hand after eleven years of nonstop campaigning). There is no doubt that the legion was the most lethal war form in the ancient world, but no one came nearer than the Carthaginians to out-performing it, and perhaps the only reason they failed was that they were less wealthy than Rome. They simply could not field enough soldiers.

What is interesting is that the Carthaginians knew the Greek way of warfare from literature and the Greek example. Hannibal dissected the campaigns of Alexander and Pyrrhus and through his father had exposure to the practical lessons gleaned from Xanthippus, a mercenary who hired himself out to Carthage and did well in the opening phase of the First Punic War. But there was nothing Hellenistic about the organization and deployment of Hannibal's army except its reliance on maneuver. It was the Carthaginian way of war (and the Carthaginian culture that it reflected) that drove the Romans to destroy the city entirely in 146 B.C.E., even after it had been reduced to the status of a third-rate power. In Fernand Braudel's words, the city's destruction represented "the final silencing of a very special voice."[49]

As Adrian Goldsworthy writes:

> If we are to learn from the past then history must first be understood on its own terms. One general point is worth emphasising, namely that each society and culture tends to have a unique view of warfare which affects how they fight and as a result how they may be beaten. This can be seen in most periods of history but the difference between the two philosophies of war has rarely been as clearly illustrated as it was during the Punic Wars.[50]

Indeed, Rome only began to decline when this situation changed, when it began to abandon discipline and drill. By the third century, the empire was recruiting from the German tribes. There is no evidence that the development was not welcomed by most citizens, who in the interim had become a remarkably civilian people, pleased to know that the Germans at least were good at fighting. By then, the state could recruit only 1 percent of its population. Cities preferred cash payments to meeting the quotas demanded of them. Powerful landowners ensured that their workers were kept out of the recruiting officers' clutches.

The extent to which the Roman army was Germanized in this period is caught by a symbolic act. The troops responsible for proclaiming Julian the Apostate Emperor in 361 C.E. were all Germans, and they elevated him in accordance with ancestral custom, raising him on a shield and acclaiming him just as they would a new chief.[51] What we witness here was a threefold change. First, on the plane of agency, the Roman citizen was no longer prepared to fight—by a law of 364 C.E., he was not even allowed to carry weapons. The state had recourse to branding its soldiers in this

period, so concerned was it to stamp out the practice of wholesale deser-
tion. The Romans would no longer defend themselves; they preferred to
contract out to German "foederati" (federated allies). By the beginning of
the fifth century, all the senior commanders had German names.

Second, the Romans had become so entrenched as civilians that they
could no longer experience war. On the subjective plane, they no longer
bred warriors or found in war an affirmation of their humanity. In part, this
change owed something to Christianity, for Christians were even more
reluctant soldiers than the pagans and were able, as did St. Augustine after
the first fall of Rome (410 C.E.), to rationalize defeat as a victory for the
city of God over the city of man.

Finally, on the intersubjective plane, the Romans could no longer tell
themselves apart from the barbarians. By the fifth century, it was difficult
to distinguish the Roman from the non-Roman because the fate of the
Roman and Germanic peoples had become inextricably interlinked. The
trouble was that as time went on, few of the Germans were trained in
Roman tactics of close order formation. The Western Empire eventually
fell when central authority collapsed. In its place emerged numerous small
estates based on a mixture of barbarian and Roman institutions, whose
prosperity depended on feudalism and, with it, a feudal way of warfare
that had little time for close order or drill.

In the East, the Western way of warfare survived for a few centuries.
The Eastern Empire was defending the Roman heritage, and the language
and vocabulary of Rome permeated its secular and religious literature and
explains the psychological aspect of its success for so long. For a few centuries, the Eastern Empire's military administration remained recognizably "Western." Emphasis was put on discipline and tactical cohesion in
battle and on well-planned logistic arrangements. Gradually, however, the
Byzantine Empire became progressively and recognizably "medieval."
The frequency of prebattle single combat in the wars with Persia in the
sixth century witnessed a return to a more heroic, less disciplined form of
warfare.[52] Success or failure began to be thought of in terms of divine
providence, not human will, another sign that the empire was becoming
medieval, not Roman. Of symbolic importance here was the siege of
Constantinople by the Avars in 626 C.E. During the siege, the patriarch
Sergius paraded about the walls, displaying an icon of the Virgin Mary
holding Jesus in her arms.[53]

The basic pattern of warfare for the next 1,000 years, at least in
Western Europe, had already been set before the empire finally collapsed
(or, as historians now prefer to claim, was transformed). Medieval warfare
was characterized by raids and skirmishes, frequently revolving around

the possession of fortified strongholds. Pitched battles were relatively rare, and the idea of the decisive battle lost its central place in the imagination. Clausewitz, the greatest analyst of the Western way of warfare, was famously dismissive of the medieval mindset: "[Medieval wars] were waged relatively quickly: not much time was wasted in the field; their aim was to punish the enemy not subdue him. When his cattle had been driven off and his castles burned, one would go home."[54]

3

The Western Way of
Warfare & the Modern Age

As a general rule, we are well advised to avoid words that end in "ism," but humanism is a word with a long ancestry. One of several difficulties is that the word has many meanings and two main ones in the dictionary. The first defines *humanism* as any system of thought concerned with human actions. This definition is associated with scientific knowledge and the extension of human thought, both of which extend the scope of human action by challenging all constraints—religious, moral, and political—that have held back human endeavor in the past. Second, humanism tends to be associated with the "rediscovery" of the Greek and Latin classics during the Renaissance. Hence the invention of the "humanities"—studies regarded as *humane,* in contrast to the formal, systemic studies in the Middle Ages in scholastic theology, canon law, and logic, which were thought to have excluded humanity and discouraged the use of scholarship that had a human interest.

The Renaissance was perhaps most important for the attitude it engendered toward the ancient world. The twelfth century had also seen a humanistic movement, but the Italian humanists of the fifteenth century found more in the classical texts than the great learning that had appealed to the medieval mind. They found a pattern of life remote in time from their own that they sought to emulate. It was not so much that this urgent and highly personal attitude toward antiquity led the humanists to rediscover much of what had been neglected or forgotten. Rather they allowed the texts of the classical world to reshape their own lives and thus entered into a *dialectical* relationship with the past.

For Aldo Schiavone, Western history involves a constant counterpoint between the ancient and modern worlds, a taking further of ancient thought. It is this act of "becoming" that makes the West "Western." Ideas persist, but material conditions change, and the discrepancy between ideas and material conditions is brought home more in the West than in any other civilization because of the great material "break" that was represented by the Fall of Rome. Other societies, especially those defined by their continuity, such as China and India, have faced no such rupture or catastrophe in their history, certainly none that have influenced them so much.[1]

In terms of ideas, the Renaissance world prided itself on reengaging the ancients in debate. In terms of *material* conditions, the humanists were aware of the remoteness of the world they evoked, as Schiavone puts it: "So much so that the impetus spurring them towards the past sprung precisely from their subtle re-elaboration of this perceived distance."[2] As a result, their admiration of the ancient world (unlike that of the Chinese for their own) was never transformed into identification or repetition. Instead, it incited them to a conversation that could be critical. It is this dual track—the continuity of ideas and discontinuity of material forces, especially technology—that established the terms of a conversation or dialogue with the past and spurred the Europeans to improve upon the Greek and Roman models they admired so much. Different material conditions, Schiavone writes, also forced a reappraisal or reinterpretation of classical ideas, and this reappraisal makes for the dynamism of Western culture: "This symmetry of abandonment and revival—virtually a contrapuntal movement between deprivation and recovery . . . has proven to be (we might say) a *style* of the Western world."[3] And that is indeed what defines the style of Western warfare.

We must read Livy, Niccolò Machiavelli insisted, if we wish to set an army in the field or conduct war successfully. Sixteenth-century military thinkers took to heart what Machiavelli wrote about reviving the concept of the legion and the importance he attached to discipline—the careful selection of recruits, the importance of extensive drill, and the hierarchical chain of command and code of military law. All were necessary to forge an army that could perform with machinelike precision.

Machiavelli's reputation as a military theorist lies primarily in his book *The Art of War* (1521), which was republished and translated several times during the sixteenth century. It puts us directly in touch with the rest of his thought. Not for him the tradition of the medieval writers who were always asking about God's intentions for man and always deriving man's nature from the answer they gave to the question. All medieval thinkers used the same method: they offered definitions and from these definitions derived conclusions about the scope of human ambition and the limits on human action. These definitions were not answers to empirical facts but questions about God's purpose. Machiavelli broke with that tradition. He wanted to know how war could make a government strong, how it could help a people win back or retain its freedom, and how it could help advance the power of a state. And in trying to answer these questions, he always appeals to the past: to the Romans (and through them the Greeks).

He can thus be said to have begun that unique discourse with the ancients. As Thomas Arnold writes, *The Art of War* is the expression of a genuine Renaissance confidence in the possibility of a perfect synthesis of ancient and modern.[4] It was the first "modern" attempt to popularize classical military thinking. And that is how the book should be read—not as an original work but as a rediscovery of the Greek and Latin classics reapplied in a new context, a new historical era. In other words, the work is a classic case of the revaluation of a tradition, one that transformed a Greco-Roman experience into a style that became distinctively "Western."

MACHIAVELLI'S LEGACY

In terms of his own world's dialogue with the past, Machiavelli had every reason to turn his attention to the demands of war, and the demands it made in turn on the societies that had recourse to it. In the fourteen years in which he served Florence as an official, his attention was largely devoted to the problems of war-making. Italy had become a battleground for the struggle for power among the great powers, whose intervention in 1494 threatened to terminate the era of independent city-states and thus displace the Italian peninsula from the center of European life.

Machiavelli's first practical or direct experience with war came in 1500, when he was appointed secretary to the two Florentine commissioners who had been assigned to oversee the mercenary army the city had engaged for the siege of Pisa. Their recalcitrance over the question of payment turned the siege, and indeed the whole campaign, into a disaster. The problem with the city-states of the age was that their citizens were reluctant to fight in person. Instead, they preferred to hire mercenaries to fight on their behalf. And although the record of the latter was not quite as disastrous as Machiavelli made out in his writings, they were essentially businessmen who showed little enthusiasm for risking their life in battle.

It was his despair of the "mercenary" style of warfare that informed Machiavelli's interest in civic history. As a humanist, he was interested in civil liberty—its gain and its loss and how it might be regained in the future. By providing insight into the scope of human action through his analysis of ancient history, he offered his readers a chance to use that insight constructively in the advancement of human freedom. And in seeing war as a subjective experience that enhanced the freedom of the warrior—and increased his self-worth—Machiavelli returned to the existential dimension of war.

Agency

Even in the early modern era, Christianity, though central to social life, is curiously absent from the discourse on warfare. When we look at the humanism of the Renaissance, John Hale tells us that its main contribution to what was written and thought about war was its imagination of a world "un-patrolled by God": to see war as an intensely human activity in a world governed by human self-determination.[5]

Success on the battlefield was no longer attributed, as it had been in the Middle Ages, to God's providence but to human ingenuity. And the dignity of human beings turned on the lessons they learned from history and how they were applied. Machiavelli was interested in history as a humanistic science. His history is not medieval or providentialist; its subject is not the emergence of universal values or the institutions of a Christian republic. And it is not post-Enlightenment either because we find no interest in historicist or determining structures and forms that dictate human actions. Machiavelli offers none of the consolations of the historicist or providentialist, only an insight into the scope of human ambition.

Subjectivity

The civic humanists can also be said to have rediscovered the democratic style that had been an enduring element of the Western way of warfare 1,500 years earlier. A democratic society, Machiavelli insisted, would allow the state to put into the field an army that was reliable even in adversity because of superior morale. In *The Art of War,* he suggested that Rome's decline began after the Punic Wars, when the republic made the mistake of switching from a citizen army to a more professional one, a process completed under the first emperors. In his interpretation of Roman history, he may have exaggerated the democratic element in the Roman constitution, but he perceived, correctly, the reason for Rome's military success and explained it in very "modern" terms. For when he wrote of Rome's triumphs, he attributed them not to mentalities but to the strength of its social and political institutions.

Morale, Machiavelli observed correctly, tends to be institutional. Soldiers who believe in the cause or fight for a community because they have a stake in the survival of both can be expected to fight much harder than others. Like many men of his generation, he was influenced by the works of the great classical authors and even those of the lesser ones such as Aelian and Vegetius. The first was a Greco-Roman writer of the second century C.E., and the second lived 200 years later. Although both lived after the demise of the citizen-soldiers of the Roman Republic, enough of the conception of the virtues of such an army persisted in their writing to inspire in their readers a disdain for mercenaries and a preference for citizen involvement in warfare. In the case of Machiavelli, we find a writer who was fascinated by how a disciplined army of heavy infantry recruited from the citizen body could be used to obtain a *decisive* result on the battlefield.

Intersubjectivity

Machiavelli's generation may have been conscious of being "modern," but what distinguished it from the generation of the eighteenth century was that the term contained only the recognition of a break with the immediate past: the Middle Ages. In rediscovering the ancient classics and in using the works of Vegetius and Aelian to discuss the tactics of their own day, they recognized the superiority of the ancient world. Indeed, the men of the Renaissance gave precedence to the ancient over all other ages. They preferred their own age to the medieval only insofar as it imitated the ancients or attempted to do so.

This looking back to the ancient world was a highly intersubjective experience, and it was liberating in one respect at least. It was based on the conviction that the classical world had been through a complete cycle of human experience and that the ancients had given an intelligent account of their experience in a corpus of classical writings. By learning from them, Renaissance man could extend his consciousness as a *moral agent*. That is why the humanists went on to create a classical curriculum that was to become the basis for Western education for the next 300 years.

But in another respect, this intersubjective dialogue was very limiting. Machiavelli notoriously ignored the importance of firearms. His ideal army is the Roman or Macedonian formation, and though artillery is discussed in his writings, its significance in battle is frequently belittled. The Swiss formations of his day could be compared, of course, to the Macedonian phalanx and the Spanish *tercio* to the Roman legion. But the introduction of firearms made them very different. And yet it was this difference that Machiavelli refused to admit. His attempt to overcome the challenge of artillery is revealing: "In approaching the enemy infantry can with greater ease escape the discharge of artillery. In antiquity they could escape the rush of elephants and of scythed chariots and of other strange weapons that the Roman infantry had to oppose. Against them they always found a remedy and so much the more easily they would have found one against artillery."[6] In the end, Machiavelli could not accept that firearms were a significant military innovation, for doing so would have required him to accept that his own age was superior to the ancient and that he would not concede. Ultimately, his own intersubjective dialogue with the past led nowhere.

Jump 200 years into the late modern era, and we find a different attitude altogether. In his *Essay on the History of Civil Society,* Adam Ferguson called Britain and Rome "the great legislators among nations." But the Romans, he insisted, had been unable to transcend their own foundations and create a society superior to the Greek city-state. They had merely perfected their own system, not transcended their own reality. They had not changed or even seen the need to. The Romans, Ferguson added "could ill be persuaded that a time might come when refined and intelligent nations would make the art of war to consist in a few technical forms; that citizens and soldiers might come to be distinguished as much as women and men; that the citizen would become possessed of a property which he would not be able or be required to defend."[7]

Hegel—the other great writer on civil society (though he differed from Ferguson on many of its aspects)—was also critical of Rome and the ancient world in general. He did believe that the Romans had put forward a more developed concept of the rights of the private citizen in their legal codes and thus involved citizen and state in a true community of values, and he also believed that they had originated a sense of ethical community, but he criticized them for not being able to develop it. In time, Rome came to manifest the worst excesses of private selfishness.

Hegel's contemporary, Clausewitz, also believed that the citizen's willingness to defend the community could be taken as a sign of a major break with the past, an enhancement of what Hegel called "the ethical health" of the nation. Clausewitz felt confident enough to conclude that in terms of war-making, "the history of antiquity is without doubt the most useless. . . . We are in no position to . . . apply [it] to the wholly different means we use today."[8] By which he meant that in material terms, the modern age had left the premodern world far behind. But it had not transcended the classical *spirit* of war or the conception of the military art that the Greeks and Romans had pioneered.

THE LATE MODERN ERA AND THE RECOVERY OF NERVE

In discussing the Western way of warfare in the modern era, it is important to begin with the first of three defining historical processes that forged the modern consciousness as we understand it today. What distinguished the modern way of warfare was the way that Western societies reconceptualized war, and that owed much in turn to the Industrial and French Revolutions as well as the Enlightenment. It remained definitively Western (i.e., it continued to draw its inspiration from the Greeks), and it did so because it was intensely humanistic, although a modern understanding of humanism now prevailed.

To begin with, the Enlightenment put a high premium on *human agency*. The great Enlightenment thinkers saw history as a conflict between the rival forces of superstition and reason. Each era had its dominant style, with either reason or superstition in the ascendant. Few periods were without a mixture of both, however, a fact that led Immanuel Kant to conclude that though his own age was the age of Enlightenment, it was not an enlightened age. This dualistic view of history, rather than the idea of progress, characterized the mind of the Enlightenment. But the theory of progress was important because it suggested that the alternation between ages was not inescapable and that humanity could break out of the historical cycles that Machiavelli and his generation had taken for granted. It was part of the Enlightenment's *humane* vision. Of course, scientific progress—the change in material circumstances visible even to the humanists of the sixteenth century—gave the lie to an unchanging historical cycle. As Peter Gay writes, the Enlightenment philosophers, unlike the thinkers of the Renaissance, used science "to control their classicism by establishing the superiority of their own . . . age . . . and to keep their respect for their ancestors within proper bounds."[9]

The Enlightenment also changed the way the West thought about the mind. The Greeks had brought philosophy and logic to bear on the art of war for the first time, whereas the eighteenth century brought a scientific method. The Enlightenment tried to give empirical and scientific answers to the old philosophical problems and thus to bring every human activity within the range of science. Isaac Newton had explained the material world by means of a relatively few fundamental laws. The philosophers of the eighteenth century set out to apply the same methods and principles to the science of the mind.[10]

Space, time, mass, force, and momentum, the terms of mechanics, took the place of final causes, divine purpose, and other metaphysical principles such as Machiavelli's *fortuna* (chance). In explaining the scientific laws that govern the human world, the philosophers set out to measure the possibilities, not the limits, of human action. Theirs was a very different humanism from that of Machiavelli, who had met the eighteenth century halfway in arguing that ruthless energy could wrest half of existence from Providence but who had also continued to insist that the other half belonged to chance. This change could be taken as a sign of what the historian Peter Gay calls "the recovery of nerve," one of the signs of which was a "growing willingness to take risks."[11]

If the Enlightenment made warriors, like the society they served, true moral agents, it also made them more conscious of their humanity in the sense of being more attuned to what they might yet "become." Nineteenth-century warriors were more existential than the warriors of the past in one critical respect that owed much to that second historical process: the Industrial Revolution. For warriors were now concerned not only with the consequences of their actions but with the acting selves that the action expressed. Clausewitz admits as much, although he restricts his observations largely to the instrumental nature of war in claiming that conflict in his own day had become "more" like war itself in allowing war to realize its own possibilities or outer limits. Hegel had recognized that in reaching these limits, war was becoming increasingly more destructive, as could be seen from the French revolutionary wars. But both men also claimed that the destruction was positive at the same time, that these tragic upheavals were advances in human religious and political self-understanding. For Clausewitz, war was more destructive and historically significant at the same time because it was now able to realize "all its severe consequences." Even in Napoleon's bid for personal glory, Hegel claimed to see a powerful modern drive to remold the political world in accordance with the principles of free, rational self-determination.

The critical process that made both the state and individual warriors aware of their own limitless ambition, their own *subjectivity,* was the Industrial Revolution. It was important that the Enlightenment prepared the way for it by introducing mechanistic thinking into Western thought. Julien La Mettrie conceived of the true philosopher as an "engineer"; Denis Diderot compared social life to a great factory.[12] Once industrial power could be harnessed, people saw ways of struggling against the givens of human nature that had previously defined their humanity. They became human now not by remaining in harmony with nature but by challenging the natural order.

Writing in the 1850s, Karl Marx had asked whether the view of nature and social relations on which the Greek imagination and hence mythology had been based was possible in the age of locomotives and electrical telegraphs. "What chance has Vulcan against Roberts and Co., Jupiter against the lightning-rod," he asked in the *Grundrisse* (1857): "all mythology overcomes and dominates and shapes the forces of nature in the imagination and by the imagination; it therefore vanishes with the advent of real mastery over them." Marx was attempting to explain why genuine epic poetry could not survive in the age of gunpowder; he was writing of the demystifying capacities of the new forces of production.

In fact, as he himself later recognized, far from killing off myths, modern inventions embodied as well as multiplied them. Several times in *Das Kapital* (1867), he gave the larger modern machines the epithet "cyclopean." Technological progress became a myth in its own right; and it gave war an even greater *heroic* quality than it had enjoyed before in the Western imagination. For if the Greeks had edged God out of history, modern technology made his presence largely obsolete. The Industrial Revolution conferred on human beings (or so it appeared at the time) two traditional attributes of the Almighty: omnipotence and omniscience (the view of modern culture as scientific—the science of human beings—and the belief that there was nothing beyond the grasp of reason). Human self-worth increased accordingly. For now human beings thought of themselves through the *application of technology* as the source of their own actions. For the modern humanist, humanity did not receive its norms or laws either from the nature of things (as had been claimed by Aristotle) or from God (as had been claimed by the church), but established them itself on the basis of reason and will.

If human beings acknowledge their limits, they are founded on an awareness of their necessity and on human willingness to impose them on themselves. A humanistic affirmation of humanity's distinctive value was defined as the Promethean capacity to be the subject of one's own being. The conditions required for the individual to develop are indeed those of modernity, for at bottom they amount to postulating human beings as "a distinctive value" whose main discourse is not with God but with each other.

Finally, what made modern humanism "modern" owed much not only to the Enlightenment and the Industrial Revolution; it also owed a debt, perhaps a decisive one, to the French Revolution as well. For it was on that great upheaval and the way in which it helped transform a state into a nation that modern *intersubjectivity* was grounded. "The nation is prior to everything," Emmanuel Sieyes thundered. Once the nation state came into being, it became possible to put larger armies in the field, as well as armies that were better motivated and led.

It also became possible for the first time to extend the warrior ethos to the entire nation, not merely a warrior class. It became possible to extend the existential element far beyond the narrow confines of the city-state of fifth-century Athens to the nation-states of nineteenth-century Europe. This shift can be found in the writings of the greatest phenomenologist of war, Clausewitz, and it can also be found in the work of Hegel, the first philosopher since Aristotle to discuss war at length.

It is true that Clausewitz does mention the existential dimension of war in discussing the warrior as a social type. "For as long as they practise [war] soldiers will think of themselves as a guild in which regulations, laws and customs, the spirit of war [are] given pride and place." And he admits that even the citizen-soldiers of the modern age once deployed in the field will see the business of war as distinctive from civilian life. But Clausewitz sees the citizen-soldier that had emerged in the course of the French revolutionary and Napoleonic wars as a new type of soldier and war in his own era as different in character from that of the past because of the "national" element. So although he tells us that war still depends on certain moral qualities, such as courage and endurance, the courage a state can mobilize depends much on the nature of the state—hence the importance of nationalism and nation-states fighting wars. Clausewitz was the first writer to recognize that the existential elements of war—the reason that warriors are prepared to die (as opposed to kill)—were about to become subsets of a national psyche.

Clausewitz's contemporary Hegel was also convinced that the national element had affirmed the existential dimension of war and had given the West a superiority it had won instrumentally by developing, indeed pioneering a new political model: the modern state. War, he contended, was not a contingent factor of history; it was part of the human condition. In distinguishing between the general concept of war and the concrete wars of his own day, he took his readers into the phenomenological realm, and what we find there is a very clear understanding that although the concrete deals in causes and is largely instrumental, war as a historical concept is largely existential.

Indeed, Hegel is quick to tell us that war cannot be centered on utilitarian motives alone, such as the defense of life or property, for this would lead to an absurd situation. It would be impossible to demand that soldiers sacrifice both their property and their lives and at the same time declare that war is waged to preserve them. If we ask why soldiers are willing to put their lives at risk, we must look at why they find it a necessary feature of their general humanity. Thus Hegel concluded that war will only come to an end when human beings no longer have need of it to express their humanity, when no one will esteem them as warriors, and thus they will no longer esteem themselves.[13]

Throughout his life, Hegel put an emphasis not only on the existential nature of war but on the wider existential nature of life and the constant fight for recognition. Human beings are not animals, for though they too fight for self-preservation, they rise above their nature by showing a willingness to risk their lives for a nonmaterial reward such as personal honor. What distinguishes humans from nonhumans is that the former are not programmed to act by instinctual behavior. They are prepared to die for honor or a flag. The warrior who dies for honor is a moral agent because honor is something that lies beyond the instinctive realm of self-preservation. Soldiers live in the recognition of their fellow citizens, in the "soldier's tale" told of their lives after their death. And in warrior societies, they even live in the esteem in which they are held by their enemies.

War separates into two those human beings who risk all and those who fear for their lives. Both may be the same genetically, but their behavior is different, and it is socially produced. In *The Republic,* Plato showed how the warriors' role in the polis corresponds to the position of the spirit within the human soul. By then Plato's warriors, of course, were no longer the citizen-soldiers who fought the Persians but auxiliaries or "semiguardians," professionals who were trained to serve the state. What their fellow citizens recognized in their courage was the autonomy of goodness from personal interest—including self-preservation. They esteemed them and recognized their claim to precedence.

In contemporary soldiers, Hegel too saw members of a class who derived their self-esteem from the service they provided society. It is only their willingness to die that allows the state to function. In the nation-state, courage was "the act not of this particular person but of a member of a whole." Warriors were now people who realized the nature of their own freedom through courage, and their courage was manifest in their willingness to hazard their lives, not for the state or a master or a community but for a universal value: freedom. "Freedom dies for fear of dying" is one of Hegel's most telling maxims.

And he was adamant in his belief that the existential dimension of war could survive increased firepower on the battlefield, the butchery that war displayed signs of becoming in the bloodiest battles of the Napoleonic wars like Borodino (1812) and Waterloo (1815). As firepower became more intense, of course, death became more impersonal. It was no longer a matter of hand-to-hand fighting. But for Hegel, the anonymous death of soldiers on the modern battlefield was the highest sacrifice that had been demanded of any soldier in history precisely because they became part of the mass. In the tomb of the unknown warrior, he would have seen—had he survived into the next century—the apotheosis of the Western way of war.

That proposition was endorsed by Clausewitz, who had firsthand experience of the Napoleonic wars: "Very few of the new manifestations in war can be ascribed to new inventions . . . or new departures and ideas. They result mainly from the transformation of society and new social conditions."[14] Technology had not yet advanced enough in Clausewitz's day to instrumentalize war entirely. Hence his insistence that the individual foot soldier was the most *independent* of the weapons, whereas the artillery was the most dependent.[15] What made the foot soldier still supreme was the intersubjective relationship with the enemy through the activity of the *zoon politikon*.

Clausewitz was subsequently criticized for his insufficient regard for technology (he died in 1831 apparently unaware, like Adam Smith, that the Industrial Revolution had taken place). But for his own generation, war was not yet the technical phenomenon it was soon to become. Neither Clausewitz nor his contemporaries had any inkling of the technical power that would overwhelm human beings and transform the soldier into purely an instrument of state. They had no intimation of the extent to which total war would subvert individual subjectivity and challenge the warrior ethos.

Writing when he did, Clausewitz was undoubtedly right to attach so much attention in his writings to the political dimension of war and what it made possible: greater discipline under fire. In a celebrated passage, he claimed that "the French revolutionaries . . . sent their soldiers into the field and drove their generals into battle."[16] Such soldiers, fired with nationalist fervor or revolutionary zeal (the former has always been more in evidence than the latter in the last 200 years) could be employed in more imaginative ways on the battlefield. They could also be "used up" as their commanders saw fit. This development was not without terrible cost— the rise of "people's wars": "The heart and the convictions of the nation . . . are an enormous factor in the product of the powers of the state, war and fighting."[17] When Clausewitz penned these words, he could have had no inkling that within fifty years, beginning with the American Civil War, modern warfare would begin to test the resolve not only of armies in the field but of entire societies locked in battle. In the clash between nations, victory and defeat would soon become no longer technical matters to be decided by opposing forces but final conclusions about the viability of a people and its way of life.

THE END OF THE WESTERN WAY OF WARFARE?

Modern warfare reached its climax in the last month of World War II, when the United States dropped the first atomic bombs on Japan. What accounted for the public impact of the two bombing raids was the knowledge that the bomb would be improved and that a bigger and better version would be built. If the A-bomb had been dropped on New York in 1945, it would have destroyed only a few blocks of Manhattan. The first thermonuclear bomb, by comparison, would have taken out all five boroughs of greater New York City.

By the 1950s the Western way of warfare seemed to have reached an endgame. The father of containment, George Kennan, saw the nuclear standoff as an ultimate betrayal of humanism, a lack of faith in the human ability to resolve political dilemmas through reason. What disturbed him most about nuclear weapons was not that they made a nonsense of the existential dimension of war but that they could not be reconciled with the instrumental use of force either, with a political purpose directed to shape rather than destroy human life: "They reach backwards beyond the frontiers of Western civilisation to the concepts of warfare which were once familiar to the Asiatic hordes." Nuclear weapons had become a negation of the principle of life. In making war "life denying," they also made it "un-Western."[18]

Is the Western way of warfare, therefore, with its origins in the Greek conception of war, as outdated as the material conditions that inspired it? Many experts are of that opinion. Western warfare, Victor Hanson writes, started with the classical Greeks, but its very commitment to individual expression created a dynamic that almost led to the destruction of Western civilization in two world wars. The tens of millions killed in the twentieth century must be seen in some sense both as the end and as a *logical* culmination of the ferocious military tradition of the Greeks. Even earlier, Hanson had deplored the fact that the West had inherited only the ideal of the battle in heroic terms but had detached it from real fighting and ignored its real lessons. With the nuclear age, he asks, surely the West must acknowledge the end of the Western way of warfare?[19]

In an introduction to Hanson's book, John Keegan agrees that the Western way of war conceived by the Greeks as trial by combat "led their descendants into the pit of the holocaust."[20] In his own, rightly acclaimed *History of Warfare,* he develops this point at greater length. The Western way of war started with the Greeks and was irresistible against others, but against itself, against other Western nations, it produced the internecine war of 1914, which sowed the seeds for even greater destruction in World War II, a struggle that, in turn, led to the development of the atomic bomb. And what was that but "the logical culmination of the technological trend in the Western way of warfare and the ultimate denial of the proposition that war was—or ought to be—the continuation of politics by other means"?[21] Josiah Ober also agrees, finding in the way that Alexander took Tyre and the Romans Jerusalem in 70 C.E. "a strategic, professional, technological tradition . . . [in which] the seeds were sown of wars that exterminated human cultures and would come to threaten the extinction of the human race."[22]

It is plausible to see the end of the Western way of war in these terms if we talk about logic, but that too is a problem. For it is wrong to find the end of anything in its origins. The Western way as it had evolved by 1945 was not implicit in Greek practice. A genealogist does not go back in time to demonstrate how the past exists in the present or how it animates it, nor is it his or her task to map the destiny of a people. The Western way of war has been shaped by many factors, including contingent ones, which is why we cannot derive the atomic bomb from the "logic" of Greek warfare. "Only a metaphysician would seek its soul in the distant ideality of origin," Michel Foucault writes in his seminal essay on the genealogical method.[23]

The Western way of warfare evolved through dialogue with the past, but it was shaped and reshaped by different material conditions. What was constant was its humanism, but that in turn was shaped by history—premodern humanism is different from modern humanism, and postmodern humanism is different again from both. Today the West has tried to humanize war more than ever to make its practice consistent with our new moral codes. As one of Don DeLillo's characters says in his novel *End Zone,* "Nagasaki was an embarrassment to the art of war. I think what will happen in the not too distant future is that we will have humane wars."[24]

Critics of the Western way of warfare are on stronger ground when they see how it has abandoned the existential dimension. The Greeks offered warriors the realization of their own humanity. They found in war a master text by which they came to know themselves better. It defined their humanity by distinguishing a free man from a slave, a man from a woman, and a Greek from a barbarian. It is this idea of war that now appears obsolete in the Western world.

Martin van Creveld, for one, questions whether war can mean anything for Western soldiers that is existential or, in his words, *expressive* of their humanity. The Western way of warfare has become almost entirely instrumental. It is determined almost entirely by what it takes to "kill" members of the opposing side. By contrast, non-Western strategies ask a very different question: What does it take to persuade soldiers to die for their beliefs? Like the Greeks, they still find war life affirming. Clearly, the West no longer does. War no longer defines the "self," and therefore Westerners cannot kill others and retain their *self*-respect at the same time.

Why, asks van Creveld, are Western soldiers unwilling to die for their beliefs? And the answer he comes up with lies at the very heart of the Western way of war: the relationship between ends and means. Why should one lay down one's life for a state interest or political objective, as opposed to one's community and its way of life? We may say that soldiers are not just killed but "wasted." In our postmodern world, death is life-denying in every sense of the word. Others, however, still seem prepared to die for their communities or communal beliefs or for the god of the tribe. For the Hizbollah militiaman, war is life affirming in every respect. It provides the most intense experience life offers.

Once this was true of the West. As Ernst Junger wrote (quoting Nietzsche), it is not the good cause that hallows war, but the good war that hallows the cause. The Great War, he added, was the last moment in Western history in which, beyond the immediate instrumental aims of the belligerents, soldiers were able to discover themselves: "Deep under the areas where the dialectics of war are meaningful the German met with a superior force: he encountered himself."[25] Is it possible to get the "enthusiasm" back into the killing process? Is it possible to motivate soldiers in a way that would make them willing to die as they did in the past? Van Creveld doubts it. It is no longer possible, he maintains, for Western armies to fight war in a way that allows individual soldiers to keep their self-respect as human beings, for they are no longer fighting for themselves.[26]

In part, Westerners have tried to rectify this by hoping that humanitarian war reflects our wider humanity or sense of collective selfhood— the "we" principle extended further to include even our enemies. But the new humanism this attitude entails is difficult to square with success on the battlefield when the latter means incurring casualties at rates incommensurate with humanizing war for our own soldiers or when it means taking the lives of our enemies in large numbers. And it is difficult to fight wars with conviction when that means killing large numbers of people. Our soldiers are burdened with the terrible weight of bad conscience; they have become self-conscious; they are haunted by what philosopher Paul Ricoeur calls "the hermeneutics of suspicion."

4

The Death of the
Warrior Tradition & the
American Way of Warfare

For better or worse the United States has seized the future of
war and for a time the future of humanity.
—George Friedman, *The Future of War*

Writing in 1973, the historian Russell Weighey claimed that the U.S. way of warfare was merely an offshoot of the "European" and that U.S. strategic thinking was "a branch of European strategic thought."[1] It is no longer. We now recognize, Edward Luttwak writes, that with its ritualized nuclear threats and mostly symbolic maneuvers, the Cold War concealed the de-bellicization of the Europeans. War was once a core activity of European societies, but the Europeans themselves now watch from afar the wars of others.[2]

We can now see why Kant was right. War, he tells us, is natural; peace is not. Peace can only be made practical if so-called practical men recognize that what is natural is not actually in their self-interest. What made Kant's ideas so much more realistic than many of the other peace manifestos of the past was his instinctual bias for dealing in institutions, not mentalities. He sees intuitively that without social change, peace will be unobtainable. He calls for a republican constitution, by which he means a government of law, responsible to its citizens through representative institutions. Kant's ideal state is not aristocratic because in aristocratic societies the rulers lose nothing "of their banquets, hunts, chateaux, court entertainments," even in wartime. Indeed, war is "a kind of pleasure policy" providing the most stunning entertainment of all. All this has changed dramatically. The aristocracy whose values, if not its members, dominated Europe up to World War II has vanished, leaving only a memory of the warrior tradition behind. The meritocrats who run the European Union (its political class) may be less accountable than Kant would have liked, but they derive neither profit nor status from war or the use of force. Instead, they find it increasingly distasteful.[3]

But if Europe is effectively out of the war business, the United States is not. And the Americans practice war in a particular way that is beyond both Europe's capabilities and even its technological understanding. If the U.S. way of war can no longer be seen as a branch of European strategic thought, can it still be considered "Western"? As it happens, most features of the U.S. way are still familiar, as we would expect of a country whose origins are Western. The Greek model still persists. War is still a system of thought that demands discipline, initiative, and ingenuity on the part of soldiers at every level. It is still a science accessible to human reason. It still remains a democratic experience now that the Americans fight humanitarian wars. But although the U.S. style conforms to aspects of the Western model, it is vitally different in two key respects. Its emphasis on technology is ultimately not compatible with Western humanism; it is leading us into a very different, posthuman world. And its attempt to make war more humane for its own soldiers and the viewers back home is making it increasingly vulnerable to the kind of asymmetric strategies we saw demonstrated in the World Trade Center attack on September 11, 2001. That too is pushing it down a posthuman road—it has embarked on a journey that it will probably walk alone.

In short, if the instrumental dimension of the U.S. way of warfare is still Western, the existential dimension no longer obtains. War has become almost entirely an instrument for solving problems and managing crises or risks. Instrumental war is certainly more civilized in one respect. Based as it is on instrumental reason, it tends to be less emotive and more "reasonable." But to use a phrase of Max Weber's, the U.S. military has created its own "iron cage." In grounding war on a purely instrumental understanding of what is "necessary" and basing what is necessary on humanitarianism, the United States is finding itself vulnerable as never before in its history. For the first time, its humanism is not warlike but warless. It is now self-defeating.

POSTMODERN HUMANISM AND WAR

Does the West "do" war any longer? "We are talking about the use of military force—but we are not talking about war," U.S. secretary of state Madeleine Albright told reporters in 1998 after the military strikes against

Iraq, one of a series in the Clinton years to contain the most tenacious adversary of the United States.[4] On average, President Bill Clinton fired a cruise missile every three days of his presidency. U.S. and British pilots flew 200,000 air sorties between 1991 and 2001. Cruise missiles and air strikes are the preferred means for societies who no longer find it easy to live with war as a concept. Unfortunately, there are serious problems with grounding the "necessity" of military action purely on instrumental principles. Let me look at them through the prism I have employed so far in this book.

Agency

Are Western soldiers still willing to die, or are the American people still willing to let them? U.S. soldiers are humanitarian enough to kill on behalf of an oppressed group, but they are not prepared to die for its members. Is the act of dying considered a denial of agency?

In Somalia and Lebanon, U.S. soldiers suffered particularly heavy casualties in the course of a single day: 241 marines were killed in a car bomb in Beirut in 1983 (the largest single loss of life in a day sustained by the U.S. Army since the Korean War); eighteen rangers were killed in a firefight in Mogadishu ten years later. On both occasions, the United States withdrew its forces. The list does not end there. After nineteen deaths in a truck bomb at Khobar Towers in Dharan, Saudi Arabia, the United States constructed another military base deep in the Saudi desert, far away from civilian centers. It was another retreat of a kind.

Some research suggests that the body bag syndrome is exaggerated. Although American public opinion does not like incurring casualties, it does not insist either on bloodless wars. In Kosovo, the American people stood by as their country applied the decisive use of force. The air war may not have won the campaign, but it represented an enormous commitment of military power. To defeat the Serbs in Kosovo, the United States deployed two-thirds as many planes as it would now envisage using in another war against Iraq and flew one-third as many sorties as it did in Desert Storm. When governments deploy force decisively, they indicate that operations are important and by implication suggest that a military reverse might actually matter.[5]

It seems to me that such arguments, though well taken, miss the point on a number of counts. First, "zero tolerance" is real enough in the minds of those who advise policymakers, including the military. Whether the perception of casualty aversion is accurate or not, it seems to shape current U.S. military planning as well as long-term force development. In a society that is structured around the avoidance of risks in all walks of life, the military will also be encouraged to see risk aversion as its principal mission. "Force protection has become the air force's highest priority," writes Brigadier General Richard Coleman, the director of U.S. Air Force (USAF) security forces, and "conducting that mission is now as important as projecting our combat power."[6]

Second, many of the West's adversaries are fully aware that the societies they may have to fight are risk averse. Adversaries of the United States are watching it closely. Its withdrawal from Somalia was a disaster for its standing in the Islamic world, where a willingness to die for one's belief tends to be seen as a sign of moral conviction. Interviewed on ABC News, the terrorist leader Osama bin Laden made the following observation: "We have seen in the last decade the decline of the American government and the weakness of the American soldier who is ready to wage cold wars and unprepared to fight long wars. This was proven in Beirut when the Marines fled after two explosions. It also proves they can run in less than 24 hours and that was also repeated in Somalia."[7] A few years later, he drove home the point by unleashing an attack on New York.

Bin Laden's dismissive attitude was shared by other political factions in the Middle East. A few years earlier, the commander of Iran's Revolutionary Guard told a CNN anchorman that he expected the Americans to balk not only at war-related deaths but at soldiers taken prisoner in battle. If Iran were invaded, he expected to take 20,000 U.S. prisoners, but he also thought that Washington would be at the negotiating table after losing only 1,000.[8] Islamic fundamentalists (or, for that matter, anyone else) can hardly be blamed for arriving at that opinion when our unqualified respect for individual life makes it increasingly difficult to hazard life in battle. What else are they to conclude when they see the United States flying 500 sorties in 1995 (about one-third of the British sorties flown during the entire Kosovo conflict) to rescue one downed air pilot, Captain Scot O'Grady?

Concern for excessive force protection is expressed by U.S. allies as well. Many are worried that the low tolerance of casualties has become the benchmark for expectation of success in war. They are critical of the Pentagon's enthusiasm for "disengaged conflict"—the ability to use standoff weapons where possible to avoid committing ground troops. And when troops are deployed on the ground, the situation is often no better. Conservative operation procedures created problems at senior North Atlantic Treaty Organization (NATO) levels when U.S. troops were sent to Bosnia. Once they were safely ensconced in their base camps, they became "ninja turtles" in the eyes of the locals. Some described them as "prisoners of peace," locked away like prisoners of war (POWs) behind the safety of their barbed-wire fences.[9] In Somalia, the insistence of the Americans on wearing their helmets and body armor on patrol (they were called "human tanks" by the locals) and their reluctance to mount street patrols without combat support from helicopter gunships overhead produced a fatal combination. They both inspired fear and appeared to be fearful, a paradox that was an important factor in provoking a hostile response on the part of the local population.

Zero tolerance of casualties may be an example of our respect for human life, but it is also a reflection of something more profound and disturbing, our belief that a life lost is a waste. Hence the popular euphemism for killing is not "taking" life but "wasting" it. One of the principal reasons we cannot justify casualties any longer is that we can no longer make sense of the waste of life in the complex situations that demand the use of force. Our soldiers have lost the sense of tragedy that they inherited from the Greeks and that was such a central feature of Western humanism.

"It was a watershed," one State Department official observed of the Somalia fiasco, a watershed for the naive belief "that good, decent, innocent people were being opposed by evil, thuggish leaders." Like many of the soldiers sent to Somalia, this particular official could not comprehend a society in which people claimed to want peace but were not prepared to share it with other clans to attain it. "People in these countries—Bosnia is a more recent example—don't want peace. They want victory. They want power. . . . Somalia was the experience that taught us that people in these places bear much of the responsibility for things being the way they are. The hatred and the killing continues because they want it to. Because they don't want peace enough to stop it."[10] It is an opinion that reflects an idea of history defined in starkly etched colors and contrasts, rather than history's true color: gray.

Only our sense of the tragic tells us that solutions cannot always be found in life because no resolution is ever final and few causes are ever totally just. Tragedy usually involves not the clash of good versus bad but two half-truths—the fact that they are half true is what makes life tragic.

But then the United States is no longer in touch with tragedy as a way of understanding life. Some years ago, military historian Williamson Murray took an informal poll of sixty-five students in his military history courses in three different universities and found that only five had been exposed in high school or college to a single Greek tragedy. The academic world, he warns, is producing a generation of Americans who are incapable of understanding the nature of the tragic through the medium of books. One day they may find themselves disadvantaged when they are fighting people beyond their comprehension.[11]

Being ignorant of the tragic is not a problem that confronted the Greeks. The great virtue of reading Euripides' Trojan War plays (the most savage indictment of the cruelty of war to be found anywhere in the Western canon) is that problems are never resolved by scholarly argument. Precisely because Greek tragedies grew out of a chaotic world in which violence was often random and ever present, what they had to say about it should still be of interest to us. The great tragedies convey the image of a radically plural world in which there is no ultimate principle and no ultimate judge to reconcile all differences. Differences have to resolve themselves.

The American philosopher Richard Rorty describes himself as "a tragic liberal" for that reason.[12] Alisdair MacIntyre, though eschewing that description himself, comes up with a similar diagnosis. He agrees with Rorty that Westerners have lost the point of reference that allows us to judge what is tragic; that is why the work of Sophocles and Euripides is so vital, for the world they portray has no common reference point either. That life could be the site of an agon between opposing sides, each believing itself to be justified, was obvious to both playwrights. It sufficed that religion gave little explicit instruction on how to overcome such conflicts, let alone resolve them, but instead made apparent that conflict was a normal part of life. One relied on one's own arguments (not the truth) and continued the fight as long as one's argument was coherent. The force of that logic on the battlefield is what gave war its humanistic coloring.[13]

Is the problem the medium rather than the message? In a world in which the cinema to a very large extent determines our perception of the world, the sense of the tragic is largely absent. Most Hollywood fare offered on our cinema and TV screens is not in itself necessarily self-limiting, but its life-enhancing themes, usually describing triumph over adversity, do not always describe the world as it is.

The issue, writes Mark Le Fanu, hinges on the notion of seriousness and taking it seriously: "A measure of bleakness is part of the human condition and it used to be possible to reflect this in art."[14] It seems impossible to do so any longer. If we take a defining event—the war in Bosnia, which claimed over 250,000 lives in the first half of the 1990s—the war passed almost without comment in Hollywood. Those films that did emerge from the conflict had an energy and inventiveness that put them in a different league. But how many were seen in the West? Emir Kusturica's diptych about the war, *Underground* (1995) and *Black Cat, White Cat* (1998), found few takers at the box office in the West. And filmmakers would have had to have been astute indeed to catch the other great films about the war: Goran Paskaljevic's *The Powder Keg;* Srdjan Dragojevic's

Pretty Village, Pretty Flame; Stole Popov's *Gypsy Magic;* and, most memorably, Ademir Kenovic's melancholy masterpiece, *The Perfect Circle.* All of them in their different ways were compelling works of art, imbued with a concept of tragedy that would have helped decode the conflict for a Western audience, had there been one of any significant size.

Without a sense of the tragic, it is difficult to maintain a humanistic understanding of war or, for that matter, for soldiers to see themselves as warriors. Toward the end of his life, Walter Kaufman, one of the great twentieth-century commentators on tragedy, came to the conclusion that in a century that was irredeemably tragic, tragedy had replaced philosophy as the only way of understanding history. "Philosophy now seems like a dream that Plato dreamed and made a lot of others share. . . . Plato tried to tell us that the tragic poets offered disillusions, images of images, while he would show us true reality. Now we know to our sorrow that philosophy as he envisaged it was an illusion, while the tragic poets show us the reality of life."[15] Tragedy, he concluded, was at the heart of modern humanism, for it entailed a serious, committed concern for one's fellow beings and an appreciation of the fallibility of the human condition.

Kaufman himself did not merely look at tragedy as a form of art. In a book published in 1968, he identified the U.S. involvement in Vietnam as "tragic in the most exacting sense." What was tragic for him was that the suffering it produced was not merely incidental. The United States pursued the lofty purpose of defending freedom but did so with a staggering brutality. The avowedly good cause (and he had no doubt that the United States represented the forces of good and North Vietnam the forces of repression) stood in stark contrast to a war in which success was defined by "body counts" (the calculation of the number of enemies killed). The escalating interplay between power and guilt added to its tragic characteristics. Kaufman ended with this plea: "When we speak of events as tragedies, we use the word figuratively; but sometimes this is not merely legitimate but illuminating; it sharpens our perception and permits us to see what, without the benefit of literary insight, we might overlook. Not only philosophers could learn much from the tragic poets."[16] The last sentence may sound didactic, but it reflected Kaufman's belief in the contemporary and continuing relevance of tragedy in modern life.

The extent to which the West has turned its back on its own tragic heritage is confirmation perhaps that its humanism now runs skin deep. It is, of course, not a specifically American problem. It is inherent in all power, and perhaps the United States, more powerful now than ever before, merely reflects that fact more than any other country. Power, after all, is often associated with the privilege of not having to learn. MacIntyre quotes the

Australian John Anderson, who urges us "not to ask of the social institution: 'what end or purpose does it serve?' but rather, 'of what conflicts is it the scene?'"[17] As we have seen, it was the Greeks' insight—one at the heart of the humanistic approach to war—that it is through conflict and sometimes only through conflict that warriors learn what their own ends and purposes are. It is that understanding that makes them true moral agents.

Subjectivity

Not only are Western societies unwilling to demand too much of their own soldiers, but also they are increasingly reluctant to appear insensitive to human suffering. Instead, they are expected to experience humanity in both senses of the word. During the Kosovo war, for example, the director of information strategy and news of the British Ministry of Defence, when asked to name the ministry's greatest success, had no hesitation. Every time the alliance was criticized for collateral damage, accidental attacks on refugee convoys, and later the death of civilians incurred in raids on Belgrade, it was able "to get the message back on line"—to the plight of refugees on whose behalf they were at war with Slobodan Milosevic. They were able to concentrate public opinion on the humanitarian disaster that was unfolding on the ground.[18] NATO remained "on message" until the end of the crisis. As the refugees were seen streaming across the frontier to be penned in overcrowded refugee camps, the West was able to wrap its actions in a humanitarian discourse.

But that is the problem. The humanity of our soldiers has to be *seen* on television if the media themselves are not to become asymmetric assets. And today the media scrutiny of war is unprecedented and exerts a strong influence on the way Western democracies fight. Learning from its experience in Vietnam, the United States imposed strict controls on the mass media. Few gruesome pictures were shown during the Gulf War. Of the 1,104 Desert Storm photographs that appeared in the nation's three major news magazines, only thirty-eight showed actual combat, whereas 249 were catalog-style photographs of military hardware.[19] In the end, General Colin Powell terminated combat operations before they fulfilled the objective of destroying Iraq's elite Republican Guard. The media had obtained footage of carnage on the road to Basra, which they were quick to name emotively "the highway of death."[20] They also began running stories of pilots who had expressed misgivings about shooting up Iraqi troops who were powerless to defend themselves.

Real-time broadcasting was also a problem in Somalia. In February 1995, when the U.S. Marines briefly returned, they could have used nonlethal weapons such as sticky foam to enhance barbed wire and other barriers. But they were deterred from doing so, even though the weapons were not lethal, because of their fear of Somali youths getting stuck and then injuring themselves struggling to break free. As one marine officer put it at the time: "If the sticky foam had been used to cover unattended portions of barbed wire during the night, in the morning we would have found a dozen Somali youths stuck to the wire, entangled in a bloody trap. Removing the trespassers from the wire would be difficult and not play well on CNN." Of course, the West is not entirely on the defensive with regard to the news media and especially the cable channels and networks proliferating within the Western world. It would be wrong to exaggerate the extent to which a transparent media environment is a necessary handicap for military operations. Recent Chinese writing on the Revolution in Military Affairs displays a fascination with the West's ability to determine reality not only for itself but the world. In the Gulf, the West was able to use news reports from over 100 on-site reporters exaggerating the success of the Patriot missiles to keep Israel out of the war and to hold the alliance together. It made effective use of TV news releases and radio broadcasts and real-time transmissions to make the war appear more bloodless than it was.[21]

The West is also well placed to fight media wars for another, even more important reason. It owns most of the real-time cable news networks, and they tend to frame the debate in Western terms, in the vernacular of a democratic discourse. If an Arab network (rather than CNN) had been present when Iraq invaded Kuwait in 1990, it might have framed the event not as an act of aggression but as an attempt to reverse over a century of colonial humiliation. And the gradual allied buildup during Desert Shield produced such an imbalance of forces between the coalition and Iraq that an Arab news agency might have chosen to frame the debate in terms of the humiliation of a fellow Arab nation.[22] Indeed, that is what happened when the network al-Jazeera covered President George W. Bush's "first war of the twenty-first century," the war against terrorism. The newscasters showed not so much a war against Islam but the humiliation of yet another Muslim society, this time Afghanistan, a theme that had much greater resonance in the Arab world.

However, Western institutions are still seen as transparent and therefore credible. In an information age, credibility is a crucial resource, and "asymmetrical credibility is a key source of power."[23] To establish credibility, one must develop a reputation for providing correct information even when it may reflect badly on one's own side. After all, it is the perceived impartiality of Western reporters that makes their reports credible. In an age when legitimacy matters more than strict legality, Western governments can treat this credulity as a crucial resource. Given the abundance of information in the world, the ability to determine the interpretation of facts is extremely important. Political struggles, we are told, now focus less on control over the ability to transmit information than over the creation and destruction of credibility.

That is especially important not only for world opinion but for public opinion at home. For Western democracies too are becoming more interested in *legitimacy* than strict legality. Although the rule of law is a central characteristic of a democratic state, its belief in the legitimacy of an international norm and observance of that norm does not imply the state is law abiding or submissive to authority. As Ian Hird points out, often the opposite is true: "A normative conviction about legitimacy might lead to non-compliance with law when laws are considered in conflict with that conviction." Arguably, that was the case with NATO in Kosovo when the alliance acted without a UN mandate.[24]

But although the West certainly has an advantage when it comes to the transmission and dissemination of news, it suffers from several disadvantages that allow non-Western actors to maximize its own sense of unease. The fact that the global media channels are Western promotes "virtual convergence." It makes the world into a single cognitive space, a variation of the global village. The non-Western world knows much more about the United States than the United States knows about it. As Martin Libicki warns, small states may be able to use "the globalisation of perception" to cast themselves as victims even in the eyes of Americans.[25] Reading the psyche of the American people is considerably easier than reading that of the Chinese.

In fact, many non-Western societies have proved adept at exploiting U.S. sensibilities. There are many examples—the use of women and children as human shields by Somali warlords, Saddam Hussein's decision to ring his palaces with civilians to deter U.S. air strikes in 1998, or the decision by groups of Belgrade Serbs wearing "target patches" who lined the main bridges to forestall NATO air strikes in the 1999 war. The very fact that Western societies now seem to care more for legitimacy than legality is problematic. To be legitimate these days, a society must be humane. It must avoid the pain and suffering that Nietzsche (speaking for the Greeks) recognized as the necessary condition for subjectivity: to be subjective, one must experience suffering and make sense of it, not conjure it away.

Today, the strict enforcement of international law must be seen to be upheld, whatever the cost in casualties. By contrast, the enforcement of a legitimate norm demands a different set of rules. The contest in Kosovo, Michael Ignatieff writes, was so unequal and seen as such on TV, that NATO could only occupy the moral high ground by observing especially strict rules of engagement (ROEs). Even earlier, the ROEs for Operation Deliberate Force (1995) in Bosnia had posed a problem. Special instructions were issued to pilots who were involved in attacking bridges. They were expected to make a dry run over the target and attack on an axis perpendicular to it, releasing one bomb per pass. Those responsible for suppressing enemy air defenses were not permitted to conduct preemptive strikes against surface-to-air missile sites, except under strict conditions.

Fear of producing casualties also involves troops on the ground. In Somalia, the Tenth Mountain Division was trained to work in combined arms terms, usually with tanks and infantry fighting vehicles attached to infantry units. But it was not allowed to use its artillery to blast through doors or windows that might be booby-trapped. AC-130s, the gunship variant of the C130 turboprop transport, were also not available on October 3, 1993, because their previous employment had resulted in an unacceptable level of collateral damage. As Colin Powell put it at the time: "They wrecked a few buildings and it was not the greatest imagery on CNN."[26]

But it seems to me that the problems of appearing "humane" run much deeper. Modern soldiers are the products of a purely visual culture. They have spent their childhoods watching films and playing computer games. As a result they are creatures of an age that has made violence largely "virtual" and war an entertainment that raises few questions, moral or political. And the civilians who send soldiers to battle the enemies of humanitarianism are creatures of the age too. For although televised images of human suffering may impel people to act, they do not provide any insight into anything that approaches irony, conflict, or dilemma—the dilemma, for example, of having to act cruelly in the name of humanity or humanitarianism or at the very least accept the need for a human cost. That is the stuff of the tragic sense of history. Peter Euben puts it elegantly in his analysis of Thomas Pynchon's seminal novel, *The Crying of Lot 49:*

> Television rather than Greek tragedy, Pynchon suggests, is our institution of political education. But unlike tragedy, television is essentially a passive medium. Rather than energising our passions and mind, it enervates them. Rarely does television deal with moral complexity, profound suffering or people charged by the trials of their lives. Rarer still does it ... interrogate the unacknowledged cultural accommodations, polarities,

or hierarchies that bound cultural life. Television is . . . a narcotic, as numbing as alcohol and drugs, creating the homogenised culture that dissociates us. All of us see the same programmes but we see them in private, and as privatised individuals.[27]

Television's message is impoverished in another way. Television pictures are the opposite of language. They do not create analogues of the world in grammatical propositions, as does language. They do not map the world with sentences; they offer no analysis. Film, writes another contemporary American novelist, E. L. Doctorow, is time driven. It shows the outside of life; it shows behavior but not the reasons for it. "It tends to the simplest moral reasoning. . . . It implodes discourse, it deliterates thought."[28] Television tends to limit the imagination by making events so visible. People think its imagery is exhaustive, when it only gives us a glimpse of appearances such as cruelty, which often prompt public opinion to insist that their forces pull back. We experience war without understanding it. Our subjective understanding of it is not what it was.

Intersubjectivity

Of course, we are told (or tell ourselves) that we do show imagination in one critical respect: we imagine the suffering we inflict on our enemies. Our societies, it is claimed, are moving away from a humanism grounded on an excessive affirmation of self to a radically different notion of personal identity, a quest for the liberation from the ego. We find this in Jacques Lacan's declaration, "I'm not a poet but a poem." A contemporary Jungian psychologist challenges the permanence of any referent beyond the first person pronoun: "Each time the first person pronoun is uttered it projects a different entity, a different perspective and identity."[29] In an age of multiple realities and cultures, we are forced to ask questions about "the self." We are challenged to look at ourselves anew and rethink our assumptions about who and what we are. The whole thrust of humanistic psychology (Carl Rogers, R. D. Laing, Thomas Szasz) suggests that it is ultimately possible and desirable to empathize with everything human. Psychological damage is no longer to be "treated" but fixed through empathy between the therapist and patient.

What we are encountering, Richard Shweder writes, is a "post-modern humanism" that allows us to travel the world to find in other cultures expressions of our "repressed" or unexpressed selves.[30] The unity of human beings is no longer to be found in what makes us the same but what makes us different. We recognize in others our own complex selves, making the stranger for the first time fully accessible and imaginable. As Julia Kristeva claims, "Strangely the foreigner lives within us: he is the hidden face of our identity, the space that wrecks our abode, the time in which understanding and affinity found us. By recognizing him within ourselves, we are spared detesting him in himself."[31]

As a result, we are grounding our moral commitment to war no longer on abstract metaphysical principles but on a biological commitment to avoid inflicting pain on others and to punish those who inflict pain on their own citizens. Tzestvan Todorov is right to attribute this shift largely to the West. It is Western humanism taken to its logical end. Todorov, incidentally, is not claiming any superiority for Western civilization; he is merely making an observation.[32] It is only the West that has changed its own behavior in dialogue with others. Its human rights agenda is largely a product of the lessons learned from the anticolonial, antiapartheid, and other struggles that marked the Western retreat from empire.

All this may appear rather remote from the practical concerns of soldiering. But there are many people who would like to see the military empathize even more with others. Some analysts would like to see the military more actively involved in vaccination programs, the management of food centers, and the distribution of relief items. They would like to see the last vestige of the warrior ethos disappear altogether. The problem is that the military is becoming divided between those who still see themselves as warriors and those who see themselves as humanitarians. It is a danger that has been analyzed by two American sociologists of the military who take as their case study U.S. involvement in Somalia.

We must be careful, of course, about using Somalia as the only case study. It was not a war. It was described from the start as a humanitarian mission. Most of the soldiers interviewed claimed they had been told they were coming to rescue the Somalis and that they would largely be involved in relief work similar to that which had been undertaken after Hurricane Andrew in Florida the previous summer. And in a sense they were, though most of the relief work was undertaken by engineers working in rural areas, clearing land mines and building roads. By contrast, the marines in Mogadishu soon found themselves in the middle of a civil war.

Soon afterward, the cultural fault lines running through the military began to be exposed. Black soldiers were especially vulnerable. They had been drawn to the conflict by the fact that it was one of the first U.S. military missions in Africa, offering them a once-in-a-lifetime opportunity to discover their African roots. But they were soon singled out as the main object of hatred and scorn. The Somalis expected them to be able to speak their language and, when they discovered they could not, took it as a personal affront. They were also racially different. Because they were not Semitic, Somali children frequently abused them on patrol by calling them *adorn,* the Somali word for slave. Black women soldiers were especially singled out and accused of being "whores" for not covering their heads while out on patrol.

The Americans themselves repaid the compliment. Many soldiers had a low opinion of the Somalis, whom they found lazy, anarchistic, and excessively prone to argument and violence. However, they did not invent a pejorative word for the Somalis as they had for the Vietnamese. As one soldier commented, the word *Somali* was bad enough. But despite the abuse they suffered, black soldiers, especially women, were prepared to give the Somalis the benefit of the doubt. Many found the attitudes of their own white colleagues to be racist.[33]

There is much more in the study I have just quoted about internal divisions within the military between whites and blacks and men and women. But one of the key ones was between those who saw themselves as warriors (bitterly critical of the restraining orders preventing them from dealing as harshly with the Somalis as other contingents such as the Italians were allowed to) and those who put a premium on being humane.

What is even more striking, however, is that few of the soldiers who thought of themselves as "humanitarians" seem to have been aware of how they were seen by the Somalis themselves. There was much respect for their humanitarian mission but not for humanitarian soldiers, and not just because a warrior culture despised a postmodern military. Even the Somalis who originally welcomed the U.S. intervention found themselves at odds with the U.S. mission. They particularly disliked the rangers and their use of Black Hawks (helicopter transports), which flew over the city continuously, swooping down so low that they destroyed whole neighborhoods, blowing down market stalls and terrorizing cattle. The helicopters would create havoc on the streets, leaving the crowds below choking on dust and exhaust. Often women walking down the streets would have their robes blown off. Some had children torn from their arms by the powerful updraft made by the helicopters as they hovered overhead. In a word, many Somalis felt brutalized.

In an account of the famous firefight on October 18, 1993, that left eighteen rangers dead, the journalist Mark Bowden tells one story, that of a young man who had been educated in South Carolina and knew and liked Americans but found their actions increasingly offensive.

> The helicopters had become an evil presence over the city. Yusuf remembered lying in bed one night with his wife who was pregnant

when Black Hawks had come. One hovered directly over their house. The walls shook and the noise was deafening and he was afraid his roof, like others in the village, would be sucked off. In the racket his wife reached over and placed his hand on her belly: "Can you feel it?" she asked. He felt his son kicking in her womb, as if thrashing with fright.

As a lawyer who spoke fluent English, Yusuf had led a group of his villagers to the UN compound to complain. They were told nothing could be done about the Rangers. They were not under UN command. Soon every death associated with the fighting was blamed on the Rangers. Somalis joked bitterly that the United States had come to feed them just to fatten them up for the slaughter.[34]

In short, the operation in Somalia was not a true intersubjective experience for the Americans because they never understood their enemies or tried very hard to know them. In the end, the U.S. military was deeply demoralized in Mogadishu, particularly as a result of finding that the other side would not allow it to be humane and even more that its technology did not always allow it to fight humanely. That is the fate of the purely instrumental warrior. He—or she—has great difficulty in finding war life enhancing; and that goes for "humane" soldiers too.

NIETZSCHE'S LAST WARRIOR

How then should we understand the Western way of warfare today? I suggest we employ an approach pioneered by Nietzsche, the philosopher who dominates this book as he has dominated the Western imagination since his death. I suggest we turn to a genealogical method. For Nietzsche, genealogy had a number of advantages, of which three were critical.

First, it offers us a specific type of historical inquiry, one that is concerned to illuminate the present from the perspective of the past and to explain how the present has become logically possible. A genealogist studies what is particular in the present from the angle of history and offers a history of how we have become what we are. In this study, I have tried to explain why the West has lost faith in the existential idea of war and why, as a result, it tends to fight wars with so little conviction.

Second, a genealogy offers not only a history but a *critique* of the present. It is critical because it does not take the present for granted but seeks to enquire how practices have evolved historically. Nietzsche's own approach in the most developed of his books, *On the Genealogy of Morals,* offers a model that is genuinely historical because it explains the conditions under which values grow up, develop, and change. Several times he criticized his fellow philosophers for lacking a genuine historical sense by applying their own understanding of what is good or evil and for thinking that all history leads up to the present.

From this understanding, he insisted that we should not confuse the "origin" of a thing with its present "purpose." Origin and utility are different. Yes, we can trace the Western way of war back to the Greeks, but we must recognize that like all things "Western," it was "confiscated," or "transformed and rearranged for new uses" as the premodern phase of history gave way to the modern. Everything, Nietzsche tells us, is in that sense an "overcoming" or "reinterpreting" to fit the specific needs of an era so that often the original meaning or purpose of something (like morality) may have been obscured over time. The Greeks used war not only for instrumental purposes but as an existential exercise that helped them to understand themselves. Why can Westerners not do so today; and why is that not true of other cultures?

The third aspect of Nietzsche's genealogical method is that it does not seek to recount the entire history of a phenomenon. Instead, it offers an episodic approach. It restricts itself to the historical episodes that are of decisive importance in helping us understand a phenomenon in terms of what makes it *problematic*. In this study, I have tried to identify the most problematic feature of the Western way of war by a selective use of the past and to illustrate a specific problem: the increasing instrumentalization of war, which has made the warrior almost entirely redundant.

So like Nietzsche himself in *On the Genealogy of Morals,* we must turn to the beginning. What makes that particular work the most important contribution to moral philosophy since Kant is that Nietzsche sketches out a history of morality that begins at the very beginning. And this is what he has to say. Man is little more than an animal: instinctive, cruel, and not very bright. In time, stronger individuals come to the fore. They constitute an aristocracy that enslaves the others. It is cruel and instinctive and measures its own superiority in terms of its ability to be cruel and oppressive. In a word, it exults in its own strength.

Enslavement is a different matter for the slaves. Their instincts are not allowed expression but suppressed. The upshot is repression. They turn in on themselves and develop an inner life, a slave morality, an ethics of resentment. They are cleverer than the nobles because they suffer more and turn their suffering to good account. They invert the scale of values, judging weakness, meekness, and humility to be good and brute strength to be bad.

Society continues to develop. A new system of morality takes hold as priests appear and instruct the slaves on the higher religions, which all teach without exception that suffering is not in vain, though it is not entirely undeserved. The weak are made more resentful by the teaching that poverty and oppression are their reward for sin (original or real, predestined or earned). But they are also offered a consolation: God will punish the proud and forgive the sinners (the meek will inherit the earth). In subscribing to these moral codes, real value is placed beyond the world—it becomes transcendental or otherworldly.

In both cases, Nietzsche claimed, the weak prevailed over the strong. In the first case, the values of the weak, such as humility, became the basis for value overall. It had become the universal morality of Western society. "Weakness . . . [was] lied into something *meritorious*"; it is "the sublime self-deception that interprets weakness as freedom and their being thus-and-thus as a *merit*."[35] In the second case, value was located in metaphysical structures such as the moral law. The transcendental was the product not of human reason but resentment against life. As such, traditional moral codes were more life denying than life affirming. The slave morality Nietzsche so despised was a reaction against the life of suffering, against life conceived *as* suffering. In that sense, it was life denying.

Repression remained, however. It could not be conjured away, and over time the repressed became more cunning as they became more resentful. They began to reject the priests' stories as fabrications. They began to demand the truth. In time, God himself became a fiction, at which point he was replaced by the scientific method—the demand for the truth at all costs. Truth itself became the absolute value that took precedence over all others. But as people became more truthful with themselves, they became more self-conscious. They began to reject morality itself and its transcendental fictions. And so they became distrustful of every value, at which point (one that Nietzsche believed his own generation had reached) nihilism beckoned.

If we were to apply a similar Nietzschean genealogy to the warrior ideal, we might produce the following account.

1. War is a social institution, not a human one. If we compare ourselves to other animals, there is only one other species that appears to be warlike—ants. Ants wage war according to a highly organized form of life. Ant colonies even produce specific warrior types that constitute organized armies. There is one crucial difference. Individually, ants are haplodiploid reproducers, female offspring of a central queen, sharing three-fourths of their genes with their numerous sisters. In these circumstances, sacrifice in war is their best chance to perpetuate their own genes. Individual death is trivial compared with the success of an army made up

of genetic near-replicants. Humans, by comparison, reproduce them-selves. All mammals beside ourselves limit their self-sacrifice to their own offspring. It is therefore pertinent to ask, Why are humans inherently war-like, and why it is possible for them to wage war at all? The answer is not that we are programmed because of our genes; we wage war because the culture we live in requires it. War, in a word, has its historical origins. It is a product of culture.[36]

2. In the earliest organized cultures, around 6000 B.C.E., war was a product of exigency. It acted as a stabilizing agent to balance demo-graphic swings. When stress (i.e., resource shortages) emerged, hunter-gatherer societies tended to migrate. The solution was horizontal, but sedentary societies, committed to staying put, went vertical and generat-ed a new level of hierarchical control. In periods of stable population growth, the agrarian surplus was limited, as was wealth creation. It had to be defended.

3. The specialists in violence were endowed with a rank higher than the specialists in production. In periods of overpopulation, the new war-rior elite could conquer new lands on which to produce food. And when numbers fell, new laborers were appropriated by conquest or raids, which explains the ancient traffic in slaves and the repeated, coerced transfers of entire peoples (the Jewish exodus to Babylon being one of the few still remembered). The trophies of war included prisoners of war who, as slaves, were the most valuable asset of all. In short, in all agrarian soci-eties, "nobility" and war were equivalent: it was the only way of organiz-ing them properly.

4. As societies developed in more complex ways, a different warrior class emerged. In the fixed society of Homer's *Iliad,* in which social mobility was minimal (if that), a warrior's worth or value was determined by his social role. As Sarpedon tells Glaucus, as warriors they have obli-gations and duties. Their sense of their own "nobility" stemmed not from brute strength and their ability to exploit others but from the ends to which their strength was put—the security of the community, tribe, or clan. By the time of fifth-century B.C.E. Athens, the warrior's role had changed. When asked to define courage, the Athenian general Laches cited the example of the man who "stays at his post and faces the enemy," an image that calls to mind the hoplite standing in line, not the heroes of *The Iliad* yearning for individual glory.[37] Warriors are no longer willful. They have become instrumental heroes in the service of a larger social good. And they are instrumental in another sense. Plato's professional soldiers (which they were by the fourth century B.C.E., not citizen-soldiers as of old) served the state by standing down when unneeded. War was not

endemic but a policy to be adopted as the state saw fit. Achilles' brand of heroism requires a battlefield. The world of *The Iliad* is at war all the time. The world of Plato's *Republic* is not.[38] When Achilles dies, he makes clear in a speech to Lyacon that his death and his destiny are important. By the fifth century, the warrior's death may be the supreme moment in his life, but it is meaningful only for society in general. In his funeral speech, Pericles praises the soldiers who risked their lives for Athens and who in "a brief moment of time, the climax of their lives, the culmination of glory . . . were swept away from us."[39] Their supreme moment of glory is glorious, however, only because it is the supreme moment of Athens as well.

5. On one level, the state now treated its warriors as an instrument to the attainment of certain ends. On another level, warriors were subject to a more refined and complex scrutiny. Philosophy and higher religions traded in the currency of necessity. War was increasingly judged not only by its own standards but by standards *external* to itself. As a result, warriors became more human, more humane.

6. By the time the Western way of warfare was revalued and reinvented—by the Renaissance—the warrior's standing in society was still absolute, and princes still went to war for revenge and prestige. Wars were still fought to avenge wrongs against the honor and glory of the king. Primitive militarism was replaced by kingly or theocratic militarism, an ideology that continued without much change until the early eighteenth century.[40] A warrior was still a man willing to hazard his life for honor. By then, the economic causes of war were also becoming more compelling as states became more complex and populations began to grow. As war became an organizational source of power, wars were fought more and more for political reasons, and the existential worth of war, though still important, was no longer as profound. As civil institutions developed, the warrior's freedom of action was increasingly curtailed. Trade and commerce and the rise of the bourgeoisie introduced unwarlike values. As wealth grew, the balance between producers and specialists of violence tilted in favor of the former. War did not make the state strong; wealth did. Thus Alexander Hamilton in *The Federalist* famously contrasted the "industrious habits of the people" of his own day (absorbed in the pursuit of gain) "with the condition of a nation of soldiers which was the true condition of those [ancient Greek] republics."[41]

7. As a result, warriors had to internalize martial values even more: they had to see war in more utilitarian or instrumental terms. The development of firearms and technology further diminished the existential experience of war. With the rise of democracy, warriors were forced to open the ranks to the citizenry. In time, they were even forced to adopt the

citizens' language as well. For some time, the discourse of war has borrowed heavily from the civilian world—from the theater, organized sport, or the marketplace. Generals talk of what the "market will allow." If distinctive military values still predominate, the occupational incentives of the marketplace have begun to compete with normative considerations of the military. The convergence of the military and civilian worlds is almost complete. The warrior has been displaced by the soldier, and how long will the soldier survive in public esteem?

Nietzsche himself accepted that there was no going back. In *The Gay Science,* he used a particular metaphor to express this: "We have quit the land and gone on board ship and have cut off the bridge behind us—more than that, the land. . . . Alas, if you should be seized by homesickness for land . . . there is no land anymore."[42] The loss of the old world with its warrior ethos is permanent; that is the purpose of genealogy, to trace why and how it has occurred. There can be no question of even wanting to go back; we can only go forward. Nietzsche's whole genealogical approach was intended to show this fact. Any return to the warrior ideal or aristocratic principle in war is impossible. Once people are self-conscious, they cannot return to an unquestioning belief in the existential value of their trade.

Nietzsche himself put it well when he described Napoleon, the last warrior prince in European history, as "a more isolated and late born man . . . than there has ever been [in whom] the problem of the *noble ideal* is as such made flesh. . . . One might well ponder what kind of problem it is, this synthesis of the brutish (inhuman) and more than human (superhuman)."[43] One interpretation of this passage is that Nietzsche saw Napoleon as an anachronism, a man "late born," a throwback to antiquity, for even in his day this man who believed in war for its own sake was defeated by the material realities he tried to defy. Napoleon was an existential warrior through and through, for in pursuit of *glory* he was prepared to turn everything into the military: the private into the public, life into war, the individual into the collective will. He was even prepared to requisition the nation for the duration, to turn it into a supremely effective instrument of war. He failed because he overstepped himself—because he refused to accept the mundane, material, political realities that doomed his enterprise from the beginning.

War, by then, had become far more instrumental than existential. It had to be justified and directed to attainable ends. The "inhuman" instincts of the man who is driven by his instinctive drives—the man who, in Hegel's words, needs war to experience his own humanity—were becoming increasingly anachronistic. And Napoleon was recognized by his contemporaries as "inhuman," or demonic. For here was a man who ignored everything that was secondary or ephemeral in pursuit of a single goal: his own ambition. He was the most dangerous man of the nineteenth century. It was precisely this feature of his character that Fyodor Dostoyevsky captured in the person of Raskolnikov in *Crime and Punishment,* a man who identified specifically with Napoleon's criminality. He was "a real *ruler of men,* a man to whom everything is permitted," Raskolnikov proclaims appreciatively. He "takes Toulon by storm, carries out a massacre in Paris, *forgets* an army in Egypt, *wastes* half a million men in his Moscow campaign."[44]

By contrast, the "superhuman" or "overman" in Nietzsche's philosophy is the man of good conscience or true nobility. In antiquity, it was possible to combine both. By the nineteenth century, such a "synthesis" was impossible. Nietzsche tells us that the synthesis is the *problem* of the modern age, and his central ethical concern in writing *On the Genealogy of Morals* is, how is it possible to have the "superhuman" without the "inhuman"?[45] For the inhuman presupposes a warrior elite that is unmindful or scornful of civilian values. Premodern warriors affirms themselves and their lives instinctively—the world and existence were good simply for having them in it. By the nineteenth century, it was impossible for warriors to act unselfconsciously, to accept the inhumanity of war as a condition of their own existence.

Fearing just such a future, one in which there would be no place for warriors at all, Nietzsche tried to shock his readers out of their indifference by showing them a presentiment of their own fate. "Behold! I show you the *Last Man,*" he proclaims in *Thus Spake Zarathustra.* What is he? A man who has become small but happy. "'We have discovered happiness,' say the Last Men and blink."

Who are today's "last men"? Those who still work but do so in service industries (like entertainment). They have no vision of grand politics aimed at emancipating the poor or the dispossessed because politics is too much of a burden. They are ironic because their beliefs are conditional. "They have their little pleasure for the day and little pleasure for the night: but they respect health."[46] If this passage, Aaron Ridley writes, does not provoke a thrilling horror of self-recognition one should go back and read it again. It is one of many passages from Nietzsche's work that on rereading becomes more and more acute.

In our respect for heath and for life (for conserving and extending it), we have lost our taste for battle. But warrior figures are not entirely dead—they still live in our imagination. They are still to be found in what

Alvin and Heidi Toffler, echoing the commercial language of the hour, call "a niche market."[47] Niche warriors can be found in the special forces that the Western world still boasts: the rangers and Special Air Service (SAS), those who still struggle for Hegelian recognition from their peers; those for whom, in Hegel's words, war is still "an existential choice: an assertion of will which defines the self and asserts its value."[48] Their numbers may be few, but they are contemporary heroes for courting danger and for the demanding and dangerous missions they undertake.

In the technologically defined discourse on war, they still represent human agency, battling against the odds and exercising their own discretion. They are still subjective beings who experience danger by operating behind the lines and by enduring more, both physically and emotionally, than other soldiers. They are subjective because what distinguishes them form other units is "a way to *be* rather than the fulfillment of preferences or the acquisition of valued things."[49] And they are still intersubjective beings who are more likely to honor or understand the fighting qualities of their enemies in the hand-to-hand, one-on-one encounters in which they often engage.

We honor these warriors because we still acknowledge that they are the last link with our own past. They put us in touch with the power war once had to define our humanity, one it now seems to lack. But we know that their time too has probably come. War, Nietzsche claimed, turns man "into an interesting animal," but as Aaron Ridley adds, "we have to find a way of accepting ourselves as the interesting animals we have become."[50] One of the reasons we still find ourselves an interesting species is that we are still evolving. One reason that genealogy is important is that it attempts to show us how we have become what we are so that we may see what we might become. In that sense, to talk of the end of the Western way of warfare as many historians now do is mistaken. In the Roman case, the Western way ended when the Roman state contracted out its own defense to others. We have not done that yet and probably never will. Instead, we will continue to instrumentalize war still further by diminishing the human factor. And as we continue down that path, we will find ourselves increasingly distant both emotionally and psychologically from other societies who have preserved the warrior tradition or find themselves more in tune with what Clausewitz called its "true nature."

5

The West Encounters the
Non-Western World

The nineteenth century had no doubt which of the battles in the encounter between Greece and Persia had been the most decisive: "It is certain as any contingent event respecting historical events," wrote John Stuart Mill, that if there had been no Themistocles there would have been no victory of Salamis; and had there not, where would have been all our civilisation?" Mill was attempting to establish "the facts of universal history," and Salamis was seen as the most important "fact" in Western history: the first "world event."[1]

If Marathon brought the first Greco-Persian war to an inconclusive end, Salamis was the decisive engagement of the second. It was fought by Xerxes, the son of Darius, to avenge his father's defeat, and this time he was determined not only to punish the Greeks but also to subjugate them. In 480 B.C.E., a canal was dug across the isthmus of the Athos peninsula, and the 2-mile-wide Hellespont was bridged by the largest army Europe had ever seen. Although it probably numbered 180,000 combatants, not the 5 million mentioned by Herodotus, the picture the historian draws is striking. Xerxes led a multiethnic army (not just a Persian one) into Europe, an army that reflected the ethnic diversity of his empire. Herodotus could have followed his roll call of the army with its Scythian, Egyptian, Libyan, Arab, and Indian units marching to the command of one man with a list of the opposing Greek forces. Instead, with a sense of drama worthy of Homer, he tells us that against this formidable force, the Greeks opposed an idea, and the idea was decisive.[2]

Herodotus was a fine storyteller, and his narrative of the war still colors our thinking. His stirring account, however, tends to gloss over the extent to which the Greeks were divided in their response and were unusually demoralized at the beginning of hostilities. There were many counsels of despair and resignation, even in Athens, but not on the part of

Themistocles, the hero of the hour. Ever the astute politician, he was not above bribing the Oracle of Delphi, which had foretold a Persian victory. Such a defeatist stance was hardly good for morale, and Themistocles induced the priests to change their verdict and to predict instead that the Greeks would owe their salvation to their "wooden walls." The Athenians were duly persuaded to take to the sea. They evacuated their city by ship and removed themselves to Salamis, the island that the oracle had identified as the ground on which the fate of Greece would be determined.

Themistocles was not only a brilliant politician but also a brilliant tactician. The somewhat thin religious argument he used to embolden his fellow citizens was reinforced by his tactical cunning. He recognized that the narrow straits of Salamis provided the smaller Greek ships with the advantage of maneuver. The Greeks had 300 ships to the Persians' 350, but their superiority in numbers was irrelevant. Themistocles had detailed knowledge of the local typography, sea conditions, and winds, and the winds changed at a decisive moment, causing the Persians to run afoul of one another and making the Greek task of ramming and boarding much easier. The Greeks took on the invaders in detail as they sailed into the narrows and sent half to the bottom. Leaving a substantial army behind, Xerxes retired to Asia to deal with any unrest occasioned by his defeat. The Persian fleet was forced to abandon Greek waters. Never again would the Athenians and their allies fear an enemy landing south of Attica.

Emboldened by the result, Themistocles urged the Athenian captains to sail immediately for the Hellespont and destroy the bridge of ships upon which the Persians relied for their communications, but they demurred. None of them understood, as he did, the use of sea power. The Greeks had to wait another year until the Persians were finally defeated, this time on land by the Spartans at Plataea (though the war would continue for another fifteen years).

There is no disagreement in any of the Greek sources that have survived that the Persian rout was total and their defeat terrible. Hundreds of ships were sunk, and thousands of Persians killed. Aeschylus's description of the battle in his play *The Persians* is still a powerful evocation of the slaughter:

> Every warship urged its own anarchic
> Rout; all who survived that expedition
> Like mackerel or some other catch of fish
> Were stunned and slaughtered, boned with broken oars
> And splintered wrecks: lamentations, cries

Possessed the open sea, until the black
Eye of evening hushed them.[3]

When Aeschylus penned these lines in 472 B.C.E., he would have been
about fifty-three years old, eight years older than he had been when he
served in the battle. His account is therefore reflective. It is a retrospective
study free of the passion of the moment, though written with the advantage of hindsight.[4]

And Aeschylus never allows his audience to forget that it was the
Athenians, not their allies, who broke Persian power. The name Salamis
punctuates the tragedy throughout, whereas Marathon is dismissed in one
and a half lines. Even if, as one critic avers, the playwright does not reduce
Plataea to an "insignificant mopping up operation," the battle takes second
place, as perhaps it should, because the Spartans only just won it (the
Greeks had difficulty in dealing with the Persian cavalry, and their own
infantry showed an uncharacteristic lack of cohesion).[5]

In our own less romantic times, we are less inclined to see history in
such heroic terms or judge that the fate of Greek civilization (and thus our
own) really did turn on the outcome of one battle. Aeschylus's play attests,
however, to the fact that the Greeks themselves recognized that they had
achieved something remarkable. Not that they saw their victory at Salamis
as mid-Victorians like Mill did—as a breakthrough for the rational mind
against the superstitious East or the triumph of Western democracy in the
face of oriental despotism. To have understood the battle as we do, they
would have had to have shared our own point of view, derived from our
social institutions and ways of thought. As a premodern people, the
Greeks did not believe in historical turning points. What they did believe
was that they had saved not the West or rationality so much as a model:
the city-state, and a democratic city-state at that.

Employing a term from Greek tragedy, we could say that Salamis was
cathartic. It made the Athenians supremely self-confident. They were not
smarter than the Persians, nor did their soldiers display greater courage.
No one was braver than the Immortals, the elite unit of the Persian army.
But although the Athenians were not cleverer, they had to think differently. Confronted by different challenges, they had to be more *abstract* in
their thinking: to push back the boundaries of reality and discover new
possibilities in themselves.[6] At Salamis, a land power took to the sea and
defeated the Persians in an element they had made their own.

Salamis was truly decisive, for it was only in its wake that the Greeks
began to ask themselves what was distinctive about the way they fought.

The Persians, they concluded, were suited by nature to waging war on land; the sea was their own natural element. Indeed, Aeschylus implies that by venturing out onto the sea, the Persians had tempted fate. The picture he paints of Xerxes at the head of a powerful army mowing down cities in his path compares to the destruction of his fleet as the barbarians struggle in an alien element. And Aeschylus identified another point of contrast: the Greeks used the spear, the Persians the bow. The Greeks engaged their adversaries in close combat; the Persians preferred standoff weapons. In the play, the chorus anticipates that the king will bring destruction by the bow. But the result of the battle shows that the spear is more decisive.

Both accounts are myths. The Greeks took reluctantly to the sea. The Phoenicians who taught the Persians their seamanship were much better seamen. Salamis itself was practically a land battle (Themistocles lured the enemy into the narrow straits rather than fight at sea). And the spear/bow opposition, despite its poetic effect, neglects the fact that historically, neither weapon was confined to either side. But Aeschylus used the discourse of poetry to identify what he recognized as an important difference between two very different cultures. The victory of the spear over the bow is a "conceptual shorthand," but the concept is important.[7] For Aeschylus established an ethnographic approach in portraying a way of warfare dictated by cultural norms.

Herodotus, who first read his account of the wars in the theater of Athens in 445 B.C.E., followed suit. For him, the difference in the way the two sides fought owed everything to their different *political* cultures. Perhaps he exaggerated the extent to which democratic thinking in Athens had provided it with an advantage in battle. He had an ax to grind, after all. As a native of Halicarnassus, which was virtually governed by Persia, he was denied the possibilities of advancement that were open to his social equals in other Greeks cities. But for a century and a half, Athens proved as capable of taking care of itself in both land and naval warfare as it did in establishing and maintaining its common political life. Democracy served it well in war as well as peace.

War, the historian John Keegan writes, in the only definition he is willing to provide, is "killing for a collective purpose."[8] And no one did it better than the Greeks. Just as democracy, citizenship, and free expression were found nowhere else in the ancient world, so too the Greeks were matchless in the way they pioneered a way of fighting that was unique to themselves. In falling back on ethnography, Aeschylus and Herodotus formulated a humanistic understanding of war that was also unique because it gave so much focus to the *instrumental* dimension of war, to the discipline and decisiveness that magnified the power of the warrior. There is no echo of it in any other civilization except China, and even there the emphasis is different. It was the increasing instrumentalization of war over the centuries that was to become one of the trademarks of the Western way of warfare, one that explains why Western soldiers have been judged by themselves to be more *rational* than others.

THE WEST AND THE NON-WESTERN WORLD

Every culture is mutable, or metamorphic. Every culture has distinctive characteristics that are determined by history but also change because of contact with other cultures. To insist that cultures do not learn from each other is not only wrong but unhistorical. To think otherwise would be to assume that cultures are not governed by change, incompleteness, potentiality, or intentions—in a word, historicity. Indeed, the conclusion drawn by Michael Carrithers is that the relationship between cultures is the cause of change in all our lives and has been for centuries. In producing change, cultures make history, which is why human beings are the only history-making animals (other species may have a history through their evolution, but they their do not make it; we do make ours). The diversity of culture—in this case, a way of warfare—stems not from autonomy but interaction.

> People live by means of relationships, emotionally and intellectually. The speech we learn only makes sense in respect of others we learn it from, and to whom we direct it. The values and behavior we acquire are sensible only in the perspective of others or in our own imagination of others' perspectives. Indeed culture here, meaning just largely mental goods, forms of knowledge and values to live by which we have learned or created, is intelligible only in its use by people and in respect of other people. Culture in other words presupposes relationships.[9]

From the interaction of cultures, ideas and styles are translated into a unique idiom based on what they borrow and what they do not.

As a style of war, the Western way has been shaped by currents and crosscurrents born of its contact with the outside world. It is only by contact with others that the West has come to know itself. Equally, it is only in the discourse between himself and his enemy (between Achilles and Hector) that the warrior comes to know his true existential worth. As the Spanish philosopher Unamuno once wrote, a conversation is never between two people, Juan and Carlos, it is between six. It is between Juan and Carlos most obviously, but also between the man Juan would like to be in the eyes of Carlos, and the man Carlos would like to be in the eyes of Juan. But it also involves a third discourse between the man Juan knows himself to be in Carlos's eyes, and the man Carlos suspects himself to be in Juan's.

So let us look at three different encounters between the Western and non-Western worlds that helped define Western humanism. Each involves a different era of history: the premodern, modern, and late modern. All three tell us a great deal about why the West tends to *devalue* other warriors by dismissing their existential identity as "savage," "unmodern," and even (more recently) "unhistorical."

FIGHTING FOR THE ANCESTORS:
HERODOTUS AND THE SCYTHIAN WAY OF WARFARE

When did the West first encounter the non-Western world in battle? If one begins with the Greeks, then one can turn to the account of a war between two non-Western peoples, the Scythians and the Persians, in the early sixth century B.C.E. This campaign fascinated the accepted father of history, Herodotus, and what makes his account of that encounter important is that it conveyed a mindset, a way that a premodern people judged another whom they found barbarous because they differed so much from themselves. Even though the Greeks traded with the Scythians extensively, they did not understand them.

"Scythians" was the name given by the Greeks to certain central Asian tribes of Indo-European origin, who after their expulsion from northwestern Iran, settled in what is now southern Russia. They were a nomadic people whose skill as horsemen and prowess in mounted archery gave them a distinctive advantage, not only over the Persians but later the Greeks themselves (they later decisively defeated one of Alexander the Great's generals, Zopyrion, in about 325 B.C.E.). They were as skilled at hunting as they were at war. Certainly, the images we find of them in goldsmith work show them usually at peace or, at least in the intervals between wars, dressing one another's wounds, mending their bowstrings, and hunting. Even on the battlefield, they could be distracted by a running hare.[10]

In 512 B.C.E., they entered history for the first time when the Persian king Darius invaded their homeland in an attempt to secure his northern flank, before reducing Thrace and Macedonia in a campaign that was seen by historians as a prelude to the first Greco-Persian war. His army bridged the Danube River and crossed over from modern-day Bulgaria into southern Russia in the hope of bringing the Scythians to battle. To his surprise, Darius was outmaneuvered by a people who practiced a form of war as foreign to the Persians as it was to the Greeks. Nomads tended to employ simple logistics—their animals ate the grass, and their soldiers ate the animals. Animal husbandry required little management, which helped release manpower for war. The nomads of inner Asia could deploy up to 70 percent of their manpower. They could put larger armies into the field than any settled or civilized state, and they had the advantage of horsemanship, the best in the world, as well as horses that were small but hardy. The mobility of the nomads and the mobility of their wealth made it difficult to defeat them. Their whole lifestyle provided them with a permanent training in the exercise of violence and in resistance to the violence of others.

When Darius invaded their homeland, the Scythians avoided a pitched battle. Instead of engaging the Persians in close combat, they resorted to a scorched-earth policy, burning the grass so that the enemy's horses had nothing to eat. Instead of fighting, they retreated into the vastness of the steppes, drawing the Persians on and in the process making the hunter the hunted. As nomads, they had no capital city to capture and no trade routes to cut off. Instead, they vanished over the horizon, harrying the invaders in skirmishes and ambushes by mounted archers.

Darius was defeated because he could not discover their center of gravity. In exasperation, he issued a challenge to stand and fight like "men." The reply from one of the Scythian kings was made famous by Herodotus: "Know this of me, Persians. I have never fled for fear of any man."[11] But because they had no cultivated land to waste and no towns to capture, they also had no reason to engage the Persians in battle. They had nothing, Darius was told, but the graves of their fathers. Find them and attempt to destroy them, and the Persians would get their battle. In the event, they never did and were forced to retreat.

Herodotus was fascinated by this episode in military history. What made him the "father" of history is that he gave it a theme. He invented history itself by avoiding the themeless juxtaposition of events that makes up so many ancient chronicles. His history leads up to the encounter between the Persians and Greeks, and to explain why the Greeks prevailed, he found it necessary to go back in time and record other encounters between different cultures—between the Scythians and the Persians, as well as the Persians and the Egyptians. He was interested in the Scythians not for their own sake but as enemies of the Persians. Indeed, he started a tradition that has continued ever since, for when Western writers write about war, they are mostly interested in their own "way of warfare."

In describing the Scythian way, Herodotus helped define that of the Greeks. He was not only the father of history but also the father of ethnography and perhaps even of anthropology. His account is important for that reason. It is the first work that understands war as a reflection of culture. He treated the campaign as an episode in military history, and he saw the Scythians as warriors who had patented a way of war that made them unbeatable.

> In one respect . . . they make it impossible for the enemy who invades them to escape destruction while they themselves are entirely out of reach unless it pleases them to engage with them. Having neither cities nor forts and carrying their dwellings with them wherever they go; accustomed, moreover, one and all of them to shoot from horseback and living not by husbandry but on their cattle, their wagons the only houses they possess, how can they be conquered?[12]

What Herodotus found interesting was the *asymmetrical* nature that war tends to take whenever one culture confronts another and finds its strengths being exploited and turned into weaknesses.

The Greeks did not disparage the Scythians as fighters. Socrates reminds Laches in Plato's famous dialogue of that name that courage is not only the virtue of Greeks (that is, of soldiers who stand and fight in a phalanx). The Scythians showed courage when fleeing—a practice commended even by Homer in the pre-hoplite age. Plato was interested in the moral character of individual peoples and found that the Scythians considered bravery their defining characteristic.[13] What the Greeks found distasteful about their way of life was not their lack of courage but their way of war and its lack of humanism. For them, war was an end in itself, a way of life. For the Athenians, by contrast, Plato wrote in another Socratic dialogue, *Timaeus,* the origins of their state could be attributed to a goddess who loved both war and wisdom. Greek life embodied both. As a result, when their warriors like Ulysses displayed spiritedness and courage, those traits never degenerated into irrational fury. Their courage was tempered by an intelligence that did not manifest itself (as it did for the Scythians) as mere cunning but was employed to good purpose to secure their own freedom.[14] In a word, the instrumental and existential were combined.

To Herodotus, in other words, can be traced the very Western practice of treating other ways of warfare as barbarous. To be fair, he himself was not a cultural supremacist. He was far too intelligent a man to be content with local prejudice, and his own extensive travels and experience of other cultures led him to respect cultural differences. "Everyone without exception," he wrote, "believes that their own native customs are by far the best—there is plenty of evidence this is the universal human attitude."[15] But he must share some of the blame, for he set out to show the Greeks how they differed from everyone else, and difference is usually taken to be distance—both cultural and emotional.

As a good *zoon politikon* (political animal) Herodotus had little respect for the nomadic way of life. It is true that Diogenes the Cynic claimed that men first crowded into cities to escape the fury of those outside and that once locked within, turned against each other. Unconsciously, he offered the first example of "cultural pessimism" and gave birth to the idea of the "noble savage."[16] But there was not much regard for the noble savage in Greek thinking, especially for the Scythians, who were usually portrayed in Greek comedies as drunkards. It is clear that Herodotus too found them an unappealing people. The clear horror he expresses for the campaign and the sympathy he shows Darius is very much that of a humanist.

What we find in Herodotus's account is the first *humanistic* critique of the non-Western way of warfare. To begin with, we find what for John Keegan is the besetting sin of Western military thought: the belief that war is chiefly an instrument of policy. Because there was no political end for which the Scythians were fighting—no ideas or principles, only the survival of a way of life—they were considered to be inferior warriors to the Persians. For them, war meant something quite different than it did for Darius, who had invaded their land for "strategic necessity," to secure a flank before advancing further west. And they had no concept of fighting for an idea such as freedom, which was to sustain the Greeks themselves against Darius a few years later. Instead of fighting for freedom, they fought for honor—and not even their own but that of their ancestors. The weight of the dead cast a shadow over the living.

In addition, their style of war reflected a way of life but not a culture (for they had no cities and no settled agriculture). Their land was vast and featureless. It was marked by no monuments or cities that might recall even to a subsequent generation the presence of human life or the history of human achievement. There was not even evidence of agriculture ("the works of men," as Homer called them). They were even prepared to burn their own land to deny sustenance to the horses of the invading army.

Now all this may remind us of how the Athenians chose to fight their war with Sparta toward the end of the following century, when they huddled behind their wooden walls and left their farms and farmland to be burned by the enemy. And it may remind us of Themistocles' strategy for beating the Persians by removing the whole population to Salamis, leaving Athens to be burned by Xerxes' soldiers. But in the Greek mind at least, there was a radical difference between fleeing or retreating in the face of an advancing enemy and doing what the Athenians did in 480 B.C.E.—evacuating an entire city as part of an ambitiously conceived plan. The difference could be taken as a sign of strategy (outmaneuvering or outthinking an enemy) rather than tactics (doing what one always did). The Scythians, by contrast, deliberately avoided battle and preferred instead to engage in periodic raids and skirmishes where they had an advantage: *mobility*. The Greeks were mobile too but in a very different way—they were given to founding colonies and new city-states each with its own constitution. This mobility played an important part in their cultural memory—it defined them as Greeks.

But, above all, what in Greek eyes (as well as Western ones) rendered a people barbarous was their unwillingness to make anything of themselves. They left no mark on history. And in enduring, they were not prepared to hazard all. Herodotus tells us that at the battle of Marathon (490 B.C.E.), the Athenians were possessed of a madness, a zeal, that the Persians had never encountered before. The Greeks engaged the Persian army in shock combat. "When the Persians saw the Athenians running down on them without horses or bow men in fewer numbers they thought them mad, rushing to certain destruction."[17] By contrast, the Scythians had retreated; they had fought a standoff campaign, shooting arrows from the backs of fast-moving horses. And here was the crux. For in hazarding all as the Athenians had at Salamis, they showed they had everything to hazard—the barbarians had nothing.

It is one of the ironies of all nomads, of all peoples whose lives are wedded to movement, that their world appears to be static to those whose lives are rooted to a place. In the Scythians, Herodotus saw a people without diversity, as if the life of migration had exhausted their quota of restlessness. They seemed to adhere to a life that the Greeks themselves had abandoned; they seemed to have no restless notions of aspiration so central to the creative energies of people who dwell in cities. Although in reality the essence of their life, as for all nomads, was constant adaptation to new and changing circumstances, and although they owed their survival against the Persians precisely to their ability to innovate, react flexibly, and take advantage of opportunities while avoiding threats, that is *our* understanding of them, it was not that of the Greeks.

Of course, that is why traditionally the West has found the nomadic way of war to have been the most dangerous. The fundamental advantage nomads had was military superiority over the higher civilizations. For thousands of years, the nomadic mounted archer was more effective than the infantry or cavalry of civilized states. The only defense was to build walls, and they did not work most of the time. Even the Great Wall of China failed to establish a distinct frontier between the nomads and the Chinese; it became a zone in which people shifted from one way of life to another according to the empire's strength or weakness.

Today's fear of barbarians, whether in Africa or Bosnia, has its origins in the knowledge that the Western way of war only really proved superior to the nomadic way of war very late in the day. The Western way of war, like that of many other civilizations, is really only effective against other civilizations or states. But the distrust goes deeper than that. It goes to the heart of Herodotus's humanism, and it is present in the debate today whenever we encounter "nomads" who have made a desert of their own cities in Beirut, Kabul, Grozny, or Mogadishu. Fighting civilized states is one matter; fighting uncivil societies is quite another. Instead of trying to understand them, we tend to demonize or dehumanize them according to our own humanistic criteria. For us, as for the Greeks, the "warrior's honor" is grounded on an instrumental as well as an existential idea of war. Herodotus could never forgive the Scythians for denying the former. Although they might be a warrior people (a people for whom war was a way of life), they were not warriors as Homer understood the term. They were not Trojans.

The Enemy as Uncivil

To Herodotus's brilliant but spare observations, centuries of further reflections have been added. Attitudes toward the "barbarian" were further honed by the European conquest of the Americas just at the time when the Western way of warfare was reborn. "Can a savage be civil?" Samuel Parchas asked in the seventeenth century. For good measure, he also asked, could a Muslim be civil? In answer to his own question, he designed the blueprint of a gun that would fire round bullets against Christians and square bullets against Muslims—the latter clearly being seen unworthy not only of a Christian burial but a Christian death.[18] According to Sir John Smythe, a late-sixteenth-century commentator, the first men formed themselves into commonwealths to defend themselves against uncivil societies in which war was a condition of life. By contrasting their own state with that of savage or uncivil societies in their encounter with the peoples of the New World, the Europeans began asking themselves questions about the nature of civility itself.[19]

From the beginning, the Western discourse about the "other" had nothing to do with the fact that other societies were judged to be more warlike than themselves or that war was innate in their civil practices. The debate was framed very differently. Sixteenth-century Europeans had to confront the fact that if war was innate, it was innate in the human condition. Indeed, it was essential to political self-determination. War helped to preserve the independence of states. Luigi da Porto even developed a cyclical theory of history: "Peace brings riches, riches pride, pride wrath, wrath war, war poverty, poverty mildness, mildness peace, peace riches and so on."[20] In other words, in civil societies war was endemic too. But the difference was that it was applied *rationally*. It was instrumental, not only existential.

War, Sir Walter Raleigh wrote, was "the ordinary theme and argument of history," yet he was quick to distinguish savage wars from the state of war at home. What Raleigh meant was that Western societies were humanistic—they applied reason to war. Savages were "friends or foes by custom rather than by judgment." Civilized people engaged in war as a matter of choice, but savages did so because it was in their nature. Civilized people fought for particular ends (profit, honor, virtue, riches), but savages fought out of revenge. Civil societies needed peace or short interludes between wars so that social life could continue. Not so savages, who tended to acknowledge "no such virtue in leagues or formal conclusions of peace."[21]

Two centuries later, Adam Ferguson argued that in civilized states, war was "an operation of policy, not of popular animosity." It is interesting that in illustrating that point he cited a New World example, that of an American "redskin chief" addressing the (British) governor of Jamaica at the beginning of a war with Spain. The chief was astonished that the civilians in the colony, including merchants, had not been enlisted. The governor explained to him that the merchants took no part in war. "When I go to war, I leave nobody at home but the women," the chief replied. Here Ferguson assumed the moral high ground of a civilized man and explained patiently that "the simple warrior" did not realize that in sophisticated nations war and commerce were not so very much distinct and "that mighty armies may be put in motion before the counter . . . and how . . . often the prince, the nobles and statesmen in many a polished nation, might . . . be considered as merchants." The fact that only specialists carried out war made it commensurate with other, more *reasonable* (i.e., utilitarian) activities.

Ferguson observed that in Western societies, "the character of the warlike and the commercial are variously combined; they are formed in different degrees by the influence of circumstances." Through the use of instrumental violence, the West had "mingled politeness with the use of the sword. We have learned to make war under the stipulations of treaties and cartels and trust to the faith of an enemy whose *ruin we mediate*."[22]

Every era, be it premodern or modern, has defined civility differently. But Westerners, when confronted by what they consider incivility, have recourse to cultural stereotyping that is as old as Herodotus. We change, but they remain true to their origins by fighting war for its own sake or for honor, not for society but for their ancestors. "Our enemies of the future will be enemies out of the past," Ralph Peters writes. The U.S. Army, he argues, would prefer to fight soldiers, not warriors. Warriors are unpredictable because (like the Scythians), they have nothing to lose. "Do we have the strength of will as a military or as a nation to defeat an enemy who has nothing to lose?"[23]

At the heart of Peters's work is the idea that because some of our enemies have little to lose, they are not true warriors. They do not behave rationally or "according to our definition of rationality"; they are not impressed by tepid shows of force with restrictive rules of engagement. By stereotyping them as savages, Peters is really arguing that people have different *mentalities* from ourselves.

> For a generation and probably much longer we [the United States] will face no military peer competitor. . . . The violent actors we encounter often will be small, hostile parties, possessed of unexpected incisive capabilities or simply of a stunning will to violence (or both). . . .
>
> We will not deal with wars of realpolitik but with conflicts born of collective emotions, sub-state interests and systems collapse. Hatred, jealousy and greed—emotion rather than strategy—will set the tone of struggle.[24]

Because they are deemed to act in this manner, they are also deemed to lack the ability to think strategically or tactically. These attitudes are dangerous. As Colin Gray contends, the idea of strategy is not confined to the civilized world. It is wrong to regard "real soldiering" as entirely instrumental, as we do today: "Armed forces that decline to take small wars seriously as a military art form with their own tactical, operational and political—though not strategic—rules invite defeat."[25]

That was the experience of the Russians in the first of the two Chechen wars. In the first conflict, their discourse of war was one of a "civilized" confronting an uncivil people. True to their first principles, the Russian military commanders assumed that Grozny (the capital) could not be defended. They were proved horribly wrong. The Chechen leaders used the capital not as an urban center but as a strategic stronghold. As one Chechen fighter put it: "We were very happy. They came into the city because we cannot fight in an open field." And as a reporter who covered the war at the time later noted, the lack of obvious barricades and tank traps in the city when the Russian army arrived led its commanders to assume that resistance would be only token and symbolic. In fact, the Chechens "were much better tacticians than that."[26]

When pressed, they proved masters of street fighting. Instead of taking to the mountains, they engaged in a battle that was as brutal as the street fighting in Stalingrad, if on a much smaller scale. And they also used "modern" methods. They disguised themselves or their vehicles as Russian, transmitted false radio messages to mislead Russian troops, and employed decoys (dummies) to draw enemy fire. At the political level, they ran a successful disinformation campaign, portraying themselves in the Western media as victims. As a result of these tactics, they were able to multiply their combat power, a thoroughly rational technique.

In the future, Westerners must be careful not to repeat the mistakes we have made in the past in refusing to treat "uncivil" warfare seriously because it is largely existential. The British made this mistake with the Maori style of warfare and the Americans with the Native American in the nineteenth century. Some military writers at the time did acknowledge that cultural factors could have a significant influence in the way both peoples chose to fight, but for the most part they had little to say on the subject. It was easier to dismiss them as "barbarous."[27] The lesson to learn from this, Colin Gray adds, is that the idea of a way of warfare is not confined to civilized societies: it can be found in "primitive" societies too.[28]

Cortés and the Aviaries of Tenochtitlán

On November 8, 1519, Hernando Cortés and 400 soldiers marched out of the city of Iztapalapa and started across the great Niztapalapa Causeway separating the lakes of Xochimilco and Chalco. Before them was the Aztec capital, Tenochtitlán. We know the impact the city made on Cortés's mind and that of his colleagues through the account of Bernal Diaz, the historian of the Spanish conquest of the Americas. What astonished them most were not the feats of engineering used to link the lakes nor the splendors of a civilization so different from their own. They were struck instead by the beauty of the capital. For the Aztecs had created a city that outshone every other in Europe. With its canals, it conjured up Venice, but at 7,200 feet up, the quality of the light made Tenochtitlán special. The Spanish were particularly stunned by the gardens the Aztecs had created, which far outshone anything in Salamanca or even Grenada (a city captured from the Moors only seventeen years before). Especially impressive were the great aviaries with their thousands of white egrets, wrens, thrushes, green jays, green-blue herons, and brooding condors. Even Cortés, bluffing his way to power and living on a constant knife's edge, noticed the birds and took time to write to Charles V describing them.

Events took their course. The Aztecs revolted. Their king, Montezuma, who had welcomed the Spanish, was stoned to death by his own people. Cortés returned to the city from an expedition on the coast and subdued it by force of arms as he worked his way through the city relentlessly, block by block, street by street. When the inhabitants refused to follow Western practice and admit defeat, every garden, canal, and home was systematically destroyed in this, "the most beautiful city of the world" (Cortés's own words to Charles V). On June 16, 1521, in a move calculated to frighten the people, he set fire to the aviaries. It was a gratuitous act of violence that has appalled historians ever since.[29] Some see it as the destructive madness of war and others as an imperialist affront to a civilization the Spanish never really comprehended or wished to understand. In reality, it was not senseless (no violence ever is). And it was not mad. It was calculated to terrorize the population. That *was* the Western way of war, and it was demonstrably effective.

There have been many other clashes of culture since 1500. That between the New World and the Old World was the first major conflict in the modern age. The wars that began with the Spanish conquest of the Americas and ended in the European conquest of Africa three centuries later were wars fought against people with different ideas of war, conditioned in turn by different political and social values. Here was a clash of different mindsets, not just a physical collision of peoples. Each fought war in their own fashion. Such conflicts, one historian claims, were "more than mere clashes of arms, they were also clashes of culture expressed in the violence of the military idiom."[30]

How did this "clash of cultures" express itself in Mexico after Cortés's arrival? It was important that he and his men found a fluid political situation. The Aztecs had only recently taken control of central Mexico in the 1420s and had established an empire that extended across most of the region. It was a kin-based society with very limited institutions and an aristocratic elite at the top of a highly stratified state. The elite was a warrior caste who fought wars to provide the sacrificial victims required in Aztec mythology to secure the continued life of the Aztec people. They never saw war outside the context of a religious ritual. It was the lack of instrumentality that the Spaniards found most disturbing. Blood sacrifice was seen to be irrational as well as barbaric. Indeed, here was perhaps the only people in the history of a settled society who did not follow its economic instincts and take the traditional path from blood sacrifice to slavery.

The Aztecs paid for this choice dearly. Human sacrifice had occurred on a modest scale until Aztec domination. It was regarded as central to sustaining the sun, the existing order of the universe, and therefore social life itself. In abolishing blood sacrifice after his victory, Cortés starved the gods and thus destroyed both them and their myths. It proved to be not only a twilight of the gods but also the twilight of an entire people.

The uncertain control the Aztecs exerted over their subject peoples enabled Cortés to succeed against impossible odds. The empire was already in decline when he arrived and faced ruin through its inability to deal with its own internal contradictions. More sacrificial victims (perhaps up to 15,000 a year) were needed, but the sources of tribute had begun to dry up. Local peoples resented having to provide them. In turn, Montezuma could not make headway against other tribes and began losing control over his existing subjects. He spent much of his time reconquering areas that had submitted to his predecessor. These wars created further divisions that Cortés was able to exploit with success.

The Spanish owed much, in fact, to the willingness of so many subject peoples to collaborate with them, and that is how military historians have begun to interpret the Spanish victory. Today they tend to see it not so much as a triumph of the Western way of warfare as the triumph of an Indian way, using some of the methods and technology that Cortés brought with him.[31] The conquistadors found themselves cooperating in a Meso-American form of war, the principal tactic of which was to breach the opposing enemy lines and turn the enemy's flank. It was a difficult maneuver for a Bronze Age people to execute, but with their cannons, matchlock muskets, crossbows, and horsemen, the Spanish were able to push home their advantage. When fighting with their allies in Mexico, they formed the spearhead in the attack, punching a hole in the enemy's lines through which the allied soldiers were able to follow.

But the fact that the Spanish were a modern people did matter. In the end, what gave Cortés the decisive advantage was not modern technology such as firearms but the fact that a Bronze Age people were hamstrung by a Bronze Age mindset. The Aztecs lacked the Spaniards' confidence in being able to shape and manipulate the world through technology. They lacked what was the decisive factor in the reconstituted Western way of warfare that Machiavelli discussed in *The Art of War*. They lacked what one writer calls "mental toughness."[32]

For in all wars, then as now, weapons count much less than the concepts of war that permit armies to use them to maximum effect. For the

Aztecs, war was a ritual, not a continuation of politics (or even as in the case of Cortés, economics). When fighting each other, Meso-American tribes would agree to fight at an appointed time and place with an equal number of troops. Prior to the battle, ceremonies would be performed to honor the gods. Once engaged, combat tended to break up into individual duels. The main object was to capture prisoners intact, for only those not wounded were considered worthy of sacrifice to the gods.

The Aztecs had very precise rules about violence to the human body. Their swords were not made of metal and could do little damage; the Spanish, by contrast, used swords of Toledo steel to hack up the bodies of their enemies and demoralize them.[33] The Aztec way of war was ritualized, perhaps more than any other we know of in a relatively sophisticated society. It was *existential,* and for that reason they found the mutilation of bodies extremely offensive. True, they mutilated their sacrificial victims, their priests tearing out their hearts while the victims were still alive. But that was the point. Sacrifices were a ritual and mutilation very much part of the service. The Aztecs, in fact, were much nearer prehistoric people than they were the conquistadors in their fear of "blood pollution." In prehistoric society, rituals were necessary; they were a civilizing process by which one lived with death. Such societies set greater store than modern people in committing violence in a prescribed, formalized, and even theatrical fashion because any deviation from protocol implied pollution. The need to avoid pollution was a form of reconciliation with the victim and ultimately a justification or legitimation of violence.[34]

The Aztec way of warfare was ritualized in another respect. Although they were prepared to raze cities to the ground and enslave their population, more often than not they preferred to encircle cities to persuade the warriors to come out and fight. And they rarely starved enemy populations into submission or deliberately targeted noncombatants because it offended their idea of war as the preserve of warriors, not civilians. At times, they are known to have even supplied enemy cities with food so it could not be said that they had won by exploiting an unfair advantage.[35] The Spanish had no such scruples; they did not "play" at war. Cortés himself was not experienced in siege warfare, but many of his soldiers were Greeks, Genoese, and Spanish who had fought in the Mediterranean and understood its principles all too well. In war, they were willing to apply maximum pressure on the entire population, including the old, women, and children. The Western way of war allowed cities to be reduced to starvation and their citizens to despair with no sense of dishonor on the part of the warrior.

There is a third feature of the Aztec form of war that made it more ritual than instrumental. Much has been made of the environmental consciousness of the Meso-American societies, and much of what has been written is simply untrue. Not all traditional cultures are environmentally friendly. But the Aztecs recognized the intrinsic worth of the American landscape in a way the Spanish did not. Mexico "belonged" to them only in the sense that they felt completely at home in it and saw it filled with the same life that pulsed through themselves, but nothing "belonged" to them as property or as right. They filled the world, and the world filled them. Their way of warfare was the reflection of a way of life that was at one with nature. The Spanish, by contrast, did not live in harmony with the natural world; they tried to impose their will on it, to tame it for their own purposes; and that is why the destruction of the aviaries of Tenochtitlán was an especial affront to Aztec sensibilities.[36]

Indeed, what affronted the Aztecs most about their invaders was their acquisitiveness and rapacity. Cortés was the ultimate individualist, a free-booter who defied a government order and went off on an entrepreneurial mission that had not been sanctioned by Spain. And once the Spanish government swallowed its pride and recognized the conquest for its own advantage, the land was pillaged for its mineral wealth and gold, and the Indians were converted into property by right of conquest. All these factors were to play a central role in the Aztecs' defeat, but they owed that defeat—in the end—less to the Spanish than to the way in which they themselves perceived the external world.

A clue to this is given by the way the Spanish saw them. Nowhere else in the world had they encountered a society in which a state-sponsored religion ensured that art, architecture, and ritual were so thoroughly dominated by death, violence, and catastrophe. War was a method of capturing victims for the slaughter, and that offended Spanish humanism (despite the fact that the Spanish put heretics to the torch and traitors to the rack). As late as the nineteenth century, Charles Baudelaire glimpsed pictures of Aztec sculptures and concluded that they belonged to "a barbaric art"—in the sense of being totally alien to the concept of Western personality. In the next century, the Chilean poet Pablo Neruda asked much the same question: "stone in the stone / but where was man?"[37]

The contemporary Mexican writer Carlos Fuentes is also struck by one of the key texts of Aztec mythology that he finds devoid of humanism. All the gods of Western civilization have had a human form as well as a human face. In Christianity, the West even mediated God through humanity in a way no other higher religion has. The Aztecs were different. Their god, Quetzalcoatl (for whom Cortés was mistaken), provoked the hostility of other gods who handed him a gift. It was a mirror. He looked into it and screamed. He assumed that as a god he had no face. Now he

saw reflected back the face of a man. Since he had a human face, he realized he had a human destiny. He fled into exile, promising to return on a
fixed day that would shake the Indian world to its foundations. It was on
that day in Aztec myth that Cortés arrived in Montezuma's court, on
Maundy Thursday 1519.[38]

As a premodern people, the Aztecs were at a further disadvantage.
Their extraordinary fatalism stemmed from an insistence on recovering
the present through the prism of the past. They relied on prophecy and
thus fell victim to notions of destiny inextricably linked to it. As a Bronze
Age people, they lived through their senses. They could infer to a limited
extent from their own experience, but they could not go beyond it.
Centuries of cultural isolation had given them too narrow a range of
human behavior. The Spanish, by comparison, knew much about other
civilizations remote from their own. They had a stockpile of knowledge
that allowed them to be more imaginative in the way they prosecuted
war.[39] Their distaste for them notwithstanding, the Spanish were curious
about the Aztecs. They used reason to understand them, to inform themselves about the people they were fighting. They quickly discovered the
extent of discontent within the Aztec empire and the demoralization that
their appearance had produced within the enemy ranks. And they made
use of Aztec mythology. In fashioning the illusion he was a god, Cortés
recognized the importance of manipulating Aztec opinion.

Of course, the Spanish use of "reason" did not lead to any empathy or
even understanding of the culture they were about to destroy. We are
encouraged to subscribe today to the belief that self-knowledge is the goal
of existence and that it develops through knowledge of cultures and people different from ourselves. That postmodern sensibility was not part of
the mental landscape of a sixteenth-century Spaniard, especially of a man
as driven by greed as Cortés himself. The conquistadors were undeniably
brutal because Aztec culture was beyond their comprehension (except for
features such as blood sacrifice and polygamy, of which they disap-
proved). And because they were unable to communicate with it, they were
unable to bring themselves to view the Aztecs as human beings like themselves. They described their "otherness" as primitive or barbaric.

Above all, however, Cortés and his men remained faithful to the
humanistic ethos of the Western way of warfare in their sheer ambition. "It
was a miracle," concluded one conquistador, Cieza de Leon, "that these
wonderful lands have remained unknown to the rest of the world through
all of history and [were] saved by God to be discovered in our time."[40]
Here, of course, is no nineteenth-century concept of *the* time in history as
the crux on which the fate of humanity turned. The Spanish conquerors

were an early, not a late modern people. But in their account of the conquest of the New World, we can find a sense of history, as opposed to the Aztec sense of destiny, as well as a sense of human agency notably lacking in the Aztec mind.

The Spanish warriors shared the Greek sensibility for history as the story of the deeds of human beings, and they experienced a sense of pride in living out a moment that would be remembered for all time. They experienced a sense of pride in outdoing the ancients in the dialogue between the modern age and the classical world, the dialogue that constitutes Western civilization. As de Leon wrote in *The War of the Chapas* (1545), Alexander the Great had sought to conquer the world with 30,000 men, but no nation had covered such immense distances as the Spanish and in such few numbers. "Everything that has happened in the marvellous discovery of the Americas, . . ." Bartolome de Las Casas wrote, "seems to overshadow all the deeds of famous people in the past and to silence all talk of other wonders of the world."[41] In this discourse, there was something definitively humanistic that both invoked the Greeks and challenged them at the same time. The conquistadors woke to a new sense of life. They experienced an expansive sense of power over history and themselves. They believed rightly that the discovery and conquest of the New World had confirmed them as *modern* warriors.

Modern Versus Unmodern

One of the classic illustrations of this attitude a few centuries later can be found in a novel by Leo Tolstoy that he left uncompleted on his death. *Hadji Murad* describes an episode in the Russian conquest of Chechnya in the mid–nineteenth century in which Tolstoy himself took part (and about which he also wrote in his novel *The Cossacks*). Hadji Murad, the novel's hero, was one of the most effective warriors of Imam Shamil, who launched an Islamic revival against Russian rule in an attempt to mold the Caucasian peoples into an Islamic nation. In Dagestan even today, this period in history is still called "the time of the Shariah."[42]

Shamil's campaign began well, as he lured the Russian soldiers into valleys and then cut them to ribbons when they attempted to return to base. The Russians found themselves attacking fortified villages organized in depth while their supply lines became overextended. But Shamil made a mistake in copying his enemies and thus departing from a way of fighting that had served him so well. In the mid-1850s, the British and French supplied him with modern artillery pieces in the hope of tying down Russian forces in the Caucasus and so preventing them from being transferred to the Crimea, where they were engaged in a war. After the conclusion of that conflict, the supply of weapons dried up quickly. Only because of Shamil's insistence on protecting the guns did the rebels engage in set-piece battles in which they were outgunned and eventually defeated.

Long before that happened one of the imam's principal warriors, Hadji Murad, had broken with him and went over to the Russians before, in turn, breaking with them and attempting to rejoin the rebels. He was eventually killed in a heroic last stand in April 1852. It would be wrong to suppose that Tolstoy either understood Hadji Murad or that he sympathized with Muslim resistance to Russian rule. Few Russians who knew the Caucasus at first hand or, like Tolstoy, served in one of the campaigns, were sympathetic to the Muslims, and Tolstoy was not one of them.

Instead, he was committed to what he called "the truth." What matters in his novel is not the issue, the fight for independence, or even the pathos of a doomed cause, but only the hero's individual response to history. Tolstoy's Murad is not a Chechen at all but a thoroughly Western romantic hero whose tragedy derives from making a heroic but impossible last stand against history. And in Tolstoy's own understanding of history, like that of many modern writers, there is little place for free will. In *War and Peace* (1865–1869), he made fun of heroes like Napoleon who thought they could make their mark on history through their own indomitable will to power. As a historical determinist, Tolstoy believed that the measure of human freedom was declining in the world as the Industrial Revolution and Western imperialism marched on regardless of all obstacles in their path.

In Tolstoy's novel, the Russians are free to fight the campaign brutally or not and the Chechens free to fight or to surrender. But both must conform to the dictates of history, which in the mid–nineteenth century were Western expansionism and, in this case, Russian rule. Like his cause, Hadji is an anachronism. He only has one last freedom: to die courageously, his identity as a warrior enhanced. But he—and we—know that he accomplishes nothing.[43]

We may have lost that belief in historical determinism, but many of us still think in the purely instrumental terms that encouraged writers such as Tolstoy to formulate the ideas they did. If modern warriors are agents of history, then they fight on the side of modernity. Other warriors do not. As modern warriors, they are more soldiers than warriors, and technology will play a much larger role in their thinking, for it is the mark of modernity, after all.

In Transcaucasia still, the Russians see what they want to: a historically dispossessed world. Other cultures in Western eyes appear to be historical fossils or societies that are in the process of "reprimitivizing" themselves. Left behind by history, they are becoming "local" and therefore not worthy of universal interest. We may no longer, of course, believe that history has a theme or be as conscious as Cortés of writing it anew, but we do believe it shows development. We may no longer subscribe to our ancestors' unquestioned belief in progress, but we do subscribe to the belief that a people are unhistorical when they show no development. Hegel told us—and it is something most Westerners still believe even if we have never read him—that human freedom is the same thing as human consciousness of freedom. So the development of freedom is the development of consciousness, a process of thought that is *historical* because there are numerous phases in which consciousness is achieved. And what is that development in war (in our eyes at least), if not the growing importance of the instrumental?

In regarding our enemies as people from the past—the bandits, child warriors, and warlords who have reappeared from the pages of history—we see a people apparently trapped in the past, living in a different time zone from our own. Trapped in their own history or even worse, reclaimed by it, they have regressed and thus are no longer true historical agents.[44]

THE PADDLEBOATS OF WUSHONG: THE BRITISH ENCOUNTER THE CHINESE WAY OF WARFARE

In the early nineteenth century, a conflict finally broke out that had threatened to erupt from the time the Portuguese first entered the South China Sea in the sixteenth century. A European power, Britain, went to war against China. The reason was opium, a product produced in India but shipped or rather smuggled to China to pay for imports of tea. The Chinese government had issued several formal bans on this trade since the 1790s, but the sale of opium soon became the principal source of revenue for the British Empire in India and one of the major supports of its rule. When the Chinese government seized 20,000 cases of illegal opium and ordered British merchants to leave the city of Canton, war quickly ensued.

The first encounters were scarcely more than skirmishes. When British reinforcements arrived they took the war into the Yangtze estuary and into an entirely new phase. At the battle at Wushong in 1842, the British and Chinese navies collided. The British had the advantage of steam vessels, which they used both as tugs to pull men-of-war upstream and as armored gunboats equipped with heavy guns. River transportation by steam was even more effective than it was at sea (the oceangoing navy was still in the age of sails). The twisting and turning of China's rivers meant that the winds could not possibly blow from the right quarter for long since each bend in the river changed a ship's angle to the wind. And the rivers' narrow confines greatly limited the ability to tack. Drawing only 3 feet of water, Chinese junks were far more effective in these conditions than European sailing ships. Steam overcame both problems, however, and within a few years, British sea power had extended upriver 200 miles to Nanking.

What amazed the British at Wushong was that the Chinese navy used paddleboats. The British had a fleet of fourteen steam-powered boats, whereas the Chinese used five treadmill vessels powered by sailors. Surprised at being confronted by paddle wheelers, the British arrived at an inevitable conclusion. The memoirs of Commander W. H. Hall, the captain of one of the British ships, includes this entry:

> The most remarkable improvement of all and what showed the rapid stride towards a great change which [the Chinese] were daily making, as well as the ingenuity of the Chinese character, was the construction of several large wheeled vessels which were afterwards brought forward against us with great confidence. . . . The idea must have been suggested to them by the reports they received concerning the wonderful power of our steamers or wheeled vehicles.[45]

In fact, far from copying the British, the Chinese had merely revived an invention of their own from the fifth century C.E. A thousand years earlier, the Chinese navy had had hundreds of paddle wheelers, each capable of carrying up to 800 men.

Commander Hall's journal is interesting for two reasons, which help to define the image and self-worth of the late modern European warrior class. First, there is no evidence of any embarrassment about the narcotics trade he was engaged in promoting. We should not expect to find modern sensibilities in the journals of a mid-Victorian sea captain or expect him to see himself as we might do today, as an official drug runner. But what his own attitude toward the Chinese betrays is a tendency to be dismissive of other societies, an attitude that can be explained by the innate belief, often unacknowledged, that a technologically superior culture has right on its side.

Undoubtedly, the technological superiority that the West has enjoyed since the 1820s accounts for the ruthlessness with which it prosecutes war still. In Hall's case, he assumed the Chinese had copied the British models and even their techniques of waging war, to no avail, of course, because they were psychologically unprepared for European arms and techniques. In some cases, they were so unprepared that their psychological collapse made way for Western technological advancement.

In short, compounding our historical ignorance is the arrogance that follows from the fact that the West was the first to experience an Industrial Revolution. Ever since, it has tended to hold the high ground in war, as the Enlightenment permitted it to hold the high ground in history. We are still locked into a quasi-Hegelian world, tied to Hegel's vision of humankind's ascent to freedom by means of European development: through the Greeks to the Enlightenment and through the Enlightenment to the French Revolution and beyond. In the grand sweep of things, the non-Western world was not historically significant or, for that matter, very interesting. And it was inevitable that when the Europeans encountered the Chinese in battle, they saw what they wanted to see (or what they expected to find). What they found, to quote Hegel, was a people stuck in its "cultural infancy."

Second, Hall's journal shows that one can take pride even in destruction. "I never saw anything more beautiful," one British commander in China commented later in the century, "than the precision of our fire at long range."[46] But then the Victorians did not see themselves as destroying anything of value. As Martin van Creveld points out, technology is not just an assemblage of hardware: it is a philosophical system, and as such it not only affects the way war is conducted but also establishes the framework used for thinking about it. Technology, however, does more. It is based on the application of reason. It follows that the more rational a society is, the more reasonable it believes itself to be; its main object is to get the enemy to *see reason,* in this case through the ineluctable logic of fire power.[47]

War, in the Western tradition, illustrates what the American social scientist Thomas Sowell calls the importance of "cultural capital." In his own study of war, he invokes an old debate about what are deemed to be two of the principal differences between Asia and the West, the failure to copy other peoples' inventions and, worse still, the failure to properly exploit one's own.[48] The Chinese warrior was not esteemed in the West because China itself was considered to be technologically deficient. The invention of gunpowder did not lead to any revaluation of the Chinese way of war, even though by the mid–ninth century C.E., Taoist alchemical philosophers were the only ones in the world to have discovered the recipe for gunpowder. Over the next 300 years, the Chinese developed a completely new family of weapons never seen before: flame-throwing lances, exploding grenades, larger catapult-launched bombs, man-portable guns, and even the first cannon. This march from exploding powder to effective artillery was an impressive and sustained technological achievement and one that only China at the time could have pioneered. But it failed to change Chinese thinking about war as did the introduction of gunpowder in Europe.

If we look closer, however, we will find that the overall picture is a little more complex. The Chinese (unlike their Japanese neighbors) did use cannon throughout the seventeenth and eighteenth centuries. But it was the type of warfare in which the last dynasty engaged—steppe warfare—that reduced the importance of cannon in a way that was not true of Europe. Military success was measured in its ability to deploy—and sustain—armies in environments as different and hostile as the Gobi desert and the Tibetan plateau. And in this the Qing excelled. They were the first dynasty, in fact, to master steppe warfare, and their armies did not disintegrate even when operating thousands of miles from home, as did Napoleon's army in Russia in 1812.[49] For the first time, they were able to master the barbarian tribes of the north, but they could not subdue the barbarians who came by sea. It would have pained the Victorians, of course, to have recognized that they were regarded by the Chinese as nomadic warriors, little different from the Mongols and Tartars. The latter two reigned supreme from the backs of horses and the former from the decks of ships. Even today, it still takes a striking leap of imagination for Westerners to see ourselves in such an unfavorable light.

Conclusion

We have seen that Western warriors distinguished themselves from other warriors they encountered in history by a very precise set of humanistic criteria.

1. They were not "savage." War was the business of "civil" people not enslaved to their passions or pursuing their enemies out of revenge. Western warriors were rational.

2. They were "modern," and their ingenuity and inventiveness gave them a technological edge. The use of reason to solve the problems of war through the medium of technology marked Western warriors as children of an enlightened age.

3. They were progressive. To be sure, that was largely a phenomenon of late modernity. If we read Edward Creasy's book, *Fifteen Decisive Battles of the World* (1851), we find that its mid-Victorian author chose only those engagements that saw the triumph of Western ideas or values.

But the idea of progress goes as far back as the Greek enlightenment. We find it in Thuycidides' discussion of naval power: starting from myth and Minos's fleet, he moves to the projection of Greek naval power against Troy and concludes with the grand strategy of sea power pioneered by Pericles against Sparta.

The sense of superiority that the West drew from its encounter with the non-Western world still persists, but we forget that it is only comparatively recently that the West has enjoyed a decisive military advantage over others. The historian Edward Gibbon famously congratulated Europe on its cannon and fortifications, which had for the first time created an "impregnable barrier against the Tartar hordes."[50] Now the Europeans could pacify barbarous reaches of the globe, something that Adam Smith also famously told his readers was a mark of their civility.

> In modern war the great experience of fire arms gives an evident advantage to the nation that can best afford that experience and consequently to an opulent and civilized over a poor and barbarous nation. In ancient times the opulent and civilized found it difficult to defend themselves against the poor and barbarous nations. In modern times the poor and barbarous find it difficult to defend themselves against the opulent and civilized.[51]

In recent years, however, two developments have transformed the contours of Adam Smith's world. Today the barbarians can attack the opulent, as they did on September 11, 2001, when the al-Qaeda network struck at the World Trade Center. This time, "the opulent" are under threat from groups who are quite willing to resort to "catastrophic terrorism" to get across their message. This time, the barbarians have won back the advantage lost to them when the Europeans introduced firearms and drill in the seventeenth century.

And today the opulent can no longer intervene with impunity wherever they like, in part because societies like China are becoming opulent themselves. Even in the poorer parts of the world (or the more "barbarous"), Western armies have been beaten by poorly armed, poorly trained foot soldiers who have made up for what they lack in arms by the spirit with which they fight. In the streets of Mogadishu and Beirut, the Americans encountered a people whose cultural capital stood them in good stead. The Americans were chased out by their superior morale and tenacity of purpose. It was they who lacked the "human factors" that Clausewitz tells us allow armies to prevail in battle: courage and hatred being chief among them.

In short, "cultural capital" involves more than technical ingenuity, though the West is not always willing to acknowledge this in an age when its own way of warfare has become almost purely instrumental and when reliance on technology, not will or courage or stamina, has never been more pronounced. Other societies continue to place less emphasis on technology and more on will and morale. It is to those societies that we must now turn, even though the West has paid scant attention to non-Western cultures with their very different ethos of war, one that is *humanitarian* rather than humanistic.

6

The Warrior Tradition & the Non-Western Way of Warfare

It is a Platonic notion that in order to understand what something is, one must also consider what it is not. It is also a Platonic notion that what something *is* can be grasped by considering those instances that succeed in being the thing in question. One will never understand the Western way of war or its own warrior tradition without understanding other cultural traditions.

But first we have to ask why the West has expressed so little interest in or understanding of those traditions. In most civilizations, the main emphasis on making humanity responsible for its own fate usually, but not always, carried some sort of pantheistic implication. The Greek conception, by contrast, was that humanity is recognizable only in its interaction with itself. In the early years, "impiety" in the absence of organized religion was defined as an act against the harmony of the collective (the city-state). But the Greeks later discovered the order of the human psyche beyond the order of the polis, and finding the internal cosmos of more interest than the external, they began to seek its inner laws. The identification of self-consciousness, reason, and the good life reached its first full form in Socrates, who taught that man's first duty should be the ordering of himself and paid the penalty for questioning the collective "being" of the city by being condemned to death. In Western philosophy, the treatment of Socrates still remains the greatest crime against the urge to "become" what we are and the greatest blow against free enquiry into the human condition.[1]

Once self-knowledge was allowed in Western thought, the West found great difficulty in according equality to other cultures. Instead, we find a clash between a self-consciously "becoming" culture (the West) and other "being" cultures, less self-conscious perhaps but more attuned to identity in the world and less concerned with the painful clash between identity and authenticity that was to be a mark of modernity later on.[2] In its contact with the non-Western world after the fifteenth century, the West translated this critical difference into a critique of societies that denied or were believed to hold back human self-realization. Writers like Hegel were able to identify a lack of progress or historical ossification in the non-Western world. Treating history and humanity as the same, Hegel defined those societies as "historyless" because he found them lacking in human potential.

It was a critique that was to become more insistent and vocal in the Enlightenment, when the West began to redefine humanity without an antecedent faith. Faith became optional; liberty did not. In the Enlightenment, reason was deemed to teach that human beings are free to realize their potential without reference to anything outside human nature itself. The U.S. Declaration of Independence (1776) insisted that the right to liberty was "self-evident" through the exercise of reason. The French Declaration of the Rights of Man (1789) defined those rights as those of "man *and the citizen.*" Hegel made famous the idea that living reason was the self-realization of the Spirit in and through the agency of human consciousness. And he believed the non-Western world could realize its own potential by including itself in the final phase of human evolution: the Western (the final phase in the objectification of the Absolute Spirit).

In this difference between "becoming" and "being" cultures lies the essential difference between the Western and non-Western warrior ideals. Western warriors have located themselves in a humanistic discourse on war, whereas non-Western warriors have located themselves in one that is *humanitarian.*

HUMANITARIANISM AND WAR

To call war "humanitarian" is not to claim it is especially humane or that it is marked by "humanitarianism." Human life has been held cheaply until recently, and in many societies it still is. But in general, non-Western societies have sought to ritualize or restrict the damage that war does to nature and the human habitat, and generally they have fought wars in keeping with a tradition usually sanctioned by religion. Of course, Western societies are notoriously dismissive of such thinking. From the point of view of the humanist, humanitarian war deprives itself of intellectual freedom through its insistence on ritual and rules. From the point of view of the humanitarian, humanism, taking human freedom to be absolute in its claims, overestimates the rationality of "reason." From the viewpoint of history, one may include too little and the other too much.

Whatever Westerners may think of them, most non-Western ways of warfare proved highly effective against other non-Western societies. Against the West, most failed and failed disastrously. The nineteenth century saw the demise of styles of warfare as diverse as the Mameluk in Egypt, the Zulu in Africa, and the Maori in New Zealand. It was also the period when the Native American way of warfare failed to save them from total defeat in the last and most intensive phase of the American Indian wars. Only two non-Western ways of warfare have survived: the Chinese and Levantine. And if we are to understand them we must first grasp the three most important principles of the humanitarian war ethos.

Necessity

All societies ground war on necessity. To distinguish war from murder, we need to know why people have to die and why our enemies have to be killed. States may go to war to attain certain aims, and warriors may engage in battle to experience or celebrate their own humanity, but it is necessity that tells us why both are required to act in the way they do. According to the rationalist approach pioneered by the Greeks (and transmitted to Western civilization), necessity is a secular idea. Aristotle tells us that philosophy aims at the revelation of necessity, whereas poetry is concerned with the possible and history with the actual. History is instrumental: it explains why states go to war, and from reading it, one may arrive at the conclusion that some societies fight wars for ends different from others. It was Aristotle himself who concluded from his reading of the history of his own people that war was "a form of acquisitive activity." It was one way, for example, by which a society that put so much emphasis on leisure could find slaves to work.

Poetry, by contrast, presents us with images of virtuous and vicious men and women. It celebrates the ideal of courage and heroism in war and inspires the warriors to heroic acts so that they may live in the memory of men. As Epictetus remarks, "it is not through the deeds of men but through the words about these deeds that we are moved," and we are moved more by the poetic than we are by history.[3]

It is philosophy, however, that reveals not only what the vicious and virtuous are in themselves but also why they are part of the construct of humanity and the extent to which they form the historicity of culture. "Know thyself" was the ultimate Greek aim, and in forging a humanistic form of war, the Greeks set out to do just that. Self-observation means not only learning from the outside but observing from within, not only looking at one's own behavior but looking in on it. Hobbes described it as follows: "Given the similitude of the thoughts and passions of one man to the thoughts and passions of another, whosoever looked into himself and considereth what he doth, when he does *think, opine, reason, hope, fear* and upon what grounds; he shall thereby read and know what are the thoughts and passions of all other men upon the like occasions."[4] In that sense, the West has grounded war on human nature at its best and at its worse. That is why Hobbes's first book was a translation of Thucydides, for he found in the Greek historian's understanding and observation of war all he needed to know about the human condition.

Other Western writers less pessimistic than Thucydides or Hobbes have tended to overestimate the human ability to control war's passions. When these passions do spill over into the kind of internecine fighting that distinguished the last years of the Peloponnesian War, they are always attributing what happens to a "negative dialectic" rather than to war's "true nature." Other societies have refused to exaggerate the extent to which human beings can act "reasonably." They have insisted that not every agent is wholly or directly responsible for what he or she does. Moral experience is often limited. We do not always know what we are doing until we have done it—if then. We do not always act with a clear idea of ends.

Most non-Western cultures, in other words, have grounded war in necessity too, but on religious foundations: Zen in Japan, Hinduism in India, and Islam in the Middle East. What those religious systems preach is that the ground of necessity is limited. War is necessary because it is part of the human condition, but it is an evil because it disturbs the harmony of the world and the justice of God. It is therefore incumbent on those who practice it to do *only* what is necessary and no more. It is important to set limited ends. Necessity, in that respect, is social and is judged by social needs. A society in harmony with itself will be able to wage war more successfully than a society that is not.

That is the message of Taoism, one of China's three leading philosophical ethical-religious systems. The other systems, Confucianism and Buddhism, used the word *Tao* to refer to the way of right living. But in Taoism, the Tao *is* the Way: it is the universal principle in all things. Many attempts to translate the word usually fall short of the task, for the Tao is the Way of nature as a whole rather than a specific way of living within the natural order. The union with the Way is not secured by striving to achieve specified ends but rather by relinquishing desire, reducing needs, and subduing acquisitiveness. What results is a kind of lived understanding—a knowing "how" rather than a knowing "that." Taoism, therefore, requires every warrior to understand that there are strict limits to human ambition.

Thus in the *Tao Te Ching* (The Way and its power) one finds this advice to the soldier. Use arms only when *necessary:*

> Use only arms when there is no other course of action. A skilful leader of troops is not aggressive with his military strength.
>
> A skilful fighter does not become angry, This is called the virtue of non-competing.[5]

Much of this may read as mystical, but we should remember that the work from which I have just quoted was intended to be a practical manual for China's leaders. The work rejects an unqualified belief in human rationality. For in wartime, people's emotions are caught up in a manner that prevents them from living in harmony with the Way. The Chinese had a very developed understanding of the speed with which war taps into irrational forces. Unlike their Western counterparts, Chinese philosophers focused on consequences, not intentions.

In China, the warrior tradition at its most ruthless flourished in the period of the Warring Kingdoms. That great caesura in Chinese history was a constant reminder of the danger of allowing an independent warrior class to challenge the harmony of a system guaranteed by an imperial dynastic order that ruled with the mandate of heaven. The Taoist principles enshrined in Chinese military writings required war to be conducted in conformity with a set of strict prescriptions. Two common mistakes often get in the way of understanding these principles. The first is to assume that China was more pacific than other cultures, yet it was frequently aggressive against its neighbors, experienced periods of prolonged imperial expansion, and was always willing to use force, though for rigidly instrumental ends. The second mistake is to draw from these principles distilled lists that are suspiciously like the military professional's classic principles of war: offense, defense, economy of force, and surprise. The great Chinese military classic, Sun Tzu's *The Art of War,* is as much a philosophical text, a Taoist text, as a military manual. The Chinese way of warfare was humanitarian precisely because it was the product of philosophical thinking aimed from the beginning to preserve the system, not transform it. But in so doing, it remained definitively instrumental—war remained an activity of the state.

Ritual

What has often struck Western analysts is the extent to which ritual has played so important a role in non-Western warfare. Anthropologists have found it useful to distinguish between instrumental and expressive violence: to distinguish what a society finds important in terms of the relation between means and goals (its technical use of violence) and what it wants to "say," or express by the use of violence.[6] Even in the West, the use of ritual once characterized a majority of violent acts, including sacrifice, dueling, public executions, and even war. All these actions have been bound in the past by rules and proscriptions, etiquette and protocol. In war, in particular, violent action means crossing the greatest threshold of all, from life to death, and doing so in a way that legitimizes the act of killing. The taking of blood has always involved some form of ritual.

Ritual practices were not entirely unknown in ancient Greece. In the early centuries of its history, the outcome of a single battle was usually accepted. Though genuinely violent and murderous (Nietzsche correctly spoke of the "murderous little wars" between the city-states), they were usually of short duration. A battle might last for no more than a few hours, and its outcome was usually accepted. Ritual practices such as sacrifices to the gods and the burial of the dead came to vindicate and legitimate war. But in time, they were abandoned altogether. As the city-states developed into great powers, they began to fight great wars. Thucydides believed the war between Athens and Sparta the greatest conflict in history, and one of the features that made it different from those that had gone before was its unrestrained level of inhumanity.

By contrast, some of the most advanced societies preserved a ritualized way of war until well into the nineteenth century. The most famous example, as well as the most instructive, is Japan. When they first began importing European guns in the late sixteenth century, the Japanese improved upon their design. Even more impressive, they employed them more imaginatively. One daimyo (local warlord) fielded 3,000 musketeers at the battle of Nagashino in 1575 (depicted in Akira Kurosawa's film *Ran*). His use of mass musket volleys was completely innovative and was not seen in Europe for another sixty years. This dramatic engagement raised the musket (*tanegashima*) from an adjunct weapon to the key armament of early modern Japanese armies and made them the best in the world. But then the unexpected happened: the Japanese abandoned the use of guns altogether.

The main explanation is that their use was inconsistent with a *humanitarian* way of warfare. Muscular effort was considered to be at one with nature; chemical energy was not.[7] Guns made war less ritualistic and more destructive, and dying without coming to grips with the enemy was an affront to the Samurai tradition. The sword was the symbol of the samurai's position in society (only the samurai were allowed by law to carry two). The finest swords became the property of the richest warriors, and being a swordsmith was the most highly respected craft. The sword and its expert use attained spiritual importance in samurai life.

This is not to say that instrumental goals were not important for the samurai; they fought, after all, for the political ambitions of their masters. And when they revolted against modernization—the imposition of a gun culture—in the 1870s, they did so for a specific reason too: to arrest the military reforms that threatened their status. But in the seventeenth century (until the Tokugawa shogunate [1640–1868] imposed peace on the country), they continued to fight for goals by trying to attain them in a special, prescribed, and *ritualized* fashion.

In retrospect, of course, we can also see the intellectual limitations of such thinking, when the modern age finally arrived in Japan in the shape of a U.S. gunship. Respect for muscular effort also translated into a rejection of labor-saving devices. Japan had many of the ingredients of an Industrial Revolution in the eighteenth century: large cities, high literacy rates, and even a futures market. But the Japanese turned their back on a work-based revolution so as not to put people out of work. Instead of an Industrial Revolution, they experienced an industrious one, which is astonishing for a nation we now think of as one of the most technologically advanced in the world.

Social Conformity

What distinguishes non-Western thinking is the belief that if war is what human beings do and if human nature is defined by what society permits and prohibits, then it is possible to fence war in with social taboos. It is the survival of the culture that is vital. In that sense, other societies, unlike those in the West, never developed a "grammar of war" independent of the grammar of life.

The Indian way of war, for example, was tied exclusively to maintaining the Indian way of life. In India, society, being fundamentally holistic, created an extremely close interdependence among its members. The caste system imposed a series of collective obligations that left little scope for individualism as the West would understand it. The only real individualism in the Western sense of allowing free initiative is that of the ascetic, not the warrior, the second-highest caste. It is the saint who renounces this world in favor of self-enlightenment. But Hinduism is not a religion of individual self-renunciation, of losing oneself *in* the world. On the contrary, the saint or ascetic renounces the world to devote himself to his own liberation. Whereas the Western individual lives in the social world, the Indian lives outside it. In the holistic universe, renunciation corresponds to "a social state apart from society proper."[8]

Just like the ascetic, the warrior was a member of a caste with its own *dharma*, an untranslatable term usually rendered in English as "piety." This piety was not the *pietas* of Aeneas, the warrior who served Rome's destiny. It was that of a hereditary warrior aristocracy whose first duty in life was to live by its own code of honor. And that remained true of most other warrior traditions, especially in Japan and the Levant, which is why war has had so little impact on their lives. The exception—a critical one— was their encounter with the West. In many cases, the experience was so traumatic that the warrior tradition did not survive.

The Samurai as Conscript Soldier: The Apotheosis and End of the Japanese Warrior Tradition

Revaluing Tradition

All non-Western warrior traditions have faced the challenge of modernity since the mid–nineteenth century. Some (the Chinese) have been successfully revalued; others have succumbed.[9] The Japanese, like most other non-Western people, faced a crisis in the first half of the twentieth century. Two Japanese words denote the concept of the modern—*kindai* and *gendai*. The first, which appeared as early as the eighth century, has an etymology as old as the Latin word *modernus*. In the fifth century, Chinese culture had spread to the islands; a century later, Buddhism was made the official religion by imperial edict. Both helped forge the culture we know today. From the beginning, the "modern" in Japanese history was the capacity of a culture to survive and renew itself and to distance itself sufficiently from its outside "parent" so that it could maintain its unique identity.

Japanese historians use the word *kindai* not only for the early centuries of their history but also for the era that spans the dawn of the Meiji restoration (1868) to the end of World War II, an era that saw the end of Japanese feudalism and the modernization of the country. By comparison, the word *gendai* is used of the period since World War II. In other words, the "modern" means something both intrinsic to Japanese culture (the pursuit of the new, displayed especially in national inventiveness) and the adoption of a set of values that are considered to be external to the Japanese way of life.[10]

What makes the modern world so dynamic and so different from the premodern is its recognition that every value is conditional. Society will not survive long if it continues to adhere to values that are no longer creative. Institutions often have to be replaced and customs reinvented. New institutions, in turn, create new values. What makes a society modern is the recognition that it is necessary to challenge those ways of organizing social life that are no longer valuable. Only a society that can reinvent itself and its traditions will survive. So what were the values the Japanese wished to revalue after 1868? As far as the warrior ethos was concerned, there were two.

The samurai tradition. The first value was the wish to preserve the samurai ethic. The samurai were originally medieval knights who paid lip service to a chivalric code but were essentially in the business of making money. They were unusual mercenaries, however, for they combined the ritual of war with the writing of poetry, and what made them especially different was that instead of living (as mercenaries usually do) for the here and now, they were always looking back to a golden age—the Heian Period in the eighth century C.E. By the fifteenth century, imperial power had vanished. The samurai themselves became an aristocratic military class, vassals of the powerful daimyos who displayed themselves at the court of Edo, while the emperor at Kyoto presided over a life without power.

With the Meiji restoration in 1868, the state introduced new concepts of administrative rationality and efficiency. They, in turn, created a new intellectual framework that enabled the Japanese to see which aspects of the samurai way no longer had value in the modern world and which could be revalued to create a form of modernity that was distinctively Japanese. The samurai ethic was extended to encompass the whole nation, to adapt it to the demands and needs of a nation-state.

Strange as it may seem, that the peasants should be encouraged to emulate the samurai was not especially revolutionary. During the Tokugawa period, they themselves had tried to copy certain aspects of the ethical system of the ruling elite. With the Meiji restoration, they were actively encouraged to do so, swapping loyalty to the feudal master for loyalty to the emperor. One famous publication, the *Kokutai no Hongi* (*The fundamentals of our national policy*), which was intended to be an ethical manual for nationalism, taught that death for the emperor was not self-sacrifice but "a casting aside of our little selves . . . and the enhancing of the *genuine life* of the people."[11]

Zen Buddhism. The second value was religion. The survival of Japanese culture appeared to be conditional for much of the twentieth century, especially in the interwar years. It followed that modernization had to be an *existential* exercise as well as a moral one. It had to be a strategy for survival (an experience that no Western liberal society has had to confront). For that reason, Japan's modernization was not a secular experience but a religious one. Religion was not even *a* means to the end of modernization. It was *the* means. It was a way of preserving the sacramental nature of Japanese culture. As Robert Bellah writes, when religion maintains its "commitment to the source of ultimate value" (in this case, the survival of a distinctive way of life), it remains religion.[12]

Of the many different Buddhist sects, Zen was the most influential. With its definition of mutual obligations of vassal and lord, it provided the military with a distinctive code of honor. It was true that the use of the sword (the mark of the samurai warrior) was destructive. It killed and was used specifically for that end and, as such, might be considered to be at odds with one of the chief features of Buddhism: compassion. But the sword was used to defend a way of life, and the samurai honor code lay in the willingness to lay down one's life for one's master. Laying down one's life for one's master mitigated the killing power of the sword and in so doing transformed war into a *moral* enterprise.

The samurai honor code was called Bushido. It was (as with so much of Japanese culture) another import from China. It is the Japanese (*bu*) rendition of the Chinese *wu* (martial spirit). And perhaps because it was imported, it did not achieve its fullest poetic expression until much later, in the Tokugawa era, when Japan was at peace for the first time in centuries, and the samurai had been transformed into minor functionaries.

It was in this period that *The Hagakure* (1716)—the gospel of the Bushido ethic—produced an ideal for courage that was totally alien to the humanist ethos of war. For it held that warriors should assume that they were already dead. Because they should expect to die in their master's service, all that remained was the consummation of the fact. True warriors had to act in such a manner as not to dishonor either themselves or their master. In extreme circumstances, *seppuku* (ritual suicide) was merely another way of accepting death. What made this tradition distinctly unmodern was that it made few concessions to what modernity prizes most: not the transcendental but the mundane. It had no time for human calculation, consideration, or doubt and none at all for self-questioning. Ultimately, even if warriors suspected that their sacrifices were in vain, it did not matter because death was expected to absolve them of any ill deeds, provided they behaved courageously.[13]

The Bushido ethic became problematic in the early twentieth century, when Zen Buddhism and the state forged a much closer relationship than in the past. Once religion began to be associated with the rise of a militant nationalism, the generals were able to tap into moral and material resources that had not been available in the premodern era. They were able to fight a more intensive kind of warfare. With the demise of feudalism, Bushido was now expected of every citizen (including the peasants), as was self-sacrifice. Indeed, every feature of Bushido, such as generosity and uprightness, began to be proclaimed essential elements of the Japanese nation.

A Zen Primer, published in 1927, established a dubious historical connection between the two. "Warrior Zen," as Brian Vittoria calls it, became a major theme of 1930s writing, with its stress on the transience of life and the need to subjugate the "self" to a larger whole, the nation. In Japan, Zen transcended the subjective individual attitude toward salvation. It required of the soldier undivided self-sacrifice on behalf of the emperor (who, in turn, was seen as the incarnation of the selfless wisdom of the universe). The Bushido ethic also put the main emphasis not on the individual, loyalty to ideas (whether abstract or real), or a code of individual ethics, let alone a relationship with God, but on unquestioning obedience to a feudal lord, or after 1868, the emperor.[14]

These ideas seemed to conform to the peculiar spirit of self-sacrifice that the modern battlefield demanded. "Zen is a religion of willpower and willpower is what is urgently needed by warriors," one twentieth-century Zen thinker wrote.[15] As early as the Russo-Japanese War (1904–1905), foreign observers had been impressed by the remarkable courage of Japanese soldiers, even in the face of intensive firepower in the desperate, unimaginative assaults on Russian positions that so shocked the commanding officer General Nogi that he had asked (and was refused) permission to take his own life.

Reflecting on their own unexpected success over a Western power, the Japanese decided that they possessed a distinctive military ethic, summarized in the terms *seishin* (spirit) and *Yamato damashii* (the fighting Japanese spirit). Since spirit was the universally acclaimed factor that explained Japan's victory over Russia, the army leadership tended to emphasize the irrational (spirit) over the material (technology). The infantry field manual, while giving lip service to the doctrine of combined arms, in fact placed the total burden on infantry assaults to attain victory in the field. Late in 1928, the army revised one of its key doctrinal manuals, *The Essential Points of Supreme Command,* significantly deleting the words "surrender," "retreat," and "defense."[16]

Zen was important in this development because of the ideological support it gave the concept of spirit. It helped forge a code of sacrifice and extreme courage A kamikaze pilot who survived the war later explained that "the most effective thing to do was to train one's mind by Zen meditation."[17] Unfortunately, by 1945, the spirit of self-sacrifice was expected not only of pilots but the entire nation as it prepared for the expected invasion by an unforgiving United States.

Japan as a Different Modernity

In revaluing its military traditions, Japan was being very modern. Historians now recognize that Japan was indeed a modern country in the 1930s. "Structural differentiation" (to use the jargon of social science) was obvious in every institution of Japanese life, from the family to the class system. Urbanization, industrialization, and mass politics were well advanced. Japan's leaders may have gone to war in 1941 to defend Japanese culture from fragmentation and to defend it from class divisions and differences created by the country's own rapid industrial development and the desire of its more liberal citizens to integrate it even further into the world economy. But they did so—ironically—in the language of modernity, in the name of "rebuilding," "regenerating," "reawakening," and "rebirth." What is ironic to us, looking back, is that the strategy, though described at the time as antimodern, was distinctively modern in idiom. For all their talk of going back to the past, they wanted to give Japanese culture a twentieth-century face. For modernity is self-reflective. Even the wish to return to the past has to be framed in a modern way. It is part of a modern discourse.

Even the kamikaze tactic employed in the last months of World War II was not unmodern, for it still presupposed the critical importance of human agency in life. Modernity encourages people to recognize themselves as agents rather than instruments of fate or creatures of circumstance. One of the extraordinary consequences of cultural renewal—including Islamic fundamentalism—is that it invests life with renewed meaning. If the principal requirement of power is to empower ourselves, the principal requirement of value is to enhance life. If the revaluation of values (or culture) is the task, the nation-state and nationalism are the means through which it is carried out. The nation-state, in particular, allows states to tap into enormous human resources; it allows them to mobilize an entire people.

The message of Japanese nationalism was that through the will alone, the Japanese could build a new nation. Where it failed and where all other political religions failed, especially fascism and communism, was in the belief in the possibility of bridging the gap between the transcendental and the mundane. In Europe, the great political religions like Marxism were the products of the absence of religion in people's lives. They fulfilled a social need. They were not religions in the strict sense, but they caricatured the fundamental patterns of religious belief. They sacralized entire communities such as the nation or class. Like the great religions, they offered the faithful redemption from an ontological crisis.

Japanese militarism in the 1930s was also modern in the use of words like "innovation," "creation," and "self-creation." But it also shared with the political religions of late modernity another language: "hope," "faith," "transcendence," "immanence," all of which were traditional theological terms and portrayed a very modern if distorted belief that although warriors were something immanent in nature, they could escape the inexorable working of natural law (they could defy the rational, or material, circumstances of life).[18]

Post-Hiroshima Nation

By 1945, the role of the Japanese warrior class had been played out. Economic power had begun to drift to large business corporations that did well out of the war and seized the high ground of industrial production during it. The social and political functions of the aristocracy were passing to others. The military still spoke the language of the samurai; it still believed itself to be the bearer and custodian of a great historical tradition, but its way of warfare had become obsolete. The kamikaze phenomenon marked the bankruptcy of that tradition. The heirs of the samurai had failed. Japan's future belonged to others.

A whole nation cannot be made into warriors; in its attempt to do so, the high command subverted the very notion of the warrior's honor. Moreover, collective national suicide is not a strategy. One of the new generation of postwar Japanese writers to recognize the fact was Sakaguchi Ango. In an essay entitled "On Decadence," written in April 1946, he contrasted the national myth of the war with the return to genuine humanity in Japanese life. The kamikaze hero, he claimed, had been a mere illusion. Humane history had begun at the point at which the kamikazes who survived had turned to black marketeering, as the great majority did. The samurai ethic was not the problem, if it could be revalued again.[19]

Every individual could now create his or her own samurai ethic. No society not based on genuine subjective autonomy at the individual level could survive in the modern era. But, of course, this was not democratic humanism as understood in the West but collectivist humanism. Japan's recovery after 1945 was national and the pursuit of economic growth protectionist, based as it was on the understanding that the nation had to trust itself, not its allies. And the wish to avoid social inequality so important in Japanese history was distinctively collectivist as well.

Buddhism too was revalued. The day after the first contingent of U.S. troops arrived in Japan, the prime minister declared that the future lay with "the collective repentance of a hundred million people."[20] The same message was found in the work of Tenabi Hajime, one of the country's most influential philosophers, who found the redemptive theme in the work of a thirteenth-century Buddhist thinker. Later he went on to extol the peculiar Japanese path to redemption, drawing upon what he claimed to be a transcendent wisdom that was richer than that of the West because it appeared to offer a Buddhist way out of Japan's moral crisis. This message embraced the vision of negation and transcendence through conversion and an affirmative return to the world.

With its language of "rebirth" and "reinvention," redemption was both Japanese and modern at the same time. It enabled the Japanese to once again occupy the moral high ground by setting an example to the rest of the world. Hiroshima gave the Japanese nation a mission: to show others the path to wisdom or compassion. The nation's new code of ethics demanded not being better armed; instead it demanded it renounce atomic weapons.

What remains of the spirit of Bushido is to be found at work in the energy with which the Japanese have struggled to win markets and beat competitors since 1945. Indeed, the language of Japanese business is replete with the old language of war. Traditional texts on the samurai lifestyle and philosophy, such as *The Hagakure* and *The Five Rings,* still influence the views of modern Japanese in their business practices. A former U.S. treasury secretary referred to the samurai tradition as a metaphor for the fierce loyalty to group institutions and self-identity derived through participation in group activities. Others talk of the samurai ethic in the willingness of Japanese shareholders or workers to sacrifice more for the collective good than their Western counterparts.[21]

Some call it the "banalization of bushido."[22] Banal or not, the quest for economic growth has certainly served Japan well. Its successful post-war era is important for confirming what the generals did not understand in the 1930s, that Westernization and modernization are not necessarily synonymous. Western patterns of modernity are not the only authentic model, despite the fact that they still enjoy historical precedence and continue to remain the reference point for everyone else (not by virtue of the fact that the West is more modern but because it is still more powerful— both culturally and militarily).

But something more is at work. If Japan does return to the warpath, it is unlikely to reinvent itself in the way that it did in the 1920s and 1930s. The modern Self-Defense Force (SDA) is among the most highly techno-logical in the world, and for technology to function, blind obedience and a spirit of self-sacrifice are of little use. When we look at the SDA today, we find that there is little of the Japanese "spirit" that was manifest in the war in the Pacific. Japan remains a "humanitarian" society, that is, recognizably different from the humanistic West, but its humanitarian efforts are now largely directed through economic, not military, channels. The samurai tradition did not survive World War II.

SUN TZU AND THE CHINESE WAY OF WARFARE

The Way that can be spoken of is not the True Way.
—Lao Tzu

What distinguishes China from the West is that China has never had a strong warrior tradition. To understand why this was the case, we need only look at the very different Chinese understanding of war that can be found in the seven military classics. The Chinese created a body of litera-ture on war that is the most extensive of all. All seven military classics were collected and made canonical in the Sung dynasty (960–1279), and all seven became required reading for those who wished to pursue a mili-tary career. While they were neglected in the Qing dynasty (1644–1911) they were rescued from oblivion by the nationalists and taught in military academies in the 1920s. All cadets were required to study Sun Tzu, as they are today.

But although the Chinese have philosophized about war more than any other civilization, they have developed a very different understanding of its character and nature. The principal difference, Martin van Creveld points out, is that in writing about war as a phenomenon, Western philosophers and military thinkers have started with Aristotle's very instrumental distinction between ends and means. War is an instrument for obtaining an end; it is a continuation of politics by other means. For Sun Tzu, war is neither instrumental nor existential; it is the product of necessity. War is a necessary evil. It is not evil because it requires lives to be taken and sacrificed; it is an evil because it disturbs the Tao. When it occurs, it must be managed. Whereas the Western emphasis is on the use of maximum force or the decisive battle that allows one to impose one's will on the enemy, the Chinese emphasis is on the use of minimum force. Any other use was considered inherently dangerous.[23]

The underlying message is simple. Avoid war when possible; otherwise, keep it short and fight it indirectly (i.e., exploit the mistakes of the enemy and wait for it to make the first wrong move). What makes the Chinese ethos of war so different from the Western is that war is not seen as problem solving, as a way of resolving a dispute or of changing the terms of a debate. War is a necessary evil, in that human actions often leave one with no choice but to respond, but one should always remember it is disruptive, dangerous, and disharmonious. War must always be managed, not given its head.

Is there something specific to the Chinese that explains this preference for humanitarianism over humanism in war? One explanation for the difference may lie in social practices that determined the way the Chinese thought not only about war but also about life.

First, unlike in the Western world, where philosophical arguments were bitterly contested, in China the debate between rival philosophical systems was never decisive. Each acknowledged the other had insight into the Truth, each acknowledged the other represented part of the Tao (or Way). The Chinese world has never known the outright victory of one school over another. In short, its way of thinking is much less adversarial than the West's.

For example, there is an impressive absence in Chinese philosophy of anything like dialectical argumentation with the view either to establishing beliefs internal to a vision or theory or to establishing the superiority of one vision or theory over another. Often Taoist arguments have a dialectical appearance, but the concept of yin and yang, which pervades the entire Chinese tradition, Confucian and Taoist, classical and modern, is not dialectical. The polar relationship of yin and yang must be distinguished from Western hierarchies such as "being" and "nonbeing," reality and appearance, or God and the world. The yin and yang principle originally referred to the shady and sunny sides of a hill and in time came to carry metaphors such as "weak and strong" and "female and male." The relationship, however, is not dialectical because one always predominates over the other.

This absence of dialectical thinking may owe something to language. The Chinese existential verb *yu* (being) overlaps with a sense of "having" rather than the copular. Therefore *wu* (not to be) means only "not to be present." It does not mean not to exist (or to be). *Wu* does not indicate non-being but not being available. Like the yin and yang relationship, the *wu-yu* distinction suggests contrast rather than contradiction.[24]

A second interesting feature of Chinese culture is that there is no notion in its mathematics or philosophy of axiomatic demonstrations. The classic texts (the nine chapters on *The Mathematical Art* and the commentaries on them written in the third century C.E. by Liu Hui) set out mathematics but not in an axiomatic deductive form. Chinese mathematics shows much less deductive rigor than the mathematics of Euclid. In geometry, attempts were made to formulate axioms and preserve proofs by means of step-by-step deduction, but they were not systematically pursued as they were by the Greeks. The proof of Pythagoras's theorem was confined to numerical demonstrations. By the third century B.C.E., this proof had been generalized into an algebraic proof simpler than that provided by Euclid, but without the Greek mathematician's deductive rigor.[25]

The explanation for this "omission" probably lies in a lack of capacity, not a lack of mental ability. The difference may relate to the character of the Chinese writing script, which did not provide the same pool of abstract, nonnumeric symbols as the Greek or Latin alphabets, which is one reason that China uses the Western system of numerals today. But the point of most interest to us is that the Chinese were never interested in *incontrovertible* arguments. They were never interested in the "final proof" that would demonstrate the victory of one argument over another. Again, in this respect, their thinking was more "humanitarian" than humanist.

Third, in China, much less emphasis was put on new ideas and principles than on the rediscovery of old ideas or the correct interpretation of old rules. The emphasis was not on replacing one system of thought with another but securing an ancient way of life. Reason could not impugn a system; it could only make it more effective. Hence when a dynasty failed or fell, it was always replaced by another. This obsession with order and continuity is also humanitarian. In pursuing war, one remains in touch with one's ancestors. It was important that the Chinese imperial order made so much of a legitimacy that derived from "the mandate of Heaven"—a mandate that could be withdrawn. The emperor was supposed to obtain his ends through benevolence. Force was never easy to justify, for its use was an admission of failure; that is one reason that of all the great civilizations, China alone never produced a dominating warrior class until the last dynasty, the Qing (which was Manchu, not Chinese). The Manchu were a nomadic people from the north whose instincts were aggressive. They were to extend the boundaries of the Chinese empire further than ever.

The Chinese Conception of War

Such is the "humanitarian" context in which the Chinese have formulated their ideas about war for centuries and that informs the views of the most famous, as well as revered of strategists, Sun Tzu. Like all great works of literature, *The Art of War* succeeds in transcending the particular circumstances of its creation, not least because of the limpid purity of the writing. To readers alienated by Clausewitz's language, dialectical thinking, and philosophical abstractions, Sun Tzu's thoughts have a refreshing directness.

Unfortunately, we still do not know for certain when the text was produced. Recent archaeological research suggests it appeared around 500 B.C.E. Even the author is disputed. He may have been Sun Wu, a native of the state of Qi. Some authorities have even suggested the author may have been a woman (for in that period, China had a tradition of women commanders).[26] What is important is not so much the author's identity but the fact that (s)he lived in a period from which emerged all the things we associate with Chinese civilization, including the variety of its philosophical systems, Tao, Confucianism, and Buddhism.

Indeed, *The Art of War* is itself a Taoist text, and it was written at the same time as one of the great classics of Taoism, the *Tao Te Ching,* in which we can find three Taoist principles that are also central to Sun Tzu's thinking.

To begin with, we find this injunction: "Those who win five victories will meet with disaster, those who win four victories will be exhausted. Those with three victories will become warlords. Those with two victories will be kings. And those with one victory will become emperors."[27]

The West has produced a remarkable list of great captains, each remembered for their victories or decisive defeats. When Napoleon named them at St. Helena, he offered this advice: "Wage war offensively like Alexander, Hannibal, Caesar, Gustavus Adolphus, Turenne, Prince Eugene and Frederick (the Great) . . . model yourself on them. It is the only way to become a Great Captain."[28] But Napoleon himself failed because he attempted to outdo them and overreached himself in the attempt. He was far too confident in his own ability. Six years after his death, one of his marshals said of him: "Napoleon has not been conquered by men. . . . God punished him because he relied on his own intelligence alone until that prodigious instrument was strained to breaking point. Everything breaks in the end."[29]

If Napoleon (a man who won more victories than anyone else in history) had heeded that lesson, he would not have ended his career, remarkable though it was, in exile on a rock in the south Atlantic. Napoleon was an excellent example of a man who suffered from one of the classic Taoist themes: emptiness, the mastery of which is given an entire chapter by Sun Tzu in his book. The side that masters its emptiness and finds "fullness" (i.e., harmony) can exploit the emptiness of others (ambition, hubris, arrogance—all of which are taken by Sun Tzu to be manifest in bad leadership, social divisiveness, and low morale). Arrogance is punished. The message is stark and simple. War should be limited in ambition.

The close relationship between Taoist and Chinese military thought is illustrated in another of the great classic writings, this one by Zhuge Liang, which was written five centuries later than Sun Tzu's book. What is interesting about his theories is that they illustrate a second axiom that is definitively Chinese. The object of war is not to impose one's will but undermine the enemy's will, and that is best achieved through asymmetry. "Attack the strong through his strength"—do not meet strength with strength, which is the Western way.[30] Strength, after all, evaporates quickly. The strong are always overconfident. They are always overextending themselves, lengthening their lines of communication or exhausting their strength. A concept such as the "culminating point," the point at which the strength of an enemy tends to dissipate through overextension occasioned by success, may be new to the West but not to China.

Asymmetric warfare (called "unorthodox" by Sun Tzu) appeals to another Taoist concept: not emptiness but formlessness. A military force is like water. Water has no constant shape. It is "formless," and so is war. The ability to gain victory by adapting to one's opponent is genius (an idea with little appeal in the West, where the genius of a great captain is defined by his ability to get his adversary to fight by his own rules). This interest in asymmetric warfare explains why Chinese writing includes far more discussions of factors such as psychological operations, covert actions, and disinformation (the spreading of rumors) than do most Western works.

A third area of common ground between Taoism and the Chinese military classics is this: the main object of war is not winning so much as survival. There were many occasions in Chinese history when the state was strong as it was at the height of the Sung era, when the seven military classics were first codified. But as changes of dynasty showed, there were many occasions when the state was weak. Yet it survived. Survival is the most notable feature of the Chinese experience.

Outwitting or outmaneuvering an enemy and in the end surviving is everything. It is not, of course, a Western view of victory. Victory for the West means restoration of the status quo, at least, and usually punishment of the enemy who tries to challenge it. The Chinese idea of victory is surviving—winning in the long term. For in the long term, dynasties may fall, but one is always succeeded by another. The dynastic principle reflects the strength and continuity of Chinese culture. There is an old adage: "China's wars are always civil."[31] External enemies can be assimilated, or with changes of dynasty, the old guard joins the new. The liquidation of enemies is not, therefore, necessarily physical; it can be ideological. In the Chinese Civil War (1937–1949), nationalist troops captured in battle were expected to join the communists and usually did. That explains why the Chinese conceived of war as limited. Even barbarians could be absorbed. They always became Chinese, with one exception: the British, the first barbarians to come from the sea.

The Modern Era

China today is a modern culture, forced into the modern world by war, when British gunboats entered the Yangtze estuary and the British together with their French allies stormed Beijing itself twenty years later. Second, it is now a nation-state, not an empire, and the most enduring nationalist image is the humiliation inflicted on it by the Western powers in the nineteenth century, especially the unequal treaties it was forced to sign and the treaty ports it was forced to concede. Both were vitally important in making China aware of its national consciousness.

Let us take modernity first. Chinese attitudes toward war have survived, but attitudes toward technology have changed. "Weapons are instruments of ill-omen to be used only when it is unavoidable," the *Tao Te Ching* informs us.[32] At first it appears a strange observation, given that until the Industrial Revolution, Chinese technology was more advanced than that of the West. According to remarkable evidence from Szechuan province, the Chinese invented the first firearms in the twelfth century, not the fourteenth, as previously supposed. To produce a true gun, three things are needed: a metal barrel, gunpowder with a high nitrate content, and a projectile that fits exactly into the barrel so that the powder charge can exert its full propellant effect. By the early fourteenth century, the Chinese had developed mobile field artillery as well. In parallel with the development of guns, they invested great efforts in producing military rockets.

Those in use 100 years later had propulsion motors that ignited in successive stages with a range of over a mile.[33]

Unfortunately, given the Taoist emphasis on indirect warfare—on mastering the will and harmonizing war with nature—none of these inventions transformed the way the Chinese *thought* about war. As inventions of the premodern world, they were applied unsystematically. The Chinese also never experienced a scientific revolution, as Europeans did in the seventeenth century. And more important, perhaps, the Chinese never experienced a historical revolution. For in the long run, the new critical methods of historians such as Casaubon in France may have been more revolutionary than the mathematics of Newton. Mathematics, after all, was part of the Greek inheritance. Historical criticism was a new force unknown to the Greeks and reminded Newton's generation of the discontinuities between seventeenth-century Europe and Periclean Athens. R. G. Collingwood talks of a "Cartesian historiography" (after René Descartes) based, like Casaubon's philosophy, on systematic skepticism and a thoroughgoing recognition of the critical principles notably absent in the surviving historical works of the ancient world.[34]

Second, we now recognize that modernity involves revising traditions, not repudiating them. What struck the *New York Times* when reviewing a book produced for limited circulation in the People's Republic of China entitled *Can China's Armed Forces Win the Next War?* was the extent to which its authors were steeped in classical Chinese military thinking. Their interest in the past is consistent with the observation of Jiang Zemin (then chairman of the Military Commission in 1993): "We must remain true to our traditions under modern conditions."[35] Modernity not only defines the conditions but *is* the revaluation of tradition. At the heart of Western civilization is the dialogue between the ancient and modern worlds. And a similar dialogue between its ancient traditions and the external world makes modern China "modern."

Finally, a third feature of Chinese modernity needs to be stressed. Premodern societies were usually incurious about the outside world. China was curious enough to dispatch a fleet to East Africa in the fifteenth century, but toward the end of the Ming dynasty (1368–1644), it lost interest in the world and paid the price. Chinese military thinking today is very modern in that it is fascinated by U.S. writing on war. The output of books on the Revolution in Military Affairs (RMA) is so extensive that the uninformed observer could be forgiven for thinking that China had pioneered it.

In short, this is not a society immured behind its Great Wall. This is not the late Qing world, which introduced Western military academies but not military concepts, or Mao's China, which retreated behind a bamboo curtain, preaching world revolution and nuclear war. This is a society fully open to the Western discourse yet true to its own military tradition, a society that is eager to understand the Western mind, the better to exploit Western weaknesses.

Nationalism

Not only is the Chinese way of war being revalued in a modern context, it is being revalued in a national context as well. Nationalism is new in China. Because for most of its history it was a single civilization coterminous with a single state, it was one of the last major civilizations to produce a nation. There was no word even for the historical and ethnic community of the Han people before the nineteenth century. The custom of referring to their historical community by dynasty rather than country implied, in fact, that there was no Chinese nation at all.

The principal reason that China was humiliated by the Europeans after 1840 was that it could not respond nationally. Take Lin Zexu (the special commissioner for Canton) who, contrary to British propaganda at the time, was not an effete mandarin but a reforming administrator who appreciated all too clearly Britain's chief weakness—its lack of manpower. All Western societies at the time had difficulty raising armies. Until the late eighteenth century, China did not. As a result, Lin Zexu made two suggestions to defeat the British. The first was to fight asymmetrically, to ignore battles on the rivers where the enemy had an advantage in its steam-powered ships and to force its soldiers inland where the Chinese had the advantage of numbers. Second, he suggested that the Chinese follow a Maoist strategy of drawing the enemy from the natural sea into the real sea: the people. He suggested concealing soldiers among the peasants in occupied areas and fighting a guerrilla war. But that was only possible if China could tap into a national consciousness. In its absence, Lin Zexu's suggestions were much too radical for a regime that preferred defeat to the danger of arming the local population.[36]

China is only now entering a new era and attempting to produce a new conception of nationhood based on a Western model of citizenship. The critics of the regime in Beijing argue that they cannot succeed, that civil society and communism are mutually exclusive. But then again, the Chinese may well invent a specifically distinctive sense of community. The accidental bombing of the Chinese embassy in Belgrade provoked the largest public demonstrations in China since the Fourth of May movement of 1919. And a more nationalistic state is likely to remain more true to its own traditions.

The Possibility of War Between China and the United States

Culture has a tenacious hold on human life. As we enter the twenty-first century, Chinese thinking about war is not only very different from the Western; it must be if China is to have any chance of defeating the West in any future conflict. As Wang Pufeng, a member of the Institute of Military Strategy, has claimed: "In wars of the future China will face the enemy's more complete information technology with incomplete information technology. Based on the fact that sometimes superior tactics can make up for inferior technology, China will carry out its traditional warfare method of 'you fight your way, I'll fight my way, and use my strengths to attack the enemy's strengths.'"[37]

In a recent book entitled *Unrestricted War,* its authors acknowledged that the Chinese could not win a conventional war against the United States. Wang Xian Gsui, an air force colonel, amplified that conclusion in August 1999 after the Kosovo War. "War has rules but those rules are set by the West. . . . If you use those rules then weaker countries have no chance."[38] These "rules of war" are key. In a review of the book, the *Washington Post* added that here was the prospect of the use of force wholly unrestricted by legal conventions or rules. In fact, that is not necessarily the lesson to be drawn from the discussion. It is *Western* rules to which the authors object.[39]

The Gulf War reinforced the Chinese belief that they will never be able to engage the West on its own terms. The Western way involves imposing one's will on another, of meeting force with force and strength with strength, which one of the main commentators on Chinese warfare rightly attributes to the Greek tradition. The Chinese, by contrast, still put an emphasis on the indirect and unorthodox. As the author of *The Six Secrets Teachings in the Way of Strategy* says: "What is too strong will certainly break; what is too extended must have deficiencies. Attack the strong through his strength."[40] That is not a passive strategy, but it does require one to be opaque rather than transparent, to conceal one's strength and plans.

The Chinese classics stress two things: opaqueness and the unorthodox. "In martial arts it is important that strategy be unfathomable, that form be concealed and that movement be unexpected, so that preparedness against them is impossible. Where capable, feign capacity."[41] Sun

Tzu also tells his readers that in battle, one engages with unorthodox views and gains victory by being unorthodox oneself. Being unorthodox includes using psychological operations, covert measures, and disinformation (such as spreading rumors), all of which tend to undermine an enemy's will.

What is unorthodox? The ability to keep one's moves secret, adapt, exploit weaknesses, and seize opportunities. As Sun Tzu adds, "Notes [in music] do not exceed five, but the changes of the five notes can never be fully heard."[42] In war, the confrontation of the orthodox and unorthodox can never be fully realized. For the enemy determines what is unorthodox by what it chooses to do. Withdrawing to force aggressors to expand their limited supplies and dissipate their energies on hostile ground; destabilizing opponents by exhausting them, and demoralizing soldiers before engaging them in combat all have great appeal.

Sun Tzu's writing and that of other classical theorists are perhaps more popular now than in the past because they appeal to the Taoist preference for war as a way of preserving social harmony and the existing world, rather than changing it. This is an important factor for a regime trying to shore up its position in a fast-changing world. There have been many moments in Chinese history when the state was strong and aggressive and used war to extend its influence. But there have also been moments when China has found itself at war with itself or defending itself against invasion, and at such moments, asymmetry is appealing. It appeals more to the weak than the strong. The Chinese classics largely address defensive warfare and tend to stress the advantage usually possessed by the defense. In an age when China is the weakest of the great powers once again, no wonder the classics have been rediscovered.[43] They caution only to do what is necessary and no more. It is the ultimate instrumental strategy to be applied against the ultimate instrumental power, the United States.

REREADING THE *ARTHASHASTRA:* THE INDIAN WARRIOR TRADITION

Unlike the Chinese, the Indians saw war largely in existential terms. We find a magnificent portrayal of both that dimension and the warrior's honor in one of the classics of ancient Indian civilization, *The Mahabarata,* which, in turn, gave rise to one of the great stories in Alexander the Great's brief campaign in the subcontinent. His appearance came as a great rupture in Indian history, the first appearance of a

European people in the Indian subcontinent. And what alarmed the Indians most was the *ruthlessness* that Alexander showed. In his last victory at the Hydaspes River (326 B.C.E.), he killed about 20,000 enemy soldiers. His war of attrition against autonomous villages and tribes such as the Mali of lower Punjab can also be seen as an early example of ethnic cleansing. He razed most of their villages. Cruelty and violence have always accompanied war, but the deliberate and *systematic* manner in which Alexander fought his campaign was India's first introduction to the Western way of warfare.

After Hydaspes, Alexander asked the defeated King Porus how he expected to be treated. "As befits a king," he famously replied. To the Greeks, it sounded like the noble and fearless request of a true warrior, and so it was. Porus was rewarded with his life and his kingdom. But Porus was also acting in character with a warrior's code unique to the subcontinent. His defiant words were borrowed from Lord Krishna's advice to Arjuna in *The Mahabarata*. Each must live according to his dharma. It was the dharma of a *ksitriya* (warrior) to fight and embrace the consequences, as it was incumbent upon a Greek like Alexander to realize his *arête* (excellence) by outdoing his ancestors.[44]

What is dharma? It is duty or good conduct or decency (including showing mercy to one who merits it). There is no philosophical justification for war and little rationalization of it in this era in Indian history. War did not accord with a particular belief system or particular ideology but with a set of behavioral exhortations that evolved around membership in a class or caste. Every caste, whether Brahmin or warrior, had its own dharma. These ideas are found in a much later work, the *Arthashastra,* two books of which (one-fifth in all) are devoted to war. Discovered only in 1904, it was not translated into English until five years later. Its dating arouses controversy still. But it now seems fairly certain that the work dates back to the second century C.E., 500 years after the life of the first Mauryan emperor. Moreover, a computer-generated statistical analysis of the frequency with which certain linguistic particles appear in the text suggests that the work was not written by a single author but is the compendium of several texts that may have been gathered together by a single editor.[45]

To be frank, the *Arthashastra* is not a great work when compared, for example, to the classics of Chinese military thought. It is essentially a political manual for the aspiring ruler, and the strategy it advances is highly political in nature. Thus it constantly advises the use of deception and treachery. For a heroic view of war, we must turn to the great Indian epics, but they, in turn, tell of gods and heroes, not of real people. In real life, the *Arthashastra* tells us, war is not heroic. Victory is secured through intrigue. One of its principal mottoes is "intrigue is better than power."[46] In keeping with this philosophy, the book enjoins its readers to deceive their enemies into thinking their army is weaker than it is and thus induce them to abandon a strong position, thereby exposing themselves to attack.

What the *Arthashastra* and every other Indian work on war (including the Janist texts that appeared after the seventh century C.E.) make clear is that these measures are adopted by default. What is common to all Indian military writing is the idea that leaders could expect little political loyalty from their subjects. No ruler can take the loyalty of his subjects for granted. But then, unlike Plato's *Republic,* the *Arthashastra* offers no advice on how the situation can be improved through collective effort, and unlike Machiavelli, it seems unaware of how "civic consciousness" might be increased so that an astute ruler might make greater use of human resources. In fact, none of the catastrophes of Indian history, including the collapse of the Mauryan and Guptan empires or the arrival of the Mughals or the British, led any writers to follow Plato and suggest breaking with the past. Plato embarked upon his political writings, including *The Republic* and *The Laws,* in an attempt to propose something new. They were both attempts to think his way forward toward a new political order following the defeat of Athens in the Peloponnesian War.

The Indian way of war, by comparison, emphasized an unchanging social landscape in which the dharma of each group was socially conditioned and predetermined. This war culture stressed that war was more existential than instrumental. Even when great empires arose, like the Mauryan and Guptan empires, they did not survive for very long. Even when great warrior princes appeared on the scene, like Asoka (268–232 B.C.E.), their careers blazed and then fizzled out. Asoka notoriously abandoned war, it is said, because he was sickened by the loss of life in his last campaign. It is more likely that the casualty lists counted far less in his thinking than his conscience, which told him that the social order was in danger of being subverted by political ambition. For him to turn to pacifism and renounce war as he did was to put himself and his subjects back in touch with their dharma.

Hinduism was important not only for its social code but its view of life. Asoka himself became a Buddhist and for the rest of his life tried to conquer through righteousness rather than war. But Buddhism, although born in India, failed either to subvert or challenge Hinduism. And the cyclical nature of Hinduism tended to suggest that things cannot change; that in the end there is a limit to how much one can think for oneself. If one subscribes

to a cyclical rather than teleological view of history, one is likely to act differently. Hinduism claims that history does not end but repeats itself end-
lessly. It is not goal-oriented but driven by cycles that are not determined
by human beings. Equally, if one subscribes to a very strong sense of destiny or fate, why try to break with tradition? Why play up individual effort
and ingenuity? Without a sense of history, as opposed to destiny, there is
little idea of shaping the world through war or any other human act.[47]

Ultimately, however, the true importance of Hinduism lies not so
much in its religious beliefs as in the social organization it promoted.
What divided India for centuries was a caste system that was taken for
granted. That is why Max Weber was right to insist that what characterized Indian history was not the principal beliefs of Hinduism so much as
the social structure it underwrote. The caste system is unique to South
Asia, and it is to that system that we should turn to explain the warrior's
social status and self-worth. Nothing like it is to be found anywhere else
in Asia.

Caste System

Weber was interested mostly in the economic aspects of caste and the
question of economic progress or lack of it. A ritual law in which every
change of occupation or work technique might result in ritual degradation
was not capable, he suspected, of promoting economic revolution from
within. Together with what he took to be the antirationalism of Indian religion and the secular-political power of its priesthood, he concluded that
Hinduism was not favorable to rational economic activity of the kind
found in the West.

Indeed, Weber claimed that the division of society into castes and subcastes by religious belief was far different from any of the divisions associated in Europe with its medieval guilds and division of society into
classes. In Europe, social divisions were undoubtedly pronounced, but
Christianity created a shared social life that was humanistic. It encouraged
the notion of a common civic life. By comparison, the Indian caste system, while promoting social stability, weakened social cohesion. The division of society into castes was considered divinely ordained. Had Weber
been interested in war, he might have added that it promoted a unique style
of warfare that was ritualistic, social, and grounded on necessity—it was
necessarily limited by the fact that rulers could not rely on loyalties of
their soldiers among groups larger than subcastes.[48]

Indeed, it was impossible for Indian princes to put into the field disciplined armies of the kind that enabled Europe to expand beyond its own

frontiers. Political loyalties, Stephen Rosen concludes—in what is by far the best and most stimulating study of Indian military culture to have been published to date—were based on caste and occasionally on a more all-encompassing loyalty to a particular leader that nearly always vanished on his death. Death in battle or a serious check in the field could diminish his authority and usually put an end to a political dynasty.[49]

Since there was little a prince could do to make his own side more cohesive, he had to exploit the divisions of his opponent. Success, advises the *Arthashastra,* depends on good spies and reliable intelligence so that one can bribe the feudal levies of an enemy army to desert at a critical moment, before or even during a battle. And when the British arrived in India, they found they could do much the same. They discovered a patchwork of principalities and kingdoms ruled by a diverse series of maharajas and nizams. Some were Muslims ruling largely Hindu populations. Some were feudal lords, and others were more absolute rulers. Among each, they found willing collaborators.

So if we question why the British successfully defeated Indian armies time and time again, we must expect to find the answer in India's social institutions as well as Britain's, for the British were a modern people with a highly developed instrumental idea of war. It also counted for everything that the British came from outside the system. Despite differences of opinion between themselves—between London and the East India Company, and the government of India and London after 1858—despite the self-aggrandizement of East India officers and their pursuit of self-interest—loyalties to the regiment, company, crown, or country always proved tenacious. This advantage outweighed every other, including technology and economic might, and Hegel spotted it. "In India 500 men conquered 20,000 who were not cowards but who only lacked the disposition to work together."[50] Hegel was right when he wrote that the British succeeded not because they were braver or even produced better soldiers but because they were a nation-state. An army of 500 soldiers, provided it was both cohesive and well disciplined, could defeat an army of thousands.

But the British owed their success to more than just their institutional power. As a nation-state they conceptualized war differently. What explains the collapse of the Indian way of warfare in the face of adversity was the absence of a *political frame of mind.* The nation-state created a particular way of thinking about war. The Indians had no practical sense of war as "a continuation of politics by other means" because they had no firm political base, no state structure, and no Machiavelli telling them how the power of the state could be increased.

When toward the end, the Indian princes tried to copy the British, the result proved disastrous. A culture of war cannot be imposed or imported. Otherwise, it will not take root or advance beyond mimicry. Because the Indians never saw war in instrumental terms, they never developed a conceptual way of employing forces in the field. Likewise, they may have possessed guns that were just as good if not better than European models, but they did not see technology as a *problem-solving* system. They did not work out how to concentrate maximum fire on a given section of an army's line or how to train a gun crew to fire eight rounds an hour instead of four. They gave little or no thought to the problems of *battlefield management*. All that ensued, as a consequence of the reforms, was that a second-rate infantry force proved no match for a British sepoy army. As a British soldier noted at the time: "By coming forward with regular infantry they gave us every advantage we could desire. They opposed to us men that never could be made so good as our men for want of a *national spirit* among the officers."[51]

In fact, the Indian way of warfare had reached a dead end much earlier than the British arrival. The Indians had also failed to reevaluate their tradition when those other interlopers, the Mughals, arrived in the fifteenth century. Why did the Indians cling to their traditions for so long? One of the best explanations is given by Octavio Paz. To avoid ossification, he writes, every culture must have a dialectic, a dialogue within it between two forces. The West, as we have seen, had a dialogue between the modern and ancient worlds. The great moment of Indian history included just such a dialogue between two contrasting religions (both indigenous), Hinduism and its offspring, Buddhism. That dialogue, Paz writes, *was* Indian civilization. The fact that it ended in a Buddhist defeat and Hindu dominance, that the dialogue turned into a monologue, explains in part the inability of India to come to terms in time with the Western challenge.

One of the reasons India could not revalue its traditions was that when Buddhism was rooted out, its chief adherent, the merchant class, was displaced from the center of social life, which further reinforced the caste system, the position of local warlords, and with them the feudal system. The feudal era made it impossible for India to be unified by Indians until the twentieth century. India, adds Paz, did not develop; it proliferated. And that explains the extraordinary social diversity of the Indian world today.[52] As the hero of Salman Rushdie's novel *Midnight's Children* observes, "There are so many stories to tell, too many."[53] India, as the novel makes clear, is excessive and for that reason still weak.

Islam, of course, appeared just as Buddhism disappeared in India, but it failed to take its place. The dialectic between Hinduism and Buddhism had represented a contradiction within the same system of thought; that between Islam and Hinduism represented a confrontation between two systems that were both different and incompatible. That is why Pakistan was born in 1947 and why Hindus and Muslims in Kashmir are still increasingly drawn to fundamentalism. What Paz claims is that India needed another dialogue, between itself and the West, which is precisely what the British phase of India's history provided.

Hindu Revivalism

Those who do not understand a culture will not master it for long. Since the British did not understand India even when the Raj was at its height, more perceptive British commentators began to suspect that they would change very little during their "moment" in Indian history. One mid–nineteenth century writer, William Arnold, was certainly struck, as were so many, by "the extraordinary fact of British domination." It appeared entrenched and immovable. The British way of war had allowed it to conquer the subcontinent and impose Western institutions. As a Victorian writer, Arnold found it impossible to imagine that one day it would be swept away. However, he was disturbed to note that British culture had not really taken root: "It was easy to look around and think of it as gone."[54]

Marx famously thought that the United Kingdom had a double mission in India—one destructive, the other regenerating: "the annihilation of an old Asiatic society and the laying of the material foundations of Western society in Asia."[55] In reality, Britain did neither. It did not Westernize Indian society, though at one point the British thought they could. They attributed their success in subduing the subcontinent to the victory of modernity over tradition, change over continuity, contract over status, and class over caste. In the end, however, they found they could only fit into the Indian social structure as one more caste.

As a result, India has managed to remain distinctively Indian. The British moment in its history allowed its way of warfare to be revived in a modern setting as soon as the British left the subcontinent. Although India is now a nation-state (if still a weak national community), its thinking about war is still distinctive. To begin with, we find an absence of strategic thinking. What prevails instead is what George Tanham calls a "mandala" system, a system found in the *Arthashastra*. As a society, India still locates itself geographically within a series of concentric circles. The first circle is India, the second circle includes India's smaller neighbors such as Sikkim and Bhutan, and the third circle is Pakistan. As the *Arthashastra* tells us, contiguous neighbors are always enemies because they are always out to exploit each other's weakness. By contrast, one's enemies' neighbors (in this case, Russia) are invariably one's friends. Tanham's analysis of this view is particularly scathing because it betrays what Westerners would consider an uninformed (and unchanging) strategic way of thinking.[56]

Tanham also accounts for the absence of a strategic frame of mind by looking at what has survived British rule, for the British hardly touched the fabric of Indian life. India is still made up of local powers, power brokers, and authorities; state governments; and regional networks. It is still a patchwork of local and regional authorities and, in that sense, remains somewhat feudal in spirit, if not in nature.

And a new factor, Hindu fundamentalism, has been added to the equation (spurred partly by the example of Islamic fundamentalism in Afghanistan and Pakistan). In one sense, it will change little. Hinduism is not a religion. It has no prophets and no social organization. It is more a way of life, one so inclusive that there is no body of beliefs that helps concentrate thinking. Indeed, there are deep ambiguities inherent in Hindu nationalist attempts to reconcile a religious tradition whose texts are inclusive of the teachings of all religions with a nationalist ideology that is necessarily exclusive. Hindu fundamentalists have even had to invent some religious elements like a "holy script," or, in the case of the reconstruction of Vedic rituals, to limit them to particular sections of the population.

But Hindu fundamentalism is likely to amplify those specifically Indian concepts of war that still persist and have proved remarkably pervasive. Given a continued sense of destiny and a continued fatalism, Indian planners rarely plan ahead. Hinduism, Tanham believes, continues to count for much in terms of fate, traditions, and intuition, all of which play a part in decisionmaking. There is not much scope for using reason to reshape the external world or impose oneself upon it.[57]

In addition, the caste system is still important. India remains a very peculiar nation-state, and its army is more distinctive than any other in Asia. The British themselves were really only another caste who instinctively tried to perpetuate an Indian style of war, though one that was more in tune with the way they looked at the world. In the nineteenth century, the British thought in terms of race. They attributed their success in conquering India to their racial superiority, and when recruiting for the Indian army, they set out to recruit what they called the "martial races"—the peoples from the north, the Pathans, the Punjabis, and the people of the North West Frontier—all of whom were considered to be superior fighters.

The sanction for this policy came from many sources, and it was not purely a colonial invention, a product of Western racism or anthropology. The martial race discourse had some basis in the customs and self-images of many Indian communities, quite independent of the colonial encounter. Some castes did indeed see themselves as warriors, for example, the Rajputs, who were in turn a major subgroup of the Kshatriya Varna, who scorned agriculture and regarded themselves as a warrior people.[58]

In response to the Mughal invasion, the Sikhs had also militarized their religion in the early seventeenth century, and they remain a warrior people to this day. Muslim identity also was strongly martial and self-assertive, and for the British, both the Sikhs and Muslims were the preferred recruits. In the Indian army today, these attitudes continue to persist, even though identities tend to be a little more fluid. Its regiments still recruit from castes and classes as did the British before them, though most are no longer single caste. Only a few units in the infantry, such as the paratrooper brigade and the armored and artillery branches, recruit without regard to caste at all. Strikingly, the Sikhs, who have their own battalions, comprise 10 percent or more of the army, despite the fact that they constitute only 2 percent of the population. And the Rajput regiment is comprised primarily of Rajputs still. Although the Indian army is a national army, some would argue the real loyalties of the soldiers are still to caste, religion, or unit.

All these factors notwithstanding, it is difficult to claim that an Indian way of warfare still exists. The armed forces are modeled on the Western model. Much has been inherited from the British: a late-nineteenth-century general would not find himself at a loss if he were to encounter the Indian army today. But enough has been said about "Indianness" to suggest that at least one lesson taught by the *Arthashastra* would be taken to heart in any encounter with the Western world. Its way of prosecuting war is likely to be asymmetrical, though in a more instrumental fashion than in the past. In 1988, the office of the U.S. secretary of defense concluded that India would seek to deny the U.S. Navy uncontested control of the Indian Ocean and that it would use "asymmetic sufficiency" as a counter.

In the future, all India may wish to do is to pose a risk, an unacceptably high one, on a foreign navy like that of the United States, at minimal cost to itself. What India enjoys in large numbers, despite losing many to the West, is scientists and engineers, the highest number per capita outside the Western world. And what the latter may lack in government funding, they may make up in ingenuity. V1-style weapons, for example, which use global positioning satellite (GPS) guidance systems and are made of "stealth" materials such as fiberglass, which are difficult to detect on radar, could certainly prove a threat in the future. Maneuvering reentry vehicles (MARVs) equipped with GPS receivers and high-performance autopilots could fly long distances with great precision. In Indian national waters subsurface weapons such as mines could act as a deterrent. After all, the damage from mines to the USS *Tripoli* and USS *Princeton* in the Gulf War dissuaded the United States from launching an amphibious assault on Kuwait City for fear of extensive damage to its shipping.[59] In a contest between a humanistic West and a humanitarian "other," asymmetrical warfare is likely to be the future norm.

Asymmetrical warfare, of course, is very much the buzzword today. We must be cautious when we use the term, for all wars are, in part, asymmetrical. "Men do not understand [the coincidence of opposites]: there is a back stretched connection like that of the bow." It is this statement, Edward Luttwak adds, that makes Heraclitus the first Western strategic thinker.[60] Doing the unexpected, turning an enemy's strengths against itself, has been the acme of strategy for centuries. Armies have always sought to find the most effective way of inflicting maximum damage on the enemy at minimum cost to themselves. Asymmetrical strategies have always been appealing for that reason to all cultures, not just the West. The Chinese word for strategy, *chan-lueh,* conveys the same sense of fighting by one's own rules if possible. As Sun Tzu maintains, "those skilled in war subdue the enemy without battle." They try to prevent the enemy from taking to the field or to outmaneuver rather than outperform it when it does.[61]

But if asymmetry has always been a vital part of war, it has rarely been a decisive factor, in large part because Western societies have usually engaged each other in the major confrontations of the last 300 years. It is only recently that we have begun to recognize that our major adversaries in the future will be non-Western states or national communities and that we can expect that our own rules of engagement (the Western way of warfare) will come under sustained challenge.

THE ISLAMIC CHALLENGE

Soft countries produce soft men. . . . It is not the property of any one soil to produce good fruits and good soldiers too.
—Herodotus, *The Histories*

In any war with China or India in the future, the West will be confronted with an enemy that may see war differently and fight it by different rules, but both countries, as modern states, will share with the United States an instrumental bias. In any conflict with the Islamic world, the reverse is likely to be true. That is what makes it a "challenge."

The Western and Islamic worlds have been divided for centuries, and one of the things that has divided them has been war. The two major Abrahamic religions, Christianity and Islam, conquered most of the world's territory and people, including South Asia and the Americas. Only China and Japan among the major non-Western nations escaped Muslim or Christian rule. Today, Muslim theocracies are the most extreme example of societies based on nonsecular principles. Back in the early nineteenth century, Hegel characterized Islam as different from Christianity because it made "knowledge of the One" alone the unique goal of reality.[62] Not only in the post-Christian West but all other cultures, Islam is a religion that has wide appeal because it remains the language of faith for those who thirst for something better than life, something that transcends the mundane or human.

Many of those who fight in its name do so for that reason. Inevitably, that creates misunderstanding. The West tends to see the martyrdom of the faithful as fanatical. For their part, many Muslims see the West's wish to avoid human suffering and pain as grossly materialistic. They contend that in taking metaphysics out of war, the West has grounded it on a very narrow understanding of humanism. In the eyes of those for whom appeal to God is the only justification for war, humanism is a poor sanction for sacrificing life or taking it.

The Levantine Way of Warfare

Is there an Islamic way of warfare? In answering that question, let me begin with an intriguing article by John Jandora, which stresses the importance of intercultural relationships. Ideas, he tells us, cross frontiers and shape ways of looking at the world. Civilizations are never self-contained; they are porous and heterogeneous. One that he considers especially important for the future is the Levant, an area spanning the Middle East and North Africa to Afghanistan. Other writers, of course, have asserted that cultural influences can have a decisive influence on the way societies fight their wars, but Jandora has a great deal more to say about them.[63]

In the case of the Levant, he identifies a specific war-fighting tradition, beginning with the Persian defeat at the battle of Plataea in 479 B.C.E. and ending in Operation Badr—the Egyptian attack across the Suez Canal in the closing phase of the 1973 Arab-Israeli war. The main conclusion he draws from his study of eight different engagements spanning as many centuries is that the Levantine way of war tends to emphasize the use of standoff weapons against the shock action traditionally favored by the West.

At Plataea, the Persians gained a temporary advantage with missile weapons (arrows) but went on to squander it by refusing to engage the Greeks in close combat. Seven centuries later, Sassanian archers kept the Emperor Julian's Roman legions from forcing a decisive encounter in their approach to the capital city, Ctesiphon (363 C.E.). Like the Russians in 1812, the Sassanians abandoned the city and harried the Roman army along its dangerously extended lines of communication. At the battle of Al-Qadisiya (636 C.E.) 250 years later, the Sassanian army was defeated, in turn, by the Arabs, who relied on their superior archery to wear down the Persian forces, thus preventing them from doing what they did best: attacking their enemy's flanks or forcing its center by frontal assault. In all three engagements, the standoff factor was related directly to archery.

Clearly, from the examples Jandora cites, the tactic was not always decisive or successful, but it seems to be a continuous theme in the history of the region. And he traces it right up to the present day. During the Iran-Iraq War (1980–1988), the Iraqis showed a distinct preference for the Levantine tradition, seizing limited ground in the early days of the conflict and defending it rather than pushing forward for a close, final engagement. When that tactic failed and their forces were dislodged from Iranian territory, they were able to bring the war to an end by using standoff weapons such as Scud missiles against Iranian urban centers and tankers in the Gulf.

One analyst at the time was surprised to find that neither Iraq nor Iran followed an aggressive battle plan. Both their previous "patrons" and chief arms suppliers, the Soviet Union and the United States, stressed the importance of maneuver, boldness, speed, and combined operations.[64] The decisions by Iran and Iraq not to pursue these tactics may have a prosaic explanation (Iran had sent its U.S. military advisers home, and Iraq had reduced the influence of its Soviet advisers). But perhaps the choice of tactic reveals something more profound. However many U.S. or Soviet advisers were on the ground, the Levantine tradition continued to prevail. In the Gulf War (1990–1991), Saddam Hussein repeated the same strategy, digging in after taking Kuwait and awaiting a coalition attack while launching Scud missiles at Israel in the hope the Israelis would be provoked into retaliating and thus destroying the fragile allied coalition.

The virtue of Jandora's article is that he chooses to identify a *regional* rather than strictly Islamic approach in the way that the Arabs and Persians have fought their wars since the fifth century B.C.E., though he does acknowledge Islamic factors and finds an aversion to close combat in some of the military treatises that have survived from the medieval era. The Levant does seem to have a unity of its own historically and culturally. Its socioeconomic profiles are very similar, as are its architecture, religious beliefs, and typical patterns of behavior. What also distinguishes it is the fact that it is the home of three major language groups—Arabic, Persian, and Turkish—as well as of three religions that all accept the scriptural authority of the Bible. These and other continuities persist in the manner in which people of the Levant construct their ethical choices and identities through their cultural imagination (the deeply held values that provide the most strongly motivating bases for action, feeling, and thought), both in their dialectical relationship with each other and with the Western world.[65]

Ibn Khaldun and Civil Life

One of the great works of analytical sociology is Ibn Khaldun's *Muqaddimah*. Living in the fourteenth century, Khaldun began his mature life in the court of Grenada, then in decline, and ended it in the highly respected post of grand *qadi* (a government-appointed judge) of the Malaki school of law in Cairo. *The Muqaddimah* (a prolegomenon, or introduction), consists of Khaldun's original preface and the first book of his universal history (*Kitab al-Ibar*). He was far too good a historian to be content with the mere description of the society he chose to analyze. His own personal experience of the Islamic world, through which he had traveled extensively during his lifetime, led him to construct a "new science." He was aware of the originality of his approach and the fact that he was a pathfinder. For what he offered his readers was the first sociological analysis of their own world.

Human beings are thinking animals; that distinguishes them from other species. They are social animals because thought gives rise to cooperation, by which they enhance their position and security. They are urban animals too because the highest form of social cooperation is in the city, with its trades, guilds, role models, and classes. And this, Ibn Khaldun tells us, is the basis of every civilization. The larger the city, the greater the scope for cooperation between its inhabitants and the more civil or civilized life will become.

But what immediately impresses one about Ibn Khaldun is that there is no trace of Aristotelianism in his thinking. For him city-dwellers are not Aristotle's political animals, and they are certainly not citizen-soldiers. War is not an activity of the city-dweller, it is the specialty of tribes with their own distinctive model of social unity. The desire to associate starts with group consciousness, group feeling, and solidarity. It begins with the clan or the tribe with which people share common descent or by which they are adopted. When studying the Arab and Berber peoples of the western Islamic world and the nomads in the east, Khaldun found that economic conditions had created fierce tribal units bound together by the obligation that the member owed to their patrilineal kin.

In the stateless, egalitarian desert tribes of the Levant, order among various horizontally arranged and vertically nested segmented groups was also maintained by the cohesion-producing effects of permanent feuding at all levels. It was a way of life vividly captured in the Arab maxim: "I against my brothers, my brothers and I against our cousins, my brothers, cousins and I against the world." Nothing could be achieved without fighting, and fighting required the loyalty of a family or group. Conflict was the basic political dynamic, and competition was intense between rival tribal leaders and the patron-client networks that were extensions of original family bloodlines.[66]

Ibn Khaldun explained this persistence of a tribal warrior tradition in terms that are intelligible today: the intense affection everyone has for clients and allies, intensified through feelings of shame when one's neighbors or relatives are humiliated or lose face:

> They are a closely knit group of common descent. This strengthens their stamina and makes them feared, since everybody's affection for his family and his group is more important than anything else. Compassion and affection for one's blood relations and relatives exist in human nature as something God put into the hearts of men. It makes for natural support and aid and increases the fear felt by the enemy. Those who have no one of their own lineage rarely feel affection for their fellows. . . . Group feeling results only from blood relationships or something corresponding to it. . . . The purpose of group feeling, which is defense or aggression, can be fulfilled only with the help of a common descent.[67]

This concept of blood descent is all-important. It is not necessary to trace one's descent from within a family or group. Once accepted, the client or ally is eventually conceptualized as a blood kin. Rights and duties are legitimized in terms of blood relationships that in time will be accepted as real by the tribe.

The great merit of Ibn Khaldun's book for the study of military history is that he recognized that tribal loyalty dictated the way conflict was conducted. What matters in war is the cohesion of the group, not the number of soldiers on a battlefield, the brilliance of a leader's tactics, or even individual heroism, though honor is important and revered. A tribe prevails over another when it succeeds in exploiting divisions within a rival group, or when it is able to employ tricks and ruses (what Ibn Khaldun calls "the hidden factors of war") so as to amplify the divisions on the enemy side. And the examples he cites include spreading alarming news or reports, hiding in thickets or the depressions of hills, and demoralizing rather than defeating the enemy in battle. These "hidden factors" affect people psychologically and tend to generate intense fear. "Mohammed said, 'war is trickery.' An Arab proverb says, 'many a trick is worth more than a tribe.'"[68]

What of today's world? Ibn Khaldun does not deny that group solidarity could extend to the city and to a civilization in general, to a people not related to each other by patrilineal links. But in the case of cities, he tells us that cooperation is largely functional, not emotional, and it can never aspire to being as close. As a consequence, wars fought by city-dwellers are usually lackluster. War requires the type of social cohesion that can only be found in a tribal group.

One of the reasons he thinks tribespeople make superior soldiers is that cities grow in riches as they grow in size, and wealth brings with it luxury and decadence. Its inhabitants, he writes, lack zeal for a fight. Their main aim, after all, is not to affirm life in battle but to make life more congenial. And when they do fight, they prefer defense to offense. Unlike the defense of a family or property, the defense of an interest or trade inspires little willingness to die: "People have little endurance. The turmoil of the battle frightens them."

It is in this respect that Khaldun's understanding of the origin of war differs significantly from the Western, for it is almost entirely *existential*. Apart from a holy or just conflict, a jihad, whose religious sanction transcends the particularity of a social group, Khaldun tells us that war has its origin in the desire of certain human beings to take revenge on others. Each party to a conflict is supported by the people sharing its group feeling. The reason for revenge is jealousy, envy, or hostility, and the most unyielding hostility is that of a neighboring tribe, family, or warrior people, such as the Kurds or the Berbers, who were among the main peoples Ibn Khaldun studied. War can only be fought successfully by soldiers who identify with each other socially, and social cohesion can only be engendered in conditions of tribal life. No central authority keeps the peace. Human beings' security is based on trust between themselves and fellow members of the group. In an atomized society such as a state or a city, trust tends to be almost totally absent.[69]

Today the Levantine world is still distinguished by its social networks, quasi-tribes, and alliances forged on the basis of kin, common experiences, and services exchanged. It has not been able to create formidable state structures or professional armies that have much hope of defeating Western armies in face-to-face encounters in the field. What is most remarkable about the Levantine style of war since the late nineteenth century is that it has proved pretty hopeless at contact warfare between states or armies, especially when the armies have been Western (or Israeli). It is not that Arab soldiers, or other ethnic groups from the same region, are by nature unsuited to the instrumental form of war. In the Crusades, they were much better motivated, better disciplined, and better led than the Europeans (whose way of warfare in this period was not Western but medieval). But 700 years ago, their political structures were far more complex and impressive than Europe's. Today the atrophy of political society, absence of civil society, and weak political culture that obtains in most of the Levant does not enable the state to put competent soldiers in the field. No Arab army, in fact, has done well against a reasonably skilled Western army. At the battle of Tel-el-Kebir (1882) some 10,000 Egyptians surrendered to a sergeant from the Shropshire regiment armed only with a stick. In the Gulf War, remnants of an entire Iraqi company surrendered to a female reporter armed only with a pencil.[70]

But then again, what impresses one most about the indirect wars of the past twenty years in Lebanon, Chechnya, and Afghanistan is that tribal warfare has proved devastatingly successful against more sophisticated state armies, even those better trained and much better armed. Ibn Khaldun would find himself vindicated. Cities do not do war best; tribes do, and the motive of revenge and honor is much more compelling than *raison d'etat*.

What holds this form of warfare together is the community of the faithful, who in default of the civil society found in the West—in the absence of "modular man"—still find psychological and emotional security in religious faith. If the Levantine way of war is humanitarian, it is largely because war must never be allowed to threaten the security that membership of the Islamic community offers the believer. But the faith also offers its members something that the Western way of warfare no longer does: a reason for dying. In the early part of the twenty-first century, the existential dimension of war is most evident in the Levant.

Warlords and Urban Tribes

Where Ibn Khaldun erred was in thinking that the tribal ethic was unique to people who lived outside the bounds of the city. Even today, group feelings prevail in urban areas of the Levant, among neighborhoods and Sufi brotherhoods who bind themselves together in self-contained groups or networks such as Hizbollah. The Americans faced this problem in Somalia, which began to fragment in the late 1980s. Reflecting on the U.S. Army's disastrous performance in Somalia, Mark Bowden quotes a State Department official who claimed that the Somali people "were congenitally incapable of appreciating unity and peace."[71] In this case, it is clear that the loss of life in the civil war was so devastating that it made peace impossible. Security could only be found in groups led by warlords for whom conflict (as was true for the Bedouins of Ibn Khaldun's day) had become a way of life.

Even the Somali army, or what was left of it, could only function along clan lines. When it took to the field, it did so not as an integrated, professionalized force but as a series of linked clan militias. The president, Said Barre, too played the clan card as he came to rely less and less on the army and more and more on paramilitary groups based on clans. By 1992, three factions were fighting for state control, although by that time there was no state to win. It had collapsed. They fought now for individual cities like Mogadishu and Kismayu or regions in the countryside, objectives that further emphasized divisions between contending clans. And as subfactions themselves began to split further, the focus of conflict shifted more and more to local concerns.

When the Americans arrived in Somalia in 1993, they believed they could restore "hope" by addressing the problems of a failed state. The Somalis were intrigued to hear them talking of "the situation." Situations usually have solutions. The difference between a problem and a "question," however, is that in the case of the latter, local actors are invariably unwilling to resolve a crisis. As the anthropologist I. M. Lewis writes:

> Few writers have failed to notice the formidable pride of the Somali nomad . . . his firm conviction that he is sole master of his actions and subject to no authority save that of God. If they have noticed it, however, they have for the most part been baffled by the shifting character of the nomad's political allegiance and puzzled by the fact that *the political and jural unit with which he acts on one occasion, he opposes on another.*[72]

The Americans correctly identified the cause of violence in Somalia: the clan system and the rivalry it produced. But despite identifying the cause, they came up with the wrong solution. In 1993 they thought they could arrest the most intransigent clan leaders, when for every leader they arrested there were dozens of brothers, cousins, sons, and nephews waiting to take their place. Indeed, one of the ironies of "the situation" was that when their most intractable enemy, General Mohamed Farah Aideed, eventually died, his place was taken by his own son, who had come to Somalia as a U.S. Marine Reservist with the Unified Task Force (UNITAF) in December 1992. For the clans, war was not "a continuation of politics by other means" but a way of life that permitted them to position for advantage. In the case of Somalia, there was no civil society to restore and no regime to put in place.

The Americans did not understand these facts. They saw positioning for advantage as unworthy of politics. They were also critical of the warlords for refusing a fair fight. And, of course, clans did not fight fairly. Aideed tried to starve rival clans by hijacking UN supplies of food. He used terror (some of the Pakistani soldiers he captured were disemboweled and skinned), and he frequently resorted to deceit, inciting demonstrators to riot against the U.S. presence and then gunning them down so that he could accuse the United Nations of genocide. This deeply cynical and murderous figure eventually died in 1996 without uniting the Somali nation. But he did succeed in uniting it in its own imagination. On October 3, 1993, the Americans tried to seize Aideed in a military operation. Instead of a surgical strike, they found themselves engaged in a firefight, in the course of which they killed 500 Somalis and lost eighteen of their own men. The action persuaded President Bill Clinton to bring home his troops. That date subsequently became a national holiday, another irony since there was no Somali "nation-state" to defend. Whatever Aideed's own standing at home (and he was reviled by a majority of Somalis), the people of Mogadishu had felt threatened, intimidated, and terrorized by the Americans and proud of the fact that they had driven off their streets the world's greatest military power.

Warriors of God, or Social Actors?

In societies such as Somalia and Afghanistan, tribes and hill people still live in a condition of shifting indeterminacy and endemic competition. There is no overarching power structure. Instead, there is intense competition between equals. No one is powerful enough to subordinate anyone else for very long, which encourages a spirit of egalitarianism. It is not the nomadic way of life as such that is valued so much as the freedom and personal independence it brings, which is reinforced by the social message of Islam. The same freedom can be found in remote mountain villages, where men claim the right to the respect and honor due to them as warriors.

In such a social context, we must not expect to find Western-style warriors with a Western existential ethos. There is no honor in exposing oneself to a helicopter gunship or the massive firepower of a Soviet tank. Warriors are those who speak for the community, and it is in the hills and mountains, not in the open, that their virtue is tested. In the first Chechen War (1994–1995), the rebels sought to avoid open battle against Russian armor, artillery, and airpower. They wanted to fight an infantry war, soldier against soldier, and they needed and found an urban environment in which to do so. In Grozny, Russian soldiers could die as easily as Chechen fighters, and it was in the streets of the capital city that their own honor and that of the Chechen nation was vindicated.

The Russian army relied on its firepower and armor because it had no other choice. Its soldiers were poorly trained. Even basic individual and unit combat skills essential to any army were seriously underdeveloped because of catastrophic budget cuts. Most soldiers were conscripts, and those who were not had not experienced a divisional-level field exercise since 1992. To the Chechen commanders, however, the Russians lacked not only skill but honor. As one rebel commander commented: "The Russians stayed in their armor so we just stood on the balconies and dropped grenades onto their vehicles as they drove by underneath. The Russians are cowards. They can't bear to come out of shelter and fight us man-to-man. They know they are no match for us. That is why we beat and will always beat them."[73] And beat them they did, in street fighting of an intensity that had not been seen since Stalingrad.

The Russians, of course, tended to see the conflict in Chechnya as they had the conflict in Afghanistan: as profoundly unmodern. In Afghanistan, the Soviet invasion disturbed the social equilibrium and created opportunities for traditionally subordinated groups to come to the top. A Tajik leader named Massoud became one of the most influential men in the country; an Uzbek warlord called Dostum carved out a kingdom in the north; and the lowest ranking social class, manual laborers, the Hazaras, became a military force to be reckoned with. None of them, however, saw themselves as "warriors of God," "soldiers of Allah," or "martyrs of the faith." Their followers were farmers, professors, students, and business-people divided by language and ethnicity but united, not by their faith but by a passionate wish to preserve a certain way of life given meaning by Islam. In that sense, they were a resistance army like any other, and it was only the media that prevented them from acquiring a genuine human face by seeing them in exclusively religious terms.

Religion has enormous expressive value in mobilizing people to take to the streets; it helps them project wider and deeper significance onto ongoing social conflicts. Everywhere in the world, political or social elites often moralize or invest their otherwise narrow ambitions with abstract and transcendental values. Religion is a particularly useful device for sacralizing violence and thus legitimizing it. Religion is a powerful ritual force and martyrdom a useful instrument of war.

Indeed, the expressive nature of violence in the Levantine world is one of the features of its "humanitarianism." Instrumental violence is technical, whereas expressive violence is ritualistic, symbolic, and communicative. Often the two are closely related; they form a continuum. The former invokes expediency and practical action; the latter invests actions with meaning. As we are reminded by a Western sociologist speaking of life in the West: "The common characterization of violence as 'meaningless' is . . . foolish and misleading. Violence is seen not only as invested with meaning but also as a means—perhaps the most important means—of *inscribing* that meaning upon the world."[74]

Of course, Joseph Rothschild argues, it is plausible for the West today, culturally removed as it is from the World War I–style battlefields of the Iran-Iraq War, to feel that there was something distinctly atavistic in a struggle in which a million soldiers perished. But it behooves us to look at our own history more closely. In World War I, after all, it was not unknown for European armies to take up to 50 percent casualties or losses in a single battle.[75] Today, looking back from the privileged vantage point of our postmodern times, we often think of such violence as meaningless. The British still talk of a "lost generation," a generation that was sacrificed for nothing of value. We consider the young men who died at Passchendaele and the Somme, to use the jargon of the hour, to have been quite literally "wasted."

We fail to ask why many went so willingly to the front. "A sense of meaninglessness" was a common complaint of European youth in 1914, and historians talk of many young people at the time attempting to "transcend" the national tradition or finding themselves engaged in a "great unifying spiritual crusade" when they marched off with such enthusiasm to war and mounted the great suicidal frontal attacks of 1915–1917.[76] "Why do men so desire death?" Marguerite Yourcenar asked in the 1930s, and she came to the conclusion that it was a symbolic substitute for a much greater "death event": the desire to transcend the experience of nihilism and to find some greater form of meaning in life.[77] Social scientists, with a less poetic turn of phrase, write instead of the trauma of modernity, which was as demoralizing for the West then as it is for much of the non-Western world today.

Indeed, on the eve of war, many Europeans were aware of passing through a deep cultural crisis that had brought with it nihilism, expressed in the uncomfortable tension between their cultural heritage, which emphasized the purpose underlying their existence, and an inability, following the "death of God," to articulate a compelling substitute. The absence of meaning led many Europeans to demand meaning with greater intensity than ever.

In this Nietzsche, as in so much else, was their prophet. He predicted that the Europeans would resort to a form of what he metaphorically called "intoxication" or "narcotization." In a published fragment from *The Will to Power,* the work he had left incomplete on his death, we find the following: "The ways of *self-narcotization*—deep down not knowing whither. *Emptiness.* Attempt to get over it only by intoxication: intoxication . . . is cruelty in the tragic enjoyment of the destruction of the noblest; intoxication is blind enthusiasm for single human beings or ages (as hatred etc.)."[78] Following "the death of God," which he himself had proclaimed so empathically, he predicted that the Europeans would seek temporary release from their nihilism and in this quest turn to "great wars," to "strong military organisations," and above all, to nationalism. The death of God was different, of course, from the trauma of modernity for the Islamic world. For Islamic fundamentalism is carried out in the name of the ulema, the community of the faithful, not the nation-state. European nihilism in the early twentieth century demanded a national solution. The nation-state became a sacred community that demanded the sacrifice of its citizens and at the same time promised them redemption through it. It also required its martyrs by the millions. As Nietzsche claimed, modern nationalism was nothing "but the metamorphosis of the Cross."[79]

Extreme nationalism became a political religion in the 1930s, and it is as political religions that movements such as fascism and Marxism are increasingly seen by historians, a product in this case of the absence of religion in people's lives. They fulfilled a deep social need. The nation became a congregation of the faithful whose leaders spoke with unprecedented emotional power. Nazi ideology offered redemption from a national crisis. Later still, during the early years of the Cold War, both Marxism and liberalism were adhered to as religious faiths. In the United States, Julia Kristeva writes, liberalism became a de facto religious ideology "based on the affective, non-critical adherence" of those who subscribed to it.[80] Liberalism, like Marxism, gave its followers a "reserve of meaning" that could not be found in social institutions or traditions. In the course of the 1950s, America was turned into an "ism" and those who harbored different beliefs were caricatured as "un-American." In an ideological age, nations were defined by their thoughts as much as their actions, and heresy was punished with the same severity as excommunication in the past.

Only in the 1970s did attitudes begin to change. The nuclear disarmers may have been disappointed. Despite their marches and protests, governments did not disarm. They continued adding to their stockpiles of nuclear weapons. But deterrence was no longer legitimized by a people's willingness to martyr themselves (at least in the West). It was legitimized instead by the continued willingness to kill others. That was the terminology of the last phase of the nuclear era, the terminology of an age that had finally put its religious calling behind it.

If we look at the Islamic world today, we find a similar wish to inscribe life with meaning. Unlike the West, however, the modern Muslim world has not turned its back on God or the quest for self-realization through war. Take the two most radical movements of the moment, Sufism and Shiism. Both are parallel spiritual responses to the challenge of modernity. For much of the late twentieth century, Sufism languished and was considered unmodern, but it has revived. It is difficult to define because it has appeared at different times and in different societies. It is a way of life rather than a system or philosophy, and Islam and Sufism evolved together, though along different paths. Islam sought to establish the welfare of society through a body of laws known as the Shari'a, whereas Sufism offered an inner way, a form of devotion that took account of the inner spiritual freedom of the individual. Sufism is not otherworldly, however, for it inspired resistance movements, including the Dervish movements of the late nineteenth century in the Sudan and Libya in their revolt against colonial rule.[81] In Chechnya, many Wahhabis began their careers as Sufis or members of neo-Sufi movements, and Wahhabism helped sustain young Chechen fighters in both Chechen wars.

As for Shiism, it is known in the West for its "martyr complex," its devotion to terror and holy wars. Martyrdom *is* an important theme of Shiism, which began its existence with the death of Hussein, an act almost equivalent to Christ's crucifixion for Christians. In 680 C.E., Hussein, the son of Ali, the cousin of the Prophet Muhammad, was killed in what Shiites regard not as a defeat but martyrdom. Hussein did not choose to martyr himself; he was chosen for it by Allah because of his special merit.

In one sense, Shiism is like Christianity in that it looks forward to a better era, but it differs from Christianity in two important respects. First, Christians usually held themselves free of blame for Christ's death (traditionally blaming it on the Jews or seeing it as divinely ordained), but Shiites continue to believe they connived at the death of Hussein through their own cowardice and that they have been paying off the debt ever since. Second, in Shiism, the sense of personal contribution to the attainment of a better state and the belief in its imminence is much stronger than in Christian fundamentalist millenarian movements. On holy days, Shiites simulate suffering and revere martyrdom as a holy act. For most of their history, in fact, they have accepted suffering as an act of redemption. Usually, individual acts of martyrdom are the norm. Communities do not martyr themselves. Saints, like heroes, are few in number. But unlike the Western ideal of heroism, martyrdom is not a personal act. It is undertaken on behalf of the community and is deemed to be a symbol of a community's capacity for suffering. In short, Shiism has a dualistic nature that makes it difficult for Westerners to comprehend. One face is quietist, as it was throughout the colonial period. Until the 1970s, Shiites were renowned for their dogged fatalism, but there has always been in Shiism a potential for radical millenarian revolt. One day, the Shiites believe, a new Hussein will return, but this time his people must be ready for him. This time, martyrdom must be not ritual but real.

CONCLUSION

Unity, legitimacy, and revelation were the original concepts of Islam, and they were revolutionary ideas in their day, firing the Muslims with a zeal that swept all before them in the seventh century C.E. All this is behind them or seems to be.

The Levantine style of war emerged from the *disunity* of the Muslim world, which has been a feature of life for centuries and prompted Ibn Khaldun to believe the region was incapable of producing a synthesis between tribe and city and thus forging a true concept of citizenship. It also feeds on the *illegitimacy* of central government, or the authority of the city where government is to be found, in the face of fierce tribal loyalties and the allegiances of patrilineal clans. Until the state is seen as legitimate, the idea of civil society is unlikely to take root. Finally, the *revelation* of religion in the form of fundamentalism continues to marginalize the Levantine world, for it encourages the rulers to leave the faith unreformed (even in its confrontation with modernity) and thus to preserve it unchanged as a consolation for those whose lives are brutal and often short and for intellectuals whose lives have been sullied by a sense of failure.

As long as the Levantine world remains marginal or unable to adapt to the demands of a globalized world, it will continue to produce poor, frustrated, and often alienated people who make remarkably good foot soldiers. This is the social milieu in which the Levantine warrior is bred, not so much a natural born killer as one of Clausewitz's "instruments of war." As Clausewitz wrote: "War is the province of physical exertion and suffering. A certain strength of the body and mind produces indifference to them. With these qualifications . . . a man is at once a proper instrument of war." The Levantine warrior today is as strong and hardy as his ancestors who fought Alexander the Great, the only Western leader to take them on and defeat them at their own game, though his victory was ephemeral.

Westerners today are physically weaker than at any time in their history, though they live longer and are obsessively concerned with their health. Few Western soldiers would survive a month in a Roman legion. Even the U.S. Marine Corps has had to reduce its standards of physical fitness simply to make good a shortfall in numbers of enlistees. But what Clausewitz meant by "suffering" included mental endurance—the stamina and dogged determination to prevail because "custom" and religion require it. These existential elements of war explain the tenacity of tribal warriors, at whose hands time and again Western armies have faced defeat or serious embarrassment. And there is something else. Hobbes was quite wrong, Ernest Gellner wrote, when he claimed that a condition of latent war makes life "solitary, nasty, brutish and short." At any rate, it is not solitary. Anarchy leads to gregariousness and the rise of groups. Ibn Khaldun was closer to the truth when he maintained that anarchy and anarchy alone led to social cohesion.[82]

Again and again Western forces, though better equipped and organized than their enemies, have encountered this reality in person. In turn, once bloodied, they have appeared unmotivated and lacking in social cohesion of their own. In Lebanon and Somalia, coalitions of the willing have been broken on the anvil of war. Instead of asking ourselves why this is the case, we prefer to condemn the Somali and Lebanese factions for being "reactionary" or "cowardly," when neither of these epithets is true. Rarely do we bother to enquire why, at this stage in our history, our own humanism makes it impossible for our own soldiers to find the existential meaning in war that once sustained them in battle. Rarely do we ask why our own way of war has become almost entirely instrumental.

History is driving the West along a distinctive path. The West achieved its military dominance of the world at the end of the seventeenth century by marrying the concepts of discipline, decisiveness, and drill it learned from the Greeks and Romans to the technology of firepower. Today it hopes to retain this dominance by marrying the human factor to technology in a more radical way still: the symbiosis of man and machine. It is called "posthuman warfare," and it will remain distinctively Western (or, more accurately, American) because it cannot be copied by anyone else.

7

Posthuman War

Thanks to the movies, gunfire has always sounded
unreal to me, even when being fired at.
—Peter Ustinov, *Romanov and Juliet*

In his semiautobiography *Enemies of Promise,* Cyril Connolly recalls an old school friend whose relaxation was reading Homer. Later he joined his father's regiment and had himself transferred to the Indian army. Later still, he took his Gurkhas to Waziristan, still reading Homer, and was killed in action on the frontier, winning a posthumous Victoria Cross. He died every inch a warrior, on a hillside, outnumbered, putting heart in his troops by assuring them that help would reach them, knowing that help would never come, and dying covered with wounds after fighting all day. "Such was . . . the destiny of character . . . a premature and lonely death with the barren glory of a military honour."[1]

That passage has stayed in my memory for a large part of my life. The school friend Connolly remembers was a representative of a dying breed, a born warrior who could trace his roots back to Homer's heroes. Connolly's remarks are interesting, however, for several reasons of more immediate import.

The first is that no Englishman before World War I would have called a warrior's death "a barren glory." Nor would Connolly's schoolboy friend have seen it in this light. As an avid reader of Homer, he would have known that in *The Iliad,* heroism does not bring happiness. Its sole and sufficient reward is fame. And that is what made warriors "heroic," for they were not oppressed by the future even when, like Achilles, they knew that it held their approaching death.

Second, Connolly wrote *Enemies of Promise* in 1937, knowing well enough, as did most of his generation, that another war was coming in which everyone would be conscripted to fight. As it happened, the warrior

159

ethos was not quite dead. In his fascinating oral history *The Good War,* Studs Terkel transcribes countless stories of men, especially fighting men, who felt that World War II was intensely real, by far the most real and significant time of their lives. Indeed, after the war, they continued to dwell on it and relive its battles and moral certainties. Life after 1945, not war, seemed to be "barren." Many of them, when asked about their feelings about the postwar world, remarked that they seemed to be "marking time."[2]

It is doubtful today whether many people, if conscripted to fight another war, would feel this calling. Even the professional soldier who volunteers to fight sees war increasingly as a trade rather than a vocation, a job like any other, even if it differs from every other in the fear and anxiety it generates. Even if that is not true of every soldier (and we produce a few warriors still), war in the early twenty-first century does indeed seem to the rest of us rather barren, bereft of that dimension that made the warrior a human type, as Hegel understood the term, a man who through war perceives his own humanity.

Indeed, we have been encouraged since World War I to see war in such a negative, life-denying light that it is difficult to grasp the nature of the warrior's honor. It is difficult to see war as it was once understood by our forebears, as an intensely human activity that was fought, in part, not only for reasons of state but because the warrior derived value from it. War has been existential as well as instrumental. It has provided a minority of those who fought it with self-esteem—the "warrior's honor." Through their behavior, warriors not only respected themselves but were, in turn, respected by others, even, perhaps especially, by their enemies, without whom they would have been in no way special.

I wrote this book because it seemed to me that the existential dimension of war was not only very real but vital in legitimizing it as a human activity. In instrumentalizing it, as Westerners have done today, we have made it purely utilitarian. That may be a virtue in our own eyes, but it devalues war in the eyes of others. This book highlights the crisis in the Western way of war brought about by the death of the warrior. Although it breaks with the conventional wisdom that the Western way of war has come to an end, it does confirm that in the future there will be no place in it for the warrior ideal.

A glimpse of the future can be found in Don DeLillo's short story, "Human Moments in World War Three," a telling commentary on a future battlefield mediated largely through technology, for the attackers never see their human targets. For one of the characters, Vollmer, a young soldier in a laser-shooting capsule orbiting the Earth, the planet has been reduced to a series of spectacular effects devoid of human action. DeLillo writes of a world in which human agency has largely departed the field, as has human interest. The warriors of the new battlefield are disengaged, both emotionally and morally, from life on Earth. They have no intersubjective contact with their enemies; they experience nothing themselves that can possibly change their own self-worth. The "human moments" in this war (the title of DeLillo's story) are largely banal: the fact that the commanders can wear their bedroom slippers at their firing panels and can take into their capsule their own "personal preference kits."

As Nietzsche would have understood them, Vollmer and his commander are not warriors but soldiers and perhaps not even that. They have become displaced into their own weapons system and transformed into technicians. In this kind of war, there is no place for emotion, fear, courage, or even endurance. For there is nothing to endure. As Vollmer remarks, he is happy, an observation that prompts the commander to note that happiness is totally outside our frame of reference. War has become just a housekeeping arrangement, a series of more or less routine tasks.[3]

It would seem, then, at the beginning of the century that we can no longer invoke war as the medium through which we relate ourselves to the state or the community or recognize our humanity: the "we" principle, the way by which we once ontologically understood ourselves. Although standards of identity go beyond war, as a result, war has come to be criticized almost entirely by *standards external to itself*. We can still fight wars, of course, but war itself can no longer be life affirming; it can no longer fulfill an existential purpose.

From the Prehuman to the Posthuman

"Consider the cattle, grazing as they pass you by," Nietzsche wrote in his first major essay, "On the Uses and Disadvantages of History for Life," "they do not know what is meant by yesterday or today."[4] Animals have no history; they only have evolution. We have a history or, what is more important, historicity. Our understanding of what it is to be human is tied to our understanding of what we might yet "become" in history. We are not finished or perfectible beings. Our interest in ourselves is rooted in our intuitive sense that of all animals on the planet, we are the only ones still evolving. Our humanity, in other words, can be described but not defined, for it is still incomplete.

If history is humanity, we ought to ask, when did humanity begin? For the anthropologist Clifford Geertz, humanity and history took off together some 15,000 years ago during the last Ice Age. For that was not only a time of receding brow ridges and shrinking jaws but a time in which were forged nearly all those characteristics of our existence that are most graphically "human": the capacity to create and use symbols, social structures such as taboos, and the increasingly complex use of language. It was also the time when it became clear that unlike other animals, we have no instincts, only institutions.

Culture, in other words, is necessary for humanity to function optimally. Geertz puts it very well. "A culture-less human being would be 'worse' than an intrinsically talented though unfulfilled ape."[5] The old anthropological view that human nature came first and then culture followed has been stood on its head. Culture, like art and religion, molded humanity somatically. It was essential not only to its survival but also its existential realization. Human beings were human because they lived in each other's imagination, and imagination is the source of the numinous, myth and art.

What we find in the prehistoric imagination is an extension of human range. Human nature is not fixed. Human beings acquired the facets of their "humanity" in the process of constructing new social worlds, as they expanded across the globe into different environments and habitats and as they began to settle and tame the land. Giambattista Vico told us all this 300 years ago, but it was only recently that anthropologists and archaeologists began to accept that prehistory witnessed a unique development, "no less than the emergence and self-realisation of humanity."[6]

In that sense, human beings have been around for much longer than previously imagined and existed much earlier than the late Paleolithic age. In the case of art, sculptured rocks recently discovered at Kunumurra in Australia may be 75,000 years old. We know that the paintings in the Chauvet caves in France are 15,000 years older than those at Lascaux, which caused a sensation when they were first discovered. The time separating us from these artists is at least twelve times longer than the time separating us from the pre-Socratic philosophers.

But if prehistoric people were human beings, they were not *our* human beings. In that respect, when studying them, we need to grasp the difference between cultural and cognitive relativism. Differences based on the first kind require us to recognize that there are different phases of human life, as there are different social practices and morals that distance us from other peoples. The fact that we can recognize these differences means that it is possible with a little effort to get into the minds of other cultures so that we can recognize the differences *as* differences. And that permits us to understand, at the same time, that we share points in common with them.[7]

This is clearly the case with all human societies, which is why Oswald Spengler's claim that one day we would not be able to appreciate the music of Mozart or the paintings of Rembrandt never caught on, any more than his insistence that what is "out of phase" with the past will never resonate in our imagination. Such thinking leads nowhere very quickly because, if we can never recognize what is "out of phase" with us or "out of style" with us, we would only be able to understand ourselves.

Cognitive relativism is more of a problem, for it requires us to recognize that there are different ways of looking at the world, ways that are so different that we can never have more than an indeterminate grasp of what it must have been like to have been a member of such a community. We cannot see them from within; we cannot grasp their reality or what was real for them. Any view of the world is highly theoretical, and our efforts to make intelligible to ourselves the prehistoric worldview can only proceed in terms of our *re*interpreting their concepts, beliefs, and practices into our own terms. Without doing so, we could not hope to make sense of them. That is what archaeologists and anthropologists used to do. Today we recognize that we do not need to humanize them in our form to understand them.

Take the early cave paintings, for example. When experts pretend that they can see "the beginning of perspective," they are falling into a deep, anachronistic trap. The pictorial system of perspective is architectural and urban. Prehistoric "perspective" is about coexistence of the worlds of animals and human beings; it is not about the distance of human beings from animals. Is such creative explosion as that found in the Chauvet caves therefore really evidence of a human revolution and the evolution of a recognizably human way of life? Or is it further evidence of continuity in the potential of peoples to produce creative work that is recognizably "human" but that falls short of a revolutionary breakthrough (or discontinuity) in terms of their need to realize their own human potential?

Even when, thousands of years later, human beings began to settle and to build civilizations, they were much more modest in their evaluation of human life than those who were to come after them. For life to be meaningful, it was enough to know not only that the gods had retained for themselves the best (immortality) but that they had also retained control over their own creations. Through their priests, they instructed humans what to do. They explained the origin of the world and its purpose. They were simply present in too many forms and too many instances of human endeavor. They, not human beings, wrote human history.

Not that life was considered any less worthwhile, of course, because it included death, pain, and suffering, any more than it was diminished by the rhythm of birth, death, and regeneration in nature. And it was no less worthwhile because so much was preordained. But if human beings in general lived at peace with the world, it was because they saw their life not as meaningless but as marginal. Life in such circumstances could unfold in complex social structures with their priestly hierarchies and scribes. Centered largely around a royal cell, their sole purpose was to reproduce the sustenance of that household and ensure that the rituals needed to secure divine favor were carried out. As long as people lived according to those rituals, they could expect to secure life itself. In other words, in prehistory, humanity lived only in order to live, not to seek a deeper or more authentic form of life. Life in this era, the philosopher Jan Patocka writes, was rooted in the immediacy of *being* human.[8]

One of the reasons for their modest demands on life was probably a sense of chronic insecurity. In the case of Egypt, everything depended on the power and spiritual authority of the pharaohs. Egyptian rulers were living gods, the very essence of a divine order nourished by a bountiful river, the Nile. In the Old Kingdom, the pharaohs *were* human existence, the symbol of equilibrium between the forces of order and chaos and of the stability that sustained human life. The collapse of that kingdom as a result of twenty years of unremitting drought ("the great hunger" recorded by the scribes—one of the consequences, we now know, of El Niño), must have come as a terrible blow to self-confidence. When the Middle Kingdom finally established itself and civilized life returned, society had a passionate aversion to change.[9]

This aversion is captured ironically but accurately in the Jewish historian Josephus's famous denunciation of the Greeks (in his treatise *Against Apion*). Josephus was scornful of their belief that despite their comparative late arrival on the scene, they were of all peoples the most interesting. True, they were not the most recent. When Hecataeus informed the priests of the Egyptian city Thebes of his descent from a god, his sixteenth ancestor, the priests took him into an inner temple and showed him images representing 345 generations that still did not end in a god. Yet the important point is that the Greeks told these stories themselves. Although they admired the Egyptians, they recognized they themselves were very different. And Josephus, despite himself, suggested a good reason for that belief: "The Egyptians," he observed, "appear never in all their history to have enjoyed one day of freedom."

Freedom in this context can be defined as the wish to *become* something different or at least something more than what one is. Why this was not the case in Egypt can be deduced from the role played by their gods, at least until the Middle Kingdom. Like those of most other societies, they

were necessarily crude, not very spiritual, and concerned not with securing the future but the present. They were not gods so much as "the symbolic expression of the custom and consent of the political community."[10]
Only with the rise of the first empires, which extended the ruler's grasp
beyond the immediate to the distant, did the gods grow in stature and even
status, as did the rulers themselves now that their presence, like that of
their gods, was felt rather than seen.

Even so, nothing we find in the sagas of Akkad (2340–2159 B.C.E.),
the first empire of which we know for certain, is marked by the celebration of its triumphant rise or the anticipation of its continuance. On the
contrary, we find the emptiness of its views on its own future. Its people
conceived the world as essentially static and unchanging. Even though the
empire lasted a century and a half, historical incidents were treated as no
more than superficial disturbances of the established order or events that
had little significance in themselves. The past and future were wholly
implicit in the present.

Samuel Kramer echoes this finding in looking at the Sumerian literature of the second and third millennia B.C.E.: "The Sumerians held out no
comforting hopes for man and his future. To be sure, they longed for security and freedom from fear, want and war. But it never occurred to them
to project these longings into the future. Instead, they thought of them in
retrospect and relegated them to the long gone past."[11] That is clearly the
case with other civilizations as well. Their understanding of their own
"humanity" was different from ours. They were in one sense "children of
lesser gods" because they had little understanding of what they might
"become."

THE AXIAL PERIOD

If we look at the past in these terms, we find that history and with it the
"human" era (as opposed to prehistory and the "prehuman") emerged
comparatively late. If we seek to date it, we need look no further than the
"Axial Period" of world history. The term was first coined by the philosopher Karl Jaspers in the 1950s, and he employed it to mean a secularized
version of the Christian idea, according to which world history is both
divided and unified by a unique axis—the life and death of Christ. Jaspers
modified this religious conception in two ways. First, he shifted the center of the axis to 800–200 B.C.E. Second, his axis does not represent a
supernatural ingression into time but a decisive historical breakthrough by
humanity in the basic conditions of life and thought, which occurred at

this time in the world's three major civilizations—China, India, and Greece. This axis constitutes the greatest historical watershed of all in that it divides and unifies history at the same time. Everything preceding it was but a preparation for the breakthrough; all subsequent history dates back to this period.[12]

The idea of an axial age begs many questions, and we still have very few of the answers. What is interesting is the fact that, for reasons we still do not know, the world's major civilizations developed along parallel lines, even though contact between them was minimal. Only in the Americas, which were cut off from the rest of the world, did these developments not occur. In the Old World, by contrast, the great civilizations simultaneously developed a distinctive ideology or set of beliefs: Taoism and Confucianism in China, Hinduism and Buddhism in India, and philosophical rationalism in Europe. We must not forget the Levant, where there were two very important religious traditions: Zoroastrianism in Iran and the theology of the Hebrew prophets, which were to be of critical importance centuries later in the emergence of Christianity and Islam.

A contemporary of Jaspers, Eric Voeglin, called this period "the Great Leap of Being," for during it, the culture of myth sufficiently weakened in its influence to permit some completely new perspectives on life. Voeglin himself put the key date at 500 B.C.E., tracing it to the active life of Buddha, Lao Tzu (possibly), Confucius, and Heraclitus, all of whom effectively changed the consciousness of their cultures and thus the world.[13] The Axial Period, contemporary writer Marcel Gauchet adds, attests to "a radical transformation of the religious" and a "trans-valuation of the values of life." For it saw the birth of three new principles—a growing gap between the life world and the supernatural; the universalization of life values; and, above all, the growth of individuality. All bear on the invention of something new—a moral imagination in which the human is the most important actor of all.[14]

In the civilizations before then, the numinous was immanent in the social structure. It was not opposed to and did not transcend the practical. By contrast, the higher civilizations and with them the higher religions insisted on a purely human realm in which humanity encountered itself, not the gods. The more emphatically the mundane realm was differentiated from the transcendent, the more the world itself came into focus as the sphere of human action proper, in which human beings assumed exclusive responsibility for their actions.[15] Thus Plato famously criticized Homer for portraying the Trojan War as one in which the gods were largely to blame. As a philosopher, he chose to locate it squarely in the province of human ambition. And it was apt that he should have cited *The Iliad*, the greatest work of the Greek literary canon, because war and the birth of the "warrior" played a central role in what Harold Bloom calls "the invention of the human."

WAR AND THE WARRIOR

Before the last Ice Age, the world could support the human population; after it, the world began to fill up very quickly. It may seem strange to claim that the globe had difficulty supporting a world population that was smaller than that of a good-sized city today. But in a world of hunter-gatherers, no environment, however hospitable, could support more than one or two foragers per square kilometer. Agriculture arose from a demographic need to use the land more intensely. With agriculture came the first appearance of small, settled communities. Because people were living in closer proximity than they had before, a demand for strong leadership soon arose to mediate disputes over domestic matters and foraging rights. In time, settlements acquired walls to keep out marauders.

The origins of war (as we know the phenomenon today) can be traced to a particularly urgent (if recurring) problem: that of nomad invasion. The great nomadic invasions (the marauders) that were to punctuate the history of civilization for centuries to come did not really take off until the harnessed horse first made an appearance in the second millennium B.C.E. At which point, the nomads became a true warrior people who lived by war and whose invasions were devastating compared with the past, when migration, though crucial, had taken the form of long-term infiltration and gradual mixing with the local population.

This discordance between settled and nomad is one of the most depressing and most destabilizing factors of history, at least up to the modern era. Settled societies, at least those unfortunate enough to live near the warrior peoples of the central Asian steppe, never knew when and how their eruptions into history would occur. Sometimes they did not destroy the institutions that had been built up over centuries: instead, like parasites, they exacted tribute. But often, they cut a swath of destruction that required civilization to be reborn from the ashes, as animal life has frequently done following episodes of mass extinction.

In the early settled communities, their members had to defend their way of life themselves. A distinctive warrior class began to emerge only with the rise of the first empires. By contrast with the nomads, the warriors who served the empires were not a people but a social class. Only they could afford bronze weapons that were the mark of a Bronze Age people.

Later, in the Iron Age, when weapons were cheap enough to be used by all, they retained a sense of their own amour propre (self-love) by further defining their status. In other words, the warrior became a specific social type, the product of a distinctive phase in the evolution of human society.

Here too the Axial Period played a vital role. Until that period, the warriors' role was resented even by those whom they were supposed to be defending. The new armies they commanded had to be fed and provisioned, and the security they provided was often oppressive. William McNeill describes the warrior elites of the prehistoric era as "macro-parasites" analogous to micro-parasites like bacteria and viruses. Both preyed on human life and culture. The example he offers is that of the empire of Akkad, whose founder-king Sargon did not hesitate to maintain his army by raiding the surrounding countryside: "Costs to the population at large were obviously very great. Indeed Sargon's armies can well be compared to the ravages of an epidemic disease that kills a significant proportion of the host population yet by its very passage confers an immunity lasting for several years."[16]

At times the difference between the "civilized" and "barbaric" warrior elites was probably not always apparent to the peasants. Both lived off the land in different ways; both exacted "tribute." The intensity of competition between warriors and peasants for a share of the slender agricultural surplus on which the success of empire depended could at times be acute. In the Indus Valley, it was only resolved in the seventh century B.C.E. by creating a system of castes and introducing Aryan religious ideas.

The higher religions that arose in this period were crucial to defining the status of the warrior. If we turn to the first epic of war we have, written 2,000 years before Homer's *Iliad,* we find that the earlier warriors of Mesopotamia were clearly parasitic. Gilgamesh, the first warrior-hero of the Sumerian epic of the same name, has to be distracted from predations on his own people.[17] Written on clay tablets and discovered only in the nineteenth century, the poem has a recognizably "human" theme. It is the first known text on the friendship between warriors and one warrior's heartbreak at the loss of another, in this case Gilgamesh's grief for his friend, Enkiddu. But Gilgamesh himself is not a hero like Odysseus or Achilles; he is two-thirds a god, and the epic encounters that bind the two heroes together are against fabulous creatures—not like the Trojan and Greek engagement between human beings.

The Homeric heroes, by comparison, may be considered the first true warriors of the Axial Period. They too live with human loss, but their grief is not absolute as it is for Gilgamesh, and they do not seek to bring the dead back to life. They grieve, knowing that grief itself is a form of remembrance, and to be remembered for one's heroic deeds is the only true immortality as well as the only consolation for human loss.

And Homer's heroes were considered by the Greeks to have existed at the beginning of human history. Their presence permeates Greek mythology, whereas heroes are nearly entirely absent from the myths of other ancient peoples, the Sumerians included. The Greek stories of their heroes are religious in a way that accords with higher religions like Buddhism in the same period. They betray a religious sensibility that is recognizably our own. What Pascal said as a seventeenth-century Christian is as true of Homer's religion as his own: "It is dangerous to let a man see too clearly how much he has in common with the animals, without at the same time making him realize his greatness. It is also dangerous to let him see his greatness too clearly without realizing his baseness. It is more dangerous still to leave him in ignorance of both." Both the baseness and greatness of man are essential to *The Iliad*. Even if Homer's religion is different from our own, his view of human life is recognizably "human"—it accords with our own values. The Homeric hero at his most heroic, although dangerous when roused and bloodthirsty in battle, is a common "human" type grappling with the inhumanity of war.

What we find in the Axial Period is a new way of thinking about war, one that involves acknowledging that it has two clear dimensions: the instrumental and the existential. *Instrumentally,* this period witnessed the rise of the state as we know it today, a unit that emancipated itself politically as well as intellectually. For God is no longer "in" the world in terms of kings who claim not the mandate of heaven or a divine right to rule, but to be gods themselves. Sovereigns may still claim divine right or be the personified union of the visible and invisible worlds, but their role has now changed. They no longer bear witness to the presence of God so much as his absence. They may be his representative, but they are only that and nothing more. The human community is left entirely to itself. This is the political body's ontological independence: its ability to set its own laws in the form of sovereign powers. Human will is translated into legitimate power; the state becomes the source of its own legitimation.[18] And it is the state that sanctions killing.

But the warrior's honor is also vital, and the Axial Period was important in this respect too. It was vital in creating an *existential* dimension of war because it was the age in which individuality was born and, with it, individual choice and will. With the emphasis on human importance comes the wish to find one's "self" in war, to test one's courage and endurance, to *become* a hero. The Greek word *arête* seems originally to have been associated with valor in battle, and may be derived from Ares, the Greek god of war. When Socrates (who was honored not only for being a philosopher but also a brave soldier) came to define virtue, he thought of courage as one of its prime components, and he came up with the proposition that courage as virtue is *self-knowledge*.[19]

We find the epitome of this self-knowledge in Virgil's depiction of the great Roman hero, Aeneas. "Bella, horrida bella" (Wars, hideous wars), the Sybil tells Aeneas when he questions her on his descent into the Underworld. War is Rome's lot. The burden of history is a heavy one to bear, especially if the bearer of it himself is permitted only an occasional prophetic glimpse into its meaning. Aeneas is allowed just that when he descends into the Underworld and questions the Sybil in the sixth book of the *Aeneid,* Virgil's master text of the foundation of Rome.

In the Underworld, he watches his own posterity file before his eyes: Caesar, Pompey, the Scipios, and Fabius Maximus. Aeneas's recently deceased father describes them vividly in terms of their predilection for war: Silvius Aeneas, "outstanding for . . . his prowess in war"; Romulus, "the child of Mars" (the god of war); and Tullus, "stirring men up to fight who have grown unadventurous and lost the habit of victory." It is a long and splendid pageant of the heroic age of warriors. Virgil's vision of Roman history is not mere propaganda, however, for he does not simply proclaim what Rome achieved. He remains aware of the enormous suffering and loss that attends its rise to power—not only for the Romans but their enemies as well. Of the heroes who file before him, Aeneas is told, "if ever they reach the world above, what warfare, what battles and what carnage will they create between them." Indeed, Aeneas observes Rome's history to come as a long Pyrrhic victory of the human spirit. Virgil's hero is a truly human warrior. His *humanitas* is revealed in his understanding of war itself as a terrible necessity and a means to its negation, peace. And it is illuminated by a very strong sense of its instrumental and existential nature.

As a warrior, he is "pious Aeneas" because through his *pietas,* he is a servant of the state and a (reluctant) instrument of Rome's destiny. He is also a man, however, who through war finds new standards of humanity in himself, as well as greater self-knowledge (in Socratic terms). The desire for battle glory or revenge or hatred of his enemies is conspicuously absent from his conduct. He fights without the violence that makes war an end in itself; he fights without the *furor* (or fury) of his enemies that make most of them indifferent to any rational purpose; in the Latins whom he kills to establish Rome, he can even see his future fellow citizens.[20] Aeneas was to remain the ideal *humanistic* warrior type in the Western literary canon for the next two millennia.

For war, hideous or not, was the lot not only of Rome but all other Western societies. War is what they did best. Traditionally, kings were judged worthy of the title "great" only if they distinguished themselves in battle. The high points in a people's life were denoted by its victories. The decline of societies was measured almost entirely in terms of defeat in the field.

Later the nation-state owed everything to war. Violence created it: it was the Big Bang in which nationalism was conceived. War provided its foundation myths and semimythical heroes: Dusan, Arthur, and Alexander Nevsky. All this required a kind of "eternal recurrence," because wars had to be continually fought to sustain the nation and its beliefs. In the course of the twentieth century, war became more of an existential experience than perhaps ever before because it was judged by some to be the ultimate test of a community's will to survive, as well as the supreme expression of its vitality. Both instrumentally and existentially (both as an act of state and a life-affirming activity), war was probably experienced more intensely by European societies than at any time since the beginning of history, the beginning of the "human" era.

Our age, by contrast, is the first in history in which war is not considered the most revealing activity of human nature. If anything, it is considered untypical or unrepresentative of the human experience. We no longer find it fascinating, in part because the nature of war seems to have changed. It seems to have become entirely instrumental, a purely technological phenomenon with no attendant comment on social value and little if any existential appeal.

We now stand on the cusp of *posthuman* history, an entirely new era in which the possibilities of our unfinished humanity still remain to be explored. Karl Jaspers glimpsed this age too. For we find in a later work of his the idea of another Axial Period, another spiritually and materially incisive event equal in historical significance: the age of science and technology. Like the first Axial Period, it spans centuries. It was foreshadowed in the seventeenth-century scientific revolution in Europe; at the end of the eighteenth century, it entered into a period of broad growth; and in the closing decades of the twentieth century it advanced at a headlong pace.[21]

The scientific axis has extended even further in ways that perhaps even Jaspers himself, were he living today, would not have been able to grasp or comprehend. For we are about to enter a radically different age to which some have given the term *posthuman*. As a term, it is often used to mean "after humanism" and "to refer to the fact that our own view of what constitutes a human being is now undergoing a profound transformation.

We no longer think about what it is to be human in the same way we used to . . . [because of] the general convergence of organisms and technology."[22] We need to imagine the nature of war in a posthuman era, a world in which human beings will inhabit the same world as machines and in which the two will evolve together coequally and symbiotically.

It is a bold claim, but one, I believe, that is warranted. With it comes new thinking about war and its place in our lives. With it comes a new ontology of soldiering in which there is no role for the warrior. It is unlikely that in the West war itself will ever again have existential appeal or a life-affirming ethos. In the future, our combatants will be technicians divorced emotionally and psychologically from the battlefield. Wars will continue to be fought, but they will be fought without warriors. They will offer no scope, in Nietzsche's words, for soldiers to "overcome" themselves through experience of battle.

TRANSHUMAN WARFARE

> TRANSHUMAN: *We are transhuman to the extent that we seek to become*
> *posthuman and take action to prepare for a posthuman future.*
> —Tiziana Terranova, "Posthuman Unbound"

In arguing that the Western way of warfare has reached an impasse, many critics are arguing that it is no longer a humanistic experience. Soldiers and pilots have little sense of their own *agency*. When Homer sang the praise of the weapons made by the god Hephaistos for Achilles, nothing was more remote from his mind than to attribute Achilles' success on the battlefield to technological superiority.[23] Today there is a tendency to see technology not as an extension of the warrior but a substitute. Technology has become "the underlying dynamic of contemporary war" as its goal becomes not to understand but improve it.[24] No longer are human beings the measure of war; instead, machines are threatening to make soldiers redundant, emeritus, and retired before their time. It has been happening for years. As computers have continued to provide a faster, more comprehensive array of data, human operations have become more subordinate to machines than ever; as technology evolves, so have human actions.

Other writers challenge the idea that war can have a *subjective* reality any longer. Their world is one of technologically produced realities in the form of computer games and artificial awareness modules, a world in which reality is mediated largely through technology. In their dystopian visions, history (or the real) vanishes into the hyperreal (the simulation of reality). They offer us a world in which we leave the reality of history and choose that of simulation instead.

"We were involved in the most thoroughly mediated war in history," an author in *Marxism Today* complained about the Gulf War. The battlefield today is electronic. Wars are waged as ever over real territories and real spheres of influence. But conflicts between major players are now also conducted in a virtual space "with rival hypothetical scenarios 'realized' as computer simulations fight it out over the data supplied by satellites. . . . Hygienically edited highlights of the actions get replayed nightly on the news through ghostly green videos shot through the night sight viewfinders of airborne artillery. In the screen's space anything can happen but little can be verified or understood."[25]

Finally, it is claimed that war is no longer an *intersubjective* experience either. Was this not true of the Gulf War, which was played out on the television screens night after night as it was happening? The international media saturation coverage of the conflict was remarkable. It has been estimated that on average 600 million people throughout the world watched the nightly TV news reports as the war unfolded. The philosopher Jurgen Habermas later claimed that television had transformed the conflict into a video game that could be recorded by the viewers as it developed and later "replayed" time and again. The war was distinguished by "the maddeningly irresistible playback of an electronic programme."[26]

The resemblance between the computerized war games played by the public as entertainment and the computerized film of the missile attacks prompted some viewers to complain of the grainy quality and poor graphics of many of the images that appeared on their screens. Here was no community of fate with the enemy. Instead, the public was distanced emotionally and psychologically from what was happening on the ground.

In sum, we are warned of the disintegration of the warrior's personality as human agency is replaced by machines and subjectivity is mediated by them. Some warn that human personality is about to be replaced by "technological fundamentalism," that warriors are about to be displaced through nanotechnology and bioengineering into their own weapons systems. Does the decentering of the human mean the end of the humanistic view of war? Let me attempt to answer that question in terms of the threefold division of humanism that I have employed in this book.

Agency

The future of war will be irrevocably linked to machines that think for us. Already in civilian life, more and more people are thinking in computer terms. Human beings, we should remember, have been "interfacing" with machines for some time. We are already undergoing something of an ontological shift in the way we look at the world. Computer-mediated communication is already changing the world we know, just as biotechnology is changing our bodies. Both are part of a cybercultural discourse in which we talk of "programming" our careers and "interfacing" with life.

As computers have continued to provide a faster, more comprehensive array of data, human operations have become more subordinate to machines than ever. In the future, more and more information will almost certainly be filtered through computers, increasing both an operator's confidence in his or her grasp of a situation (which may, of course, be entirely misplaced) and the amount of information computers may elect to withhold to avoid overwhelming a team already working under tremendous stress. As war speeds up, so the operators may have to make faster and faster decisions. Eventually, we may have to rubber stamp the decisions made by computers.

Computers may transform our understanding of the nature of war in other ways as well. In the near future, war may no longer be a source of feelings, choices, or emotions. The warrior-technician may no longer experience the interplay of courage, fear, and endurance that is the mark of the individual. Digital reality requires absolute conformity. It requires the same screens and keyboards, models, coded language, and mental operation. As a result, information technology is standardizing war. It offers little scope for different cultural perceptions and very little for individuality of any kind. Creativity is surplus to requirement. Everyone has to play by the same rules. In a computer program, there is no room for allusion, context, alliteration, or human genius. All four tend to be factored out in computer programming.

That is not the only challenge posed by the computerization of war. Computers could well transform the soldier into a technician, a man or woman who identifies with the reality as seen on the screen. As war becomes more technical, it is also becoming more remote as experience, and the chief reason is the difference between "reality" as it is perceived by the human eye and its instantaneous, mediated representation in the electronic media. The computer has supplanted photographic representation as an exclusive frame of reference. It has elided the real and the simulated. Representation now extends beyond the real. It extends beyond perceptual appearances and traditional conceptual frameworks. It diminishes the importance of direct observation. Already in military planning, there is a tendency for machines to do the "seeing" for us, a development in keeping, of course, with the continuous improvement in cinematographic and videographic techniques. Feedback, slow motion, and time-lapse, as well as live and delayed broadcasts, have all played a part in devaluing the traditional monopoly of direct sensory perception.

This development is especially important in training before combat. In the Gulf War, 90 percent of all air units were trained on simulation systems beforehand. In simulated battles and flight patterns, the computer rather than the pilot tends to analyze the battle environment and interpret the meaning of events. The replacement of reality with high-tech simulations is an important theme in James Blinn's novel, *The Aardvark Is Ready for War,* the *Catch-22* of the Gulf War, where everything is simulation, from simulated missions flown by the pilots against computer-generated simulation targets to the simulated battles fought in simulated battle environments.[27]

Simulation has a way of shielding the senses from a reality that is less than comfortable, and the reality of war and the real fear of death are the most undesirable realities. That is why, throughout Blinn's novel, its hero shields his senses from the war by videotaping as much as he can around him. What matters is not performing well in combat so much as looking good in the combat simulations of cyberspace.

Clausewitz would not have understood this world. For him, physics was important, but cyberspace is not bound by the laws of physics. The new digital space is "beyond" the space that physics describes. The cyber-realm is not made up of physical particles but "bits" and "bytes." Cyberspace is not ontologically rooted in those physical phenomena that defined the Newtonian universe. It was those physical constraints that Clausewitz argued introduced restraint into war in the guise of "friction." For our real self has a body that dies. Our real self feels pain. The social bonds we forge in the real world and on which we depend are very different from those of the virtual world. A cyberself that dies in cyberspace is no big deal, and even a world obliterated when a host computer crashes is transient. Both person and world can be rebooted. The difference between the real and virtual world is simple but profound: the social bonds forged in cyberspace, though important, are not vital.

There are other problems posed by the use of cyberspace in war. Virtual reality (VR) claims to offer us a sense of "being there" by giving the eye what it would have received if it were there. We are told that it can make the artificial as realistic or even more realistic than the real. Flight simulation, which is the most sophisticated and longest-standing application of the technology, is indeed more realistic than the experience of flying a real plane. Pilots can learn more on a simulator than they would in the air, for the former permits them to experience all sorts of uncommon situations that in the real world they might never encounter, let alone survive. But, of course, although VR can enhance the experience of flying a plane, it cannot reproduce the "feeling" of flying into a barrage of antiaircraft fire. It cannot reproduce the battlefield experience: the knowledge that in the real world, weapons kill. One of the striking aspects of the Allied bombing of Baghdad in December 1998 was the number of pilots who complained after the mission that they had experienced fear.[28] Fear is the one element of a bombing mission that cannot be simulated.

All this should remind us that the real world builds in constraints on our actions. The cyberworld does not. Because our lifespan is limited, we demarcate our lives into places that provide us with a sense of rootedness: where we were born, where we live, and where we are likely to die. It provides us (to use a Clausewitzian term) with a "center of gravity." We also have memories and a history. We encode our memories in our experience. We cannot eradicate them without destroying our identity (one of the terrors of amnesia). Finally, we are born fragile beings who suffer pain. We know we will die, which is why we seek to avoid suffering and danger.

In the VR world, none of these inhibiting factors apply. Virtual reality offers no rite of passage. It produces no experiences that will mark us for life. Instead, it offers us total safety. Because we are not in danger, we feel little if any anxiety. As users, we are not at risk. We can go beyond the limits because there are no consequences, physical or emotional, to our actions. Virtual reality is dangerous for that reason: it challenges our assumptions concerning authentic reality. When a mission is accomplished, one switches off the screen at the click of a button or mouse. One day we may not know what to do when the reality on the screen fails to conform to the reality we experience firsthand.

The soldiers who took part in the 1993 raid on Mogadishu discovered this problem. Late in the afternoon on October 3, 140 elite U.S. soldiers abseiled from helicopters into a teeming market neighborhood in the heart of the city. Their mission was to abduct two lieutenants of a Somali warlord and was supposed to take them an hour. Instead, they found themselves pinned down in a long and terrible night in a hostile city, fighting for their lives against thousands of heavily armed Somalis. Two of their high-tech helicopters were shot down. When the unit was rescued the following day, eighteen U.S. soldiers were dead and more than seventy badly injured.

When they were later interviewed, nearly all the survivors commented upon the fact that they had felt they were involved in a movie (the experience of today's visual soldiers who are trained on screens and spend their childhood playing computer games). They had to keep convincing themselves that the blood and death all around them were real. They all described feeling out of place, as if they did not belong there, and experienced feelings of disbelief, anger, and ill-defined betrayal. "This cannot be real" was the common complaint.[29] Is this likely to be one of the consequences of training soldiers in "virtual" reality? Will it make war increasingly "unreal" even for the soldier?

Subjectivity

How far can we take the symbiotic relationship between human beings and machines? Our military scientists are already working on schemes to integrate pilots into a computerized aircraft that is capable of reading their brain waves and following their eye movements and, on the basis of both, determining whether they are fit to fly a plane or not. "Tactical planning management" systems are being designed that will allow a computer to communicate with a pilot and determine whether to fly a plane itself. The intention is to create a "virtual computer space" that the computer and pilot will inhabit together. Microchips are being developed that, when implanted in a pilot's brain, can be activated through neural electrical stimulation. In turn, they will result in quicker reaction times, better communication, and possibly improved control and greater reliability. But will they do so at the cost of transforming pilots into the machines they are flying?[30]

The problem with "technologically enabled identities" disengaged from ethnicity, gender, and all the other identities that have hitherto defined our humanity is that they threaten to do away with the human subject. That would be problematic because if the subject is not present to itself, there is even less reason to believe the world is present to it. Will our soldiers and pilots find themselves living in a sanitized environment cut off from anything that is distressing? We have not yet reached that threshold, but we are doing what we can to make war less stressful for ourselves. The word is an important one. It was the stress of modern life that produced modern heroes. For Baudelaire, who coined the word *modernity,* the ordinary person became a hero for the first time because modernity was so difficult to endure: people had to experience the stress of living in new cities; to endure the stress of the assembly line; and, of course, as conscripts, to experience the stress of war on the industrialized battlefields of Europe.

We must go beyond the standard interpretation of stress linked with specific events, such as the death of a relation or a crisis in a person's

career. We are encouraged to think this way because contemporary
research into stress is almost entirely focused on psychological symptoms
and causes and almost entirely ignores its social origins. Unlike today's
psychotherapists, however, early sociologists like Georg Simmel and
Emile Durkheim were much more interested in stress that was related to
the way people responded to the society around them.

Today we live in an era in which stress is being deconstructed. That
word too is particularly apt. Since first appearing in English in 1973, it has
become ubiquitous. And unlike many of the words in common use, such
as *downloading* and *interface,* the origins of *deconstructed* do not lie in
the world of computers. It originates instead in one of the most abstruse
French philosophical theories. In literary criticism, it describes the task of
reading a text closely and analyzing the author's hidden voice. What is not
there is as important as what is. In the case of war, the hidden subtext
seems to be the military's wish to factor out anxiety.

If stress can be eliminated or reduced, the human subjectivity of the
warrior will be transformed. We are already being encouraged to believe
that we should go beyond our own humanity, as if humanity grounded on
our physical bodies is a limitation to our development. A recent popular
account of postbiological man, for example, treats the human condition as
an affliction. Human beings, we are told, are beings with "cheap bodies"
subject to disease and disability, with "erratic emotions" and "feeble mentalities." They are "battlegrounds of warring impulses, drives and emotions" with only a limited capacity for intelligence.[31] Those who dismiss
the human body as a "battleground" of conflicting emotions will wish to
reengineer it on the field of battle. Freeing the warrior from some of the
constraints of the body might lead to faster impulses and the elimination
of battle fatigue and posttraumatic stress. That is the promise of pharma-
cology.

In civilian life, the rise of psychiatric pharmacotherapy is one answer
to the problem of treating so-called minor affective disorders such as anxiety, compared with the major ones such as clinical depression and schiz-
ophrenia. What we are witnessing is the chemical engineering of person-
alities and an increasing reliance on mood-altering medication. Can this
also be applied to war?

It is worth pointing out, perhaps, that the connection between chemical persuasion and war is not new. When he came to look back on his
novel *Brave New World* in the late 1950s, Aldous Huxley was even more
persuaded that the future was indeed happening as he had predicted twenty years earlier. Religion, Marx declared, is the opium of the people. In
Huxley's dystopian vision of the future, the situation is reversed: opium,

or in this case "soma," is the people's religion. Like religion, it has the power to console and compensate for anxiety. Writing over twenty years later, Huxley cited an eminent biochemist who had playfully suggested that the U.S. government should make a free gift to the Soviet people of 50 billion doses of meprobamate, at the time a popular tranquilizer. His suggestion, though made in jest, had a serious point to it. In a contest between two populations, one of which was being constantly stimulated by threats and promises and constantly directed by propaganda, while the other was no less constantly being distracted by television, which of the opponents was more likely to come out on top?[32]

Significantly, the first major attempt to reduce anxiety in war followed a few years later. Soldiers in the past had often drunk themselves into oblivion before a battle, and Vietnam was no exception. Alcoholism, not drug addiction, was originally the main problem of indiscipline in the ranks. But Vietnam was the first war in which army doctors prescribed tranquilizers on the combat front. In the same way, many soldiers self-prescribed marijuana, opium, and heroin to deal with the stress they were facing. Vietnam, David Grossman wrote, should be regarded as history's first "pharmacological war."[33]

Unfortunately, drugs cause symptoms to remit, but they do not make pathologies disappear. In Vietnam, the use of drugs combined with the shortness of the tour of duty (twelve months) merely delayed the reaction to combat stress. The (ab)use of drugs in Vietnam merely served to delay the soldiers' inevitable confrontation with pain, suffering, guilt, and grief. That is why on their return home, the incidence of trauma was so extensive, with 20,000 suicides and 40,000 registered drug addicts among the veterans in New York City alone. Vietnam was unique for that reason—it was the first war in history in which an army disintegrated off the battlefield, not on it.

The drugs of the future, of course, will be far more reliable than the antidepressants issued in the 1970s or ministered to pilots in the Gulf War. Once we have a detailed map of the brain's components (something that we are quickly developing), we will be able to manipulate our consciousness directly with targeted drugs. It may be possible to select moods at will. The potential for altering moods is probably greater for neuroscience than it is for genetics because genetic engineering has proved very difficult in practice, whereas brain manipulation is turning out to be surprisingly easy. And it is much easier than relying on counseling after the event to correct pathological symptoms.

But the problem with prescribing mood-altering drugs is that we have not even begun to ask the major questions. Is the key to human happiness really selective serotonin re-uptake inhibition? Should our moods be controlled medically, and what is the risk of pathologizing an ever-wider range of our actions? Is anxiety a disease, an illness, a syndrome, or a symptom? If anxiety is the result of a concrete event, such as someone shooting at us, should we try to eliminate or control it with drugs? Should we expect psychiatry to cure the human condition? How wise is it to block all mental anguish, including anxiety? Surely it is so common that it must have evolved for a reason. On the one hand, it is admirable that society should be trying to ensure that in a decade or two, anxiety, depression, and other affective neuroses will be optional, an experience like physical pain that we may choose to avoid. On the other hand, there is a danger in trying to eliminate low mood states without any clear idea of what unrecognized purpose they might serve. A parallel with physical pain points out the danger. We know that pain warns us when something is wrong. Abolish the capacity to feel it, and we lose essential information vital to our physical and mental well-being. Is the same true of anxiety, even on the field of battle?

Such concerns, if they are addressed at all, do not seem to be holding back the military. The U.S. Army has at least three drugs under development with which it hopes to lower the level of anxiety of its own troops or to make them less risk-averse. In the future, the capacity to act heroically, take risks, and lead from the front may become more of a function of chemical factors than a soldier's cultural, religious, or intellectual heritage. Fear of death may remain in the conscious mind, but there may be no psychological support to make it real. Were that to happen, it would alter profoundly the military ethos, for if we reduce fear, we also reduce the support that comes from affirmations of solidarity and friendship, which traditionally have made war life affirming as well as deadly.

Intersubjectivity

Is war also changing in the area of human intersubjectivity? At the heart of war is the relationship between soldiers and their adversaries. How soldiers treat their enemies is the basis of the ethics of war. In discussing this question, I am especially influenced by the thoughts of Hans Jonas, a German Jew and pupil of Martin Heidegger and one of the most prominent thinkers of his generation. Shaped by his exile from Nazi Germany and the murder of his mother in Auschwitz, his own deeply personal work was the attempt of a Jewish student to make sense of twentieth-century history. Indeed, his work has a unifying theme. Our own mortality is at the root of our moral responsibility to safeguard humanity's future.

Ethics, he tells us, requires us to take responsibility for our own actions. It is all the more important when through the use of technology human power to do harm (as well as good) is increasing all the time. We must accept that we have a responsibility to others (we share the planet). Since first splitting the atom, we have also had a responsibility for those not yet born. It was for that reason that Jonas insisted that ethics is grounded in ontology. It can be traced not only to the being of man but is at the base of *being* in general. Our first duty is ontological: to recognize that human responsibility matters because the idea of humanity matters. Since in human beings the principle of purposefulness has reached its highest peak through the freedom to set ends and the power to achieve them, in the name of that principle, we must become the first object of our own obligation.

Until his death in 1993, Jonas continued to insist that we cannot surrender that responsibility to technology without surrendering our humanity, which, in turn, is derived from history and metaphysics. History is the record of our attempts to problematize the human condition. It tells us what is possible and what is not. It tells us that human nature cannot be perfected, though human behavior can be improved. Morality tells us the ground of our humanity: the life we ought to lead and the duties we owe each other.

Of the many challenges that Jonas identified, he thought three to be more important than the rest. The first is the environment: Do we have a right to destroy the habitat in which we live? The second is biotechnology: Do we have the right to reengineer ourselves, and what are the consequences? The third is war, and of the three it is the oldest, for it can be dated back to 1945: Do we have the right to threaten the existence of humanity itself? Like the other questions, it requires a moral answer, for nothing in biology forbids the suicide of a species in an atomic war. It is our beliefs—and our beliefs alone—that enjoin us that life is to be lived.

We cannot abdicate that responsibility, Jonas insists, to technology, which refers back neither to history nor to morality. It is not responsible for us. It is morally blind. No machine or computer can help us fulfill our responsibilities; we alone are responsible for ourselves. We cannot surrender agency without turning our back on the moral life. That is why ethics, including the ethics of war, enjoins us to act in a way that preserves the capacity for responsibility itself. If we transfer decisionmaking to computers or targeting to self-programming machines—if we seek to distance ourselves from the consequences of our own actions by mediating reality through technology—will we impoverish ourselves existentially? Will we diminish ourselves as human beings?[34]

Is this the other historic crossroads to which the protagonists of future war have taken us? Are we in danger of dehumanizing modernity by surrendering responsibility for our actions? Automation is threatening to do this for work, and technology is threatening to do the same with war. As Jonas reminds us, the technological challenge is without precedent. Our efforts so far in war have posed external threats to our existence, especially the ultimate threat of an atomic war. Now we pose an *existential* threat to ourselves, as well as the intersubjective experience that has always made war an ethical activity. For nonhuman nature, Jonas argued, is indifferent to itself and also to the human beings who have designed it. Though the latter may be subjects who posit ends and act in the light of purposes, nonliving organisms are mere objects: matter in motion. Eventually, human beings may become objects of their own mechanical creations.

In this light, the future is frightening indeed, for sometime quite soon we may allow the machines of war to make their own decisions. The fear of brilliant bombs that retarget themselves without human interaction appears in John Carpenter's science fiction film *Dark Star* (1974), in which the intelligent bombs of the spaceship have to be argued out of detonating themselves prematurely. In real life, will weapons systems with sufficient artificial intelligence be able to "learn" in combat situations, conceptualize problems, and work out the answers so that human tactical and strategic thinking can begin to be phased out?

What the above analysis shows, I believe, is the attempt by humanity—and Western humanity at that—to grapple with a new kind of humanism mediated through machines. This is the world of posthumanism, in which human beings inhabit the same world as machines, the two evolve coequally, and the relationship between them is increasingly symbiotic. It seems clear that we have not even begun to grasp the significance of either development or that we wish to. We are not at ease with our new man-machine selves; we cling to the old humanism. Can we do so for much longer?

POSTHUMAN WARFARE

Science fiction: the body's dream of being a machine.
—J. G. Ballard, *A User's Guide to the Millennium*

One of Nietzsche's most profound observations was that, of all animals, humanity's nature is not fixed. It constantly changes. It is a mark of being human to be able to *transcend* being human, to be open to untold nonhuman possibilities. The fundamental question, which is an ethical question, is how are we humans to think beyond our humanity? For technology is reinventing humanity as much or almost as quickly as we are inventing new technology. We are different because of the machines we invent and our relationship with them. The process is symbiotic. Human beings do not adapt genetically to their environment as other animals do. Human evolution is oriented toward placing outside ourselves what in the rest of the animal world is achieved inside by species adaptation. From the invention of primitive tools to the atom, we have used machines to exteriorize and understand ourselves, and we are doing so more than ever.[35]

We share our life with machines; we depend on them more and more for the decisions we make. Writers are beginning to call it the posthuman condition.

> Beyond the [present,] genetic engineering and nano-technology . . . offer us a possibility of literally being able to change our bodies into new and different forms . . . postbiological humanity can be achieved within the next 50 years.
>   Think about it. The entire thrust of modern technology has been to move us away from solid objects and into information space. Man the farmer and Man the industrial worker are quickly being replaced by Man the knowledge worker. . . . We are less and less creatures of flesh, blood and bone pushing boulders uphill; we are more and more creatures of mind-zapping bits and bytes moving around at the speed of light.[36]

More mainstream writers are no less enthusiastic about the future; many are of the opinion that we will evolve substantially; that we will come to understand our humanity very differently from the way we do today. As science discovers more about the genetic structure of the body, so it forces us to perceive ourselves and our bodies in a new light. Biochemical researchers now define human life in terms of the genetic structure of a germ cell. Others using the metaphors of technology and computer science encourage us to see ourselves as manufactured parts that can be reengineered and reprogrammed at will. Biotechnology, Francis Fukuyama writes, will allow us to accomplish what social engineers of the past failed to do. "At that point we will have definitively finished human history because we will have abolished human beings as such. And then a new post-human history will begin."[37]

Hyperbole apart, there does seem to be a significant transformation taking place in the way humans interact with machines and technology. Not all the claims of the posthuman condition are exaggerated or present only fit themes for science fiction. What is happening is not a replacement of human beings, of course, but a taking further of humanity. As such, it is quite in tune with the Western way of warfare because it still prompts us to ask what it is to be human.

Nietzsche remains the favorite philosopher of our age. One reason for the renewed interest in his work is that he tells us that evolution through machines is not an overcoming of the human condition but an extension of it. We should recognize that machines are part of our humanity, not an alternative to it. And what we should be trying to "overcome" is not our humanity but our baser natures. Nietzsche would have considered any attempt to locate the "other" human outside of the human condition to be fatally misguided, as misguided, in fact, as the totalitarian societies in the twentieth century who thought they could create a perfectly harmonious society—or machine—by reducing the citizen to a cog in a wheel.

In terms of the future of war, the posthuman condition will have profoundly serious consequences for the way we see ourselves, our enemies, and war in general. Even more, it spells the end of the warrior as Hegel's social type. One of the first people to anticipate this change was the social philosopher Theodor Adorno toward the end of World War II. Adorno had fled Germany together with several thousand other intellectuals in the 1930s. In 1944, he was fortunate to find himself in the United States, safely beyond the range of German airpower. England was not so fortunate, however. It came under attack from Hitler's secret weapons, his V1 missiles, in the closing stages of the war.

Adorno may have left Germany, but he brought with him his German philosophical heritage. When he read of the missile attacks, he was immediately reminded of Hegel's theory of history:

> Had Hegel's philosophy of history embraced this age, Hitler's robot bombs [the first cruise missiles] would have found their place . . . as one of the selected empirical facts by which the state of the World Spirit manifests itself directly in symbols.
>   . . . I have seen the World Spirit not on horseback but on wings and without a head and that refutes, at the same stroke, Hegel's philosophy of history.[38]

Hegel had made fashionable a new theory of history: that every period has its own particular character, or spirit, and that changes of consciousness could be identified as they occurred. Hegel happened to be living in the town of Jena when Napoleon passed through in 1806 before defeating the Prussian army in a decisive battle the following day. In a letter to a friend he wrote, "This morning I saw the Emperor Napoleon, that World Spirit riding through the town to a parade. . . . It is a marvellous feeling to see such a personality dominating the entire world from horseback."[39]

Although Napoleon's victories were world-shattering events, Hegel believed the real instruments of change to be not the armies but the changing spirit of the age. It was the real motivating force. Armies were merely a means to an end. The end was human freedom, the ability of human beings to make their own history by pursuing the ideas that inspired them to act. In that sense, ideas made the battles possible.

As technology became more sophisticated, however, Adorno predicted that the civilian would find it increasingly difficult to experience war as a social phenomenon. In Hegel's philosophy, modern war had been the expression of a national spirit. But modern technology—in this case Hitler's V1—had begun to erode the direct relationship between the citizen and war in a way that was making it impossible for the citizen to experience war as it had traditionally been understood, as a world historical act, as an event in world history. War no longer told a story of how progress was made, tyranny defeated, and freedom dearly bought. To put it crudely, technology had begun to supersede ideas.

Adorno went on to add that the disproportion between bodily strength and the energy of machines had begun to affect "the hidden cells of experience." With cameramen at the front, the war had become mediated through the camera lens and further removed from experience; it had created "a vacuum between men and their fate in which their real fate lies." The cinema newsreels of the invasion of Guam and the Marianas gave the impression "not of battles but of civil engineering and blasting operations undertaken with immeasurably intensified vehemence." War was becoming something quite different from anything that had been experienced before.

Even English writers, not given to such metaphysical speculations, recognized that something had changed. In an essay entitled "The Decline of the English Murder" (1946), George Orwell attributed a tawdry and sensational "thrill kill" to the fact that the two perpetrators—an American G. I. and an English ex-waitress who had killed a complete stranger merely for the sake of it—were committed to trial "to the tune of the V1 and convicted to the sound of the V2."[40] He was speaking, of course, symbolically. He saw the crime as the presage of a future in which murder would lack meaning except as an entertainment; those who did the bombing were totally removed from the fate of those they bombed, which had not been the case earlier on in the war. The same point was made more forcefully twenty years later by Evelyn Waugh, who saw the V2 missiles in a completely different light from the bombers of the Blitz. The great historical drama that had been played out over the skies of London in 1940 had given way to an experience devoid of meaning to the Londoners on the ground. The Londoners still had to endure the barrage, but they no longer felt linked with their attackers, as they had to the air crew of the Messerschmitt bombers, in a community of fate.[41]

On the other side, the Allied bombing after 1943 was so extensive that it was difficult for the British to imagine what they were achieving in their own nighttime raids. One that was on a much greater scale than the Blitz destroyed the city of Darmstadt in fifty-one minutes on September 11–12, 1944. By then, bombing had become a "routine." The pilots who flew the heavy bombers, according to one writer, were businessmen. They did a job. They called themselves "aerial taxi drivers" or "freight engineers." They returned from their missions eight hours later "bored in a way no one was ever bored before."[42]

Even on the ground, war was changing, or was beginning to, as it became more mechanized and "mechanical." The poet Keith Douglas, who served as a tank commander in North Africa before being posted to Burma, recorded how tank battles resembled wars in space or even at times a silent movie, "quite unrelated to real life." So deafening was the noise inside and outside the tanks that the crews lost all sense of direction. The battles began with the enemy tanks appearing as blotches on the landscape, shimmering in the desert heat. The actual engagements were remote and impersonal, and the crews only knew whether their side had prevailed after the outcome had already been decided. In the words he scribbled across the page facing the opening of his manuscript (the text was published posthumously in 1946), Douglas added a few words that were a kind of personal epigraph:

> I look back to a period spent on the moon
> Almost to a short life in a new dimension.[43]

That was Adorno's main contention. The experience of any social phenomenon requires not only a sense of purpose (why the war is being fought; what its ends are) but also a sense of community with the enemy (which requires that the community share a common language). In the case of a "language of war," there must be enough agreement about the possibilities and rules, about what matters and how much, and about what will and will not do—about what it is all for—for serious argument to begin and for war to remain a humanistic discourse.

Argument makes war instrumental, and humanism makes it existential. Together they make war a humanistic experience. It was war's "humanity" that Adorno feared would be subverted by modern technology. If that was true of Hitler's "secret weapons" in World War II, it was even more true of nuclear weapons. And to appreciate why, we need to look no further than Stanley Kubrick's film *Dr. Strangelove*. By the 1960s, it was only as a black comedy that nuclear war could be apprehended. War could break out by accident, computer error, or, in the case of the film, the ravings of a single maverick colonel. For Kubrick, the World Spirit is manifest in Slim Pickens's Major T. J. (King) Kong, whom we see at the very end of the film riding a bomb, not a horse like Hegel's hero, prior to single-handedly setting off a global thermonuclear war.

But it is not necessary to go back to 1945 to appreciate the endgame that the Western way of warfare has reached. The crisis was evident to many writers much earlier, who were the first to glimpse the arrival of a nonhumanistic age—or a "posthumanistic" era. The posthuman soldier has been with us for some time, if only in our imagination.

Agency

We have been dreaming of the man-machine symbiosis for some time now. Take the case of the first dystopian vision of the twentieth century, Yevgeny Zamiatin's *We,* which was published in the early 1920s. The story, set in a walled city of the future, is told by D503 in a series of diary entries, fragments that begin and end abruptly and characteristically leave much unsaid. The narrative is fragmented because there is no single personality behind it. D503 is literally a man without a personality, or rather he has a schizophrenic personality, divided between his identityless identity as a "number" of the state.

Zamiatin's society is one in which the machine is all-important. As D503 proudly explains, "Our poets no longer soar in the empyrean. They have come down to earth. They stride beside us to the stern mechanical march of the music plant." "The poet of the new epoch will rethink in a new way the thoughts of mankind and re-feel its feelings," Leon Trotsky claimed in the 1920s. In Zamiatin's book, the citizens find a bizarre beauty in the regularity of mechanical repetition. Watching a gang of laborers bending and unbending "like the levels of a single huge machine," D503 is struck by the poetry of the sight. "It was the highest, most stirring beauty, harmony, music."

Fully committed to the state, D503 embraces the conception of himself as a machine. He speaks happily about his brain as a "gleaming mechanism" and boasts about the way the "table of Hours" governs the citizens' lives: "Why it transforms each one of us into a figure of steel, six-wheeled hero of a mighty epic poem. Every morning with six-wheeled precision, at the same hour and the same moment we—millions of us—get up as one. At the same hour, in million-headed unison, we start work; and in million-headed unison we end it." Zamiatin's hero, however, is not Homer's, and the "mighty epic poem" is not *The Iliad*. For at the end of the story, D503 is saved by an operation that removes his ability to imagine anything. With his imagination gone, the path to machinelike perfection is open. The ultimate machine in *We* is the city itself, a sterile world constructed out of glass, as flawless and transparent as reason. Reason has devised a nightmare world, and reason protects it.

The posthuman warrior, like the posthuman society, has also been with us for some time in our imagination. In 1898 H. G. Wells wrote one of his most famous works, *The War of the Worlds*. It tells of the invasion of Earth by a race of Martians more intelligent than the human race. Although clearly more intelligent, however, they are also more deadly because they are more calculating. Their strength comes from their machines, from the lethal use of weapons such as poison gas and the death ray, the depersonalized instruments of mass destruction.

Wells's novel is important because it is the expression of an era, one that was soon to see the introduction of poison gas on the battlefields of the western front. His novel is a telling description of a continent hell-bent on war. In a brilliant note toward the end of the book, after the Martians are unexpectedly destroyed by human bacteria against which they have no immunity, Wells goes further and suggests that at some point in the future, human beings themselves may become machines.

As one of the novel's characters, the Artillery Man, declares after looking into one of the Martians' abandoned machines: "Just imagine this: four or five of their fighting machines suddenly starting off—heat rays, right and left, and not a Martian in 'em. Not a Martian in 'em but men—men who've learned the way how." The triumph the Artillery Man envisages is sobering indeed. For he anticipates an age in which the most advanced stage of human evolution will be marked by the transformation of man, not into a more authentic human being but into a machine, or in this case a Martian.[44]

The man-machine symbiosis has been alive in the collective imagination ever since. In the early years of the twentieth century it did indeed seem that modern warfare would require soldiers to increasingly subordinate their human selves to the demands of machinery. It was not particularly surprising that so many artists who took part in World War I should have concluded that Wells's trajectory into the future would be realized long before the twentieth century came to an end. For the Futurists, the war appeared to have produced what writers such as Emilio Marinetti always dreamed of, "the metalization of the human body." For Ernst Junger, the man of steel was a soldier whose physique had been mechanized or in part displaced into his body armor. The paintings of Oskar Schlemmer show geometric people, at once fragmentary but also immutable, made whole by geometry or by "design"—people who become their own machines. The figures resemble robots frozen in their tracks, as though their mechanism has run down. They are idealized visions of human beings in a machine age and as such have something of the appearance of machines. In depicting them thus, he was implying the influence of machines on human beings need not necessarily be dehumanizing.[45]

Human beings and machines, in fact, have been "interfacing" for some time at least in art. How far can the symbiotic relationship between person and machine be taken? If we look back at the geometric figures of the Bauhaus period, we also see that they may have been a presentiment of the soldiers of the future, who will have cognitive prostheses such as sound enhancers to make their hearing more acute and zoom lenses to make their vision more precise, both small enough to be implanted. They may also be fitted with memory chips of precoded information.

One of the most productive areas of cyberpunk science fiction—particularly the work of William Gibson and Bruce Sterling—are the characters whose brain implants (silicon chips attached to the nervous system) can download new information. Science fiction has been dealing for some time with the increasing miniaturization of technology and looks forward to a greater integration between machines and organic tissue. At some point in the future, we will be able to download information into the human brain through microchips linked to computers. We can already use brain implants to move a cursor around a computer screen without using a mouse or keyboard, and over 15,000 blind people have been given chips that allow them to "see." One day, we may be capable of sending signals to and from the human body in order to operate or interact with computers. The next step will be to download information from other people through computers. There will then be no more need of radios or telephones in the field. Soldiers connected to a central computer will be able to communicate with each other without human speech. They will also know what the other knows, see what the other sees, and remember another's memory. Such an ability will raise fundamental questions about what it means to be human. The human brain guarantees a unique single individuality. Link it to other brains, both human and machine, and what becomes of the individual then?

In addition, if emotion is the stepchild of neural and cognitive science, rapid progress is being made in understanding the chemical and electrical substates of emotion. It is not impossible to imagine that soldiers will be implanted with chips that will be capable of sending controlled electrical signals to the relevant brain centers so as to enhance courage or determination and produce artificially enhanced mood states. Science will be able to feed an already advanced improvement in our understanding of new disciplines at the frontiers of biology, such as behavioral genetics, evolutionary psychology, and cognitive neuroscience. In all three fields, we are increasing our understanding of human nature and how to mold it to the purposes of society or the state.

For some, these possibilities offer the promise of a better future; for others, a nightmare vision of what is to come. One reason, Sterling suspects, that the posthuman condition appeals to many in the military is precisely the fact that it seeks to deny the human. It offers instead "a complete and utter triumph of chilling analytic cybernetic reality over chaotic, real life human desperation."[46] Colonel Frederick Timmerman, the U.S. Army's Director of the Center for Army Leadership, talked in the 1990s of future warriors "transforming and extending the soldier's physiological capabilities" and thus achieving "the superman solution."[47] Both these visions would have depressed Nietzsche, for neither offers a chance to "overcome" our humanity—only to change it. Overcoming requires great deeds, and projects, and perhaps even wars in which warriors come to "know" themselves for the first time. Becoming posthuman does not because it is driven by factors extraneous to our previous "humanity."

Subjectivity

One of the most interesting things about us as a species is our insistent search for an understanding of ourselves. It is a search strongly rooted in our intuitive sense that of all species on the planet, we are the only ones who are still evolving. Our humanity can be described but not defined. Phenomenologically, our increasingly embedded relationship with technology (hooked into VR machines and Internet relationships) does genuinely extend intentionality into the world. It does change us for good or ill. It ensures that we will not be replaced but continue to develop. We will continue to have a history and to make it ourselves.

Take, for example, our sense of time and space, both of which have altered as a result of the technology we have designed. The speed of communications and computerization have extended our control of time. As our access to the space of others through television and electronic surveillance has increased, so the public-private divide is less pronounced than ever. Our sense of self is being transformed.[48] Similarly, our humanity is enhanced, not diminished, by the new "anthropology" that looks at the cyborg (the symbiotic relationship between the human and machine) and the relationship between industrial and "post-organic" societies or "organically human and cyber-psychically digital life-forms as reconfigured through computer software systems."[49] One school focuses on ethnography (the boundary between human and machine) in the belief that the "anthros" in anthropology (the human-centered) is no longer sufficient to encompass today's social reality. Human and social reality, in fact, is as much the product of machines as ourselves; technology is increasingly becoming an agent in social production. In art, for example, computer designs and graphics now constitute another eye.

> Some theorise that what is happening is a blurring and implosion of categories at various levels, particularly those modern categories that have defined until recently the natural, the organic, the technical. . . . New discourses for biology, for instance, do not conceptualise living beings in terms of hierarchically organised organisms but according to the language of communications and systems analysis. . . . Pathology is the result of stress and communications breakdown, while the immune system is modelled as a battlefield. . . . In sum, . . . the boundaries between nature and culture, between organism and machine, are ceaselessly redrawn according to complex historical factors in which discourses of science and technology play a decisive role.[50]

The machine age raises a first-order question: What does it mean to be human? We have already broken the barrier between animal and human as we have come to recognize that humans share common behaviors and even mentalities with the animals around us. The traditional distinction between the organic and the machine has collapsed as well. Machines can now execute human actions and beat us at chess and may soon be able to outthink us in other areas too. Certainly, we are no longer alone with our thoughts.

Cyberspace too has challenged another boundary: between the physical and nonphysical. We talk of a new range of "spaces" not tied to the body. Chemists talk of "molecular space" and mathematicians of "topographical" spaces. Chaos theorists and physicists studying the galaxy talk of "phase spaces." Cyberspace offers us a chance to extend human actions into the nonphysical realm, a realm for the imagination, or as some cyberbuffs call it, a new realm for the self.[51]

Even the Internet, Sherry Turkle writes, "has become a significant social laboratory for experimenting with the construction and reconstruction of self that characterises post-modern life."[52] Her early fascination with the impact of computers on how we think about our own minds was prompted by a student who complained that a Freudian slip was nothing more than an "information processing error." It was in that moment that she realized that she was witnessing an important new phenomenon— computers were beginning to alter the way we think about ourselves. They had begun to extend our humanity.

When Turkle talks of a "decentred self" she does not ignore the ultimate reality that we are tied to our bodies physically and ontologically. But the Internet makes explicit a process that has been going on for some time. We ourselves stem from relationships such as a family or profession. The "social" is the source of our capabilities and mentalities, as I remarked at the beginning of this chapter. This is the sense of Descartes' insistence that, first and foremost, we are immaterial beings or social beings. We have no instincts, only institutions. That has been known to philosophers for centuries. The Internet merely makes it explicit as never before. In the future, we will probably relate more and more to machines, not only to the existing networks with which we commune: the kinship networks of our family, the social networks of our friends, and the professional networks of our work associates.

There may well be a down side, however, which takes us back to Zamiatin's *We*. Is his vision all that removed from a programmed society made possible by quantum advances in genetic engineering now that the genome has been finally decoded? In the future, a warrior class may be genetically determined. Soldiers may be chosen because of their genetic code. By eliminating artificial forms of inequality based on tradition and culture, we could set up a new hierarchical order based on the genetic makeup of the individual. If genes for criminality and homosexuality exist (as is claimed), why not a gene for bravery or heroism, a gene for the warrior? At the very least, we could envisage genetic screening that would permit a new warrior type, not Hegel's warriors determined by human consciousness but the warriors of the future determined by biology.

Or if soldiers are sent into battle where they may be exposed to chemical and biological agents, why not artificially make them immune by genetic reprogramming? Or, perhaps, Zamiatin's future will be realized in another manner. As war is simulated more and more, as soldiers come to live increasingly in a sanitized, antiseptic virtual world, so they may escape into the standardizing that simulation delivers. So too we may see the standardized behavior of an entire military generation or the production of unimaginative soldiers incapable of improvising or learning from direct experience in the field. If the two version are combined—if genetic screening is operational and virtual war becomes more predominant—we could end up with standardized soldiers drawn from a smaller gene pool. What then happens to human subjectivity?

Intersubjectivity

If there is an intersubjective dimension of posthuman warfare, it is likely to be grounded less in our relationship with other human beings than our relationship with machines. In war, cruise missiles give the illusion that the age of intelligent machines has arrived already. Indeed for Paul Virilio, it is the first "seeing" machine. It sees for itself and as only a machine can. It is true it has a remote camera that takes the operator through to the point of impact. But the vision machine integrated in the missile is different. It is equipped with detection radar and built-in mapping systems. The radar constantly surveys the ground to check the coordinates. It films the target and chooses a window in a building through which to go. The cruise missile, in other words, is endowed with a gaze, even though it is an automatic one. What happens when the cruise missile can reprogram itself? What happens when it begins seeing for itself?[53]

In his novel *Kaleidoscope Century* (1995), John Barnes imagined the development of "brilliant" weapons even before the term had been coined—missiles that went after the most important thing on the battlefield sometimes independently of their programmers: smart bombs that could think for themselves and make decisions in a split-second.[54] Artificial intelligence may indeed change the contours of warfare on the ground. How this may happen has been outlined by Keith Laumer, another science fiction writer who has produced a fictional evolution of unmanned tanks, which is probably as convincing as that any scientist could predict. His "Bolo" series of vehicles begins development in General Motors' division in 1989. It has the power to perform a number of operations in unmanned mode through preprogrammed instructions. The follow-on model appears in 1995 and needs only one crew member to operate its sophisticated onboard fire control system. The Mark XV version no longer requires a crew at all. The first self-aware Bolo Mark XX model is finally introduced after much resistance from high-level military officials who fear it will wreak havoc on its makers. By the time of the Mark XXX version, human tactical and strategic thinking no longer plays a part in combat. The machines have begun to make their own decisions.[55]

Laumer was extremely conservative in his thinking; his story ends in the twenty-fifth century. The fact is that self-aware machines will probably appear before the end of the twenty-first century. What their advocates hold out is the vision of weapons systems with sufficient artificial intelligence to "learn" in combat situations, to conceptualize problems and work out the answers so that human tactical and strategic thinking will begin to be shared with noncarbon forms of life.

The implications of this development would be profound indeed, especially if intelligent machines or complex systems grow increasingly like us; if they are able to reproduce themselves, repair, and adapt to new environments; and if they are endowed with the characteristics of organic life. Will they be able to think for themselves and communicate with other synthetic beings? Will they be able to think out solutions to problems and even think ahead? Will they give the appearance of "understanding," whether they have such an ability or not? As Manuel de Landa writes: "In adversarial situations being forced to treat a machine as an intentional system may be considered as a good criterion for mechanical intelligence. In the case of predatory machines not only would we have to fight them on the intentional plane but we may also assume that they would treat us, their prey, as predictable assemblages of beliefs and desires. It would be, then, a clash of 'minds' or of 'irrational wills.'"[56] Were this scenario to occur, it would constitute a new kind of intersubjectivity. We might find ourselves battling synthetic systems as intelligent or even more intelligent than ourselves. We could program them with our DNA so that they would be part human, part machine. We could even endow them with an understanding so that we would be forced to think of them as sentient beings.

CONCLUSION

The battlefield or battle space I have been describing is one that we can expect to see emerge sometime by midcentury. What I have offered the reader is not a prediction of the future, but an account of how the Western way of warfare has evolved to the point at which it has taken us to the threshold of the posthuman age. We should be much more interested, in fact, not in anticipating developments to come so much as understanding the present crisis in military thinking, which is what the transhuman moment captures—the present could last a long time yet. All we know for certain is that in the laboratories of the United States, scientists are working away to bring us posthuman warfare.

We are still too near to new developments such as cyborgism, nanotechnology, and genetic engineering to grasp the full potential of this transformation. Accordingly, I have confined myself largely to the new cybernetic world of war, which has already diminished the importance of the warrior still further. And it is fitting that this word, coined by Norbert Wiener in the 1950s, should derive from the Greek word for steersman (a man who uses his knowledge of science, the direction of the winds and currents of the sea, to steer his boat more effectively). For there is nothing in cybernetics that precludes us from understanding more about ourselves. As Paul Edwards contends, cybernetic science has become a primary source of meaning for us, for it uses formal and mechanical modeling practices that in turn provide some of the categories and techniques by which we have come to understand our own humanity.[57]

But cybernetic warfare has little, if anything, to tell us about the warrior as a human type. Instead, we may conclude that the posthuman age will see the final close of a unique chapter in war. It will transform the nature of war. We will no longer be able to claim (like Nietzsche) that the warrior's ability to find war life affirming is what makes us "interesting as a species"; nor will we be able to follow Hegel and argue that he who has not risked his life "may well be recognized as a person but has not attained the truth of this recognition as an independent self consciousness."[58]

It is to be hoped that in the virtual communities and information orders that are growing up, society may find forms of human intercourse that make it less prone to warfare. It is also to be hoped that the posthuman era will demand that we invent new concepts of what it means to be human, that we think in radically new ways by rethinking what we are and what befalls us. But the West will still fight wars. All we can predict, probably for certain, is that when it comes to the way we practice war, we will have returned full circle to the prehuman era. Once again, war will be fought in the absence of warriors.

Notes

CHAPTER 1

1. Ruth Benedict, *The Chrysanthemum and the Sword* (Boston: Houghton Mifflin, 1989). For the samurai poems, see Marguerite Yourcenar, *That Mighty Sculptor, Time* (New York: Farrar, Straus and Giroux, 1992), pp. 73–75.
2. Joseph Conrad, *The Secret Agent* (Oxford: Oxford University Press, 1983), p. 34.
3. David Gentilcore, "The Fear of Disease and the Disease of Fear," in William G. Naphy and Penny Roberts, eds., *Fear in Early Modern Society* (Manchester: Manchester University Press, 1997), p. 190.
4. *The Washington Post,* August 27, 1998.
5. Anton Blok, "The Meaning of 'Senseless' Violence," in Anton Blok, ed., *Honour and Violence* (Cambridge: Polity Press, 2001), pp. 103–114.
6. Ibid., p. 113.
7. Arthur Danto, "Some Remarks on *The Genealogy of Morals,*" in Robert C. Solomon and Kathleen M. Higgins, eds., *Reading Nietzsche* (New York: Oxford University Press, 1988), pp. 13–14.
8. See Christopher Coker, *War and the Twentieth Century* (London: Brasseys, 1994), p. 27.
9. Cited in Catarina Blomberg, *The Heart of the Warrior: Origins and Religious Background of the Samurai System in Feudal Japan* (Richmond: Curzon Press, 1995), p. 193.
10. Franz Fanon, *The Wretched of the Earth* (London: Penguin, 1967), p. xiii.
11. Theodor Adorno, *The Jargon of Authenticity* (Evanston, Ill.: Northwestern University Press, 1973), p. 67.
12. Fanon, *The Wretched of the Earth,* p. 15.
13. Pierre Hassner, "The Bourgeois and the Barbarian," in Gwyn Prins and Hylke Tromp, eds., *The Future of War* (The Hague: Kluwer Law International, 2000), p. 67.
14. Michael Ignatieff, *The Warrior's Honor: Ethnic War and the Modern Conscience* (New York: Henry Holt, 1997), pp. 3, 5–6.

15. Barbara Ehrenreich, *Blood Rites: Origins and History of the Passions of War* (London: Vintage, 1997), p. 2.

16. *The Times,* September 13, 2001.

17. Robert Kaplan, *The Ends of the Earth: A Journey at the Dawn of the Twenty-first Century* (London: Papermac, 1996), p. 30.

18. Martin van Creveld, *The Transformation of War* (New York: Free Press, 1991), p. 27.

19. Ralph Peters, *Fighting for the Future: Will America Triumph?* (Mechanicsburg, Pa.: Stackpole Books, 1999).

20. Ibid., p. 52.

21. Frank Kermode, *History and Value* (New York: Oxford University Press, 1990), p. 134.

22. Don DeLillo, *Mao 2* (London: Vintage, 1992), p. 235.

23. Janine Chanteur, *From War to Peace* (Boulder, Colo.: Westview Press, 1992), p. 92.

CHAPTER 2

1. Bernard Knox, *The Oldest Dead White Males and Other Reflections on the Classics* (New York: W. W. Norton, 1993), p. 28.

2. Friedrich Nietzsche, "Homer's Contest," in Walter Kaufman, ed., *The Portable Nietzsche* (London: Penguin, 1976), pp. 32–39.

3. Ibid., p. 33.

4. Harold Bloom, *The Western Canon: The Books and Schools of the Ages* (London: Macmillan, 1996), p. 6.

5. Robert Calasso, *Literature and the Gods* (London: Vintage, 2000), p. 65.

6. R. J. Hollingdale, *Nietzsche: The Man and His Philosophy* (Cambridge: Cambridge University Press, 1999), pp. 74–75.

7. I. Finley, *Ancient History: Evidence and Morals* (London: Pimlico, 2000), p. 3.

8. J. P. Vernant, "Introduction," in Vernant, ed., *Problemes de la guerre in Grece ancienne* (Paris: Mouton, 1968), p. 10.

9. Knox, *The Oldest Dead White Males,* p. 98.

10. Jan Patocka, *Heretical Essays in the Philosophy of History* (Chicago: Open Court, 1996), pp. 35–41.

11. Cited in Christian Meier, *The Political Art of Greek Tragedy* (Cambridge: Polity Press, 1993), p. 215.

12. Victor Davis Hanson, "No Glory That Was Greece: The Persians Win at Salamis, 480 BC," in Robert Cowley, ed., *What If? Military Historians Imagine What Might Have Been* (London: Macmillan, 1999), p. 33.

13. Julia Kristeva, *The Crisis of the European Subject* (New York: Other Press, 2000), p. 116.

14. G. E. Lloyd, *Demystifying Mentalities* (Cambridge: Cambridge University Press, 1990).

15. G. E. Lloyd, "Democracy, Philosophy and Science in Ancient Greece," in John Dunn, ed., *Democracy: The Unfinished Journey* (Oxford: Oxford University Press, 1992), p. 52.

16. Anthony Gottlieb, *The Dream of Reason: A History of Philosophy from the Greeks to the Renaissance* (London: Allen Lane, 2000), p. 110.

17. Marcel Detienne, *The Masters of Truth* (New York: Zone Books, 1999), pp. 104–105.

18. Ibid.

19. Cited in Doyne Dawson, *The Origins of Western Warfare: Militarism and Morality in the Ancient World* (Boulder, Colo.: Westview Press, 1996), p. 47.

20. Victor Davis Hanson, *The Wars of the Ancient Greeks and Their Invention of Western Military Culture* (London: Cassell, 1999), p. 27.

21. Paul Woodruff, *Thucydides on Justice, Power and Human Nature—Selections from the History of the Peloponnesian War* (Cambridge: Hackett, 1993), p. 42.

22. Ibid., p. 41.

23. Plato, *The Republic,* trans. Francis Cornford (Oxford: Oxford University Press, 1971), p. 61.

24. See Graham Shipley, "The Limits of War," in Graham Shipley and John Rich, eds., *War and Society in the Greek World* (London: Routledge, 1993), p. 10.

25. John Wickersham, *Hegemony and Greek Historians* (Boston: Rowman and Littlefield, 1994), p. 44.

26. Josiah Ober, *The Athenian Revolution: Essays on Ancient Greek Democracy and Political Theory* (Princeton, N.J.: Princeton University Press, 1996), p. 66.

27. Cited in Ehrenreich, *Blood Rites,* pp. 149–150.

28. Carl Von Clausewitz, *On War,* ed. Michael Howard and Peter Paret (London: Everyman, 1993), p. 132.

29. Cited in Gary Sheffield, *Forgotten Victory: The First World War: Myths and Realities* (London: Headline, 2001), p. 130.

30. See Alisdair MacIntyre, *After Virtue* (London: Duckworth, 2000), pp. 121–130.

31. Cited in Robert Carroff, "War and the Hebrew Bible," in Graham Shipley and John Rich, eds., *War and Society in the Greek World* (London: Routledge, 1993), p. 26.

32. Jonathan Shay, *Achilles in Vietnam: Combat Trauma and the Undoing of Character* (New York: Simon and Schuster, 1994), p. 103.

33. See Paul Veyne, *Did the Greeks Believe in Their Myths? An Essay on the Constitutive Imagination,* trans. Paula Wissing (Chicago: University of Chicago Press, 1988).

34. Jasper Griffin, *Homer: On Life and Death* (Oxford: Clarendon Press, 1983), p. 73.

35. Ibid., p. 177.

36. Friedrich Nietzsche, *On the Genealogy of Morals,* ed. Keith Ansell-Pearson (Cambridge: Cambridge University Press, 1995), p. 25.

37. Meier, *Athens,* p. 33.

38. Hanson, "No Glory That Was Greece," p. 33.

39. Cited in Philip Selborne, *The Principle of Duty* (London: Sinclair Stevenson, 1994), p. 97.

40. Stephen Houlgate, *Freedom, Truth and History: An Introduction to Hegel's Philosophy* (London: Routledge, 1991), p. 198.

41. Cited in Gottlieb, *The Dream of Reason,* p. 205.

42. Griffin, *Homer: On Life and Death,* p. 15.

43. See the interpretation of "Of War and Warriors" (section 10) of *Thus Spake Zarathustra,* Part 1, in Stanley Rosen, *The Mask of Enlightenment: Nietzsche's Zarathustra* (Cambridge: Cambridge University Press, 1995), pp. 102–108.

44. Arnold Toynbee, *The Hannabalic War* (Oxford: Oxford University Press, 1965), p. 436.

45. Robert Cowley and Geoffrey Parker, eds., *The Osprey Companion to Military History* (London: Osprey, 1996), p. 29.

46. Josiah Ober, "Hoplites and Obstacles," in Victor Davis Hanson, ed., *Hoplites: The Classical Greek Battle Experience* (London: Routledge, 1993), p. 192.

47. Finley, *Ancient History,* p. 43.

48. Ibid., p. 68.

49. Fernand Braudel, *The Mediterranean in the Ancient World* (London: Allen Lane, 2001), p. 223.

50. Adrian Goldsworthy, *The Punic Wars* (London: Cassell, 2000), p. 368.

51. John Moorhead, *The Roman Empire Divided, 400–700* (London: Longman, 2001), pp. 19–20. See also Arthur Ferrill, *The Fall of the Roman Empire: The Military Explanation* (London: Thames and Hudson, 1986).

52. Gafey Greatrex, *Rome and the Parthian Wars 502–513* (Leeds: Classical and Medieval Texts, Paper and Monograph No. 37, 1998).

53. Moorhead, *The Roman Empire Divided,* p. 175. See also John Haldon, *Warfare, State and Society in the Byzantine World 565–1204* (London: University College Press, 1999), pp. 45–46.

54. Carl von Clausewitz, *On War,* trans. Michael Howard and Peter Paret (London: Everyman, 1993), p. 710.

CHAPTER 3

1. Aldo Schiavone, *The End of the Past: Ancient Rome and the Modern West* (Cambridge, Mass.: Harvard University Press, 2000), p. 31.

2. Ibid., p. 208.

3. Ibid.

4. Thomas Arnold, *The Renaissance at War* (London: Cassell, 2001), p. 60.

5. John Hale, *War and Society in Renaissance Europe* (London: Fontana, 1985), p. 32.

6. Agar Gatt, *A History of Military Thought: From the Enlightenment to Clausewitz* (Oxford: Oxford University Press, 1987), p. 7.

7. Adam Ferguson, *Essay on the History of Civil Society* (Cambridge: Cambridge University Press, 1995), p. 159.

8. Gatt, *History of Military Thought*, p. 9.

9. Peter Gay, *The Enlightenment: An Interpretation,* vol. 2: *The Science of Freedom* (London: Wildwood House, 1973), p. 125.

10. Isaiah Berlin, "Science and the Mind," in J. F. Lively, ed., *The Enlightenment* (London: Longman, 1967), p. 138.

11. Gay, *Enlightment,* vol. 2: *Science of Freedom,* p. 12.

12. Berlin, "Science and the Mind," pp. 140–141.

13. Schlomo Avineri, "The Problem of War in Hegel's Thought," in Jon Stewart, ed., *The Hegel Myths and Legends* (Evanston, Ill.: Northwestern University Press, 1996), p. 132.

14. Cited in T. Blanning, *The French Revolutionary Wars 1787–1802* (London: Arnold, 1996), p. 125.

15. Cited in Hans Maier, "Potentials for Violence in the Nineteenth Century: Technology of War, Colonialism, and the 'People in Arms,'" *Totalitarian Movements and Political Religions* 2, no. 1 (Summer 2001): 17.

16. Blanning, *The French Revolutionary Wars,* p. 125.

17. Maier, "Potentials for Violence," p. 18; Victor Davis Hanson, *Wars of the Ancient Greeks* p. 8.

18. Cited in Stefan Rossbach, *Gnostic Wars: The Cold War in the Context of the History of Western Spirituality* (Edinburgh: Edinburgh University Press, 1999), pp. 216–217.

19. Victor Davis Hanson, *The Western Way of Warfare: Infantry Battles in Classical Greece* (Oxford: Oxford University Press, 1989), p. xiii.

20. Ibid.

21. John Keegan, *History of Warfare* (London: Pimlico, 1996), p. 391.

22. Josiah Ober, "Hoplites and Obstacles," p. 192.

23. Michel Foucault, "Nietzsche, Genealogy, History," in Paul Rabinow, *The Foucault Reader* (London: Penguin, 1991), p. 81.

24. Don DeLillo, *End Zone* (London: Penguin, 1986), p. 81.

25. See my discussion of Junger in *War and the Twentieth Century: The Impact of War on Modern Consciousness* (London: Brasseys, 1994), pp. 118–125.

26. Martin Van Creveld, "War," in Robert Cowley and Geoffrey Parker, eds., *The Osprey Companion to Military History* (London: Osprey, 1996), pp. 497–498.

CHAPTER 4

1. Russell Weighey, *The American Way of Warfare: A History of U.S. Military Strategy and Policy* (Bloomington: Indiana University Press, 1973), p. 408.

2. Edward Luttwak, "Peace in Our Time," *Times Literary Supplement,* October 6, 2000, p. 9. See also Michael Howard, *The Invention of Peace: Reflections on War and International Order* (London: Profile, 2000), p. 104.

3. Ibid.

4. *New York Times,* February 28, 1998.

5. Ivo Daalder and Michael O'Hanlon, *Winning Ugly: Nato's War to Save Kosovo* (Washington, D.C.: Brookings, 2000).

6. Cited in John A. Genty, "Military Force in an Age of National Cowardice," *Washington Quarterly* 29, no. 4 (Autumn 1998): 179.

7. Cited in Sean Edwards, *Mars Unmasked: Changing Force of Global Operations* (Santa Monica, Calif.: Rand Corporation, 2000), p. 17.

8. Cited in Paula A. De Sutter, "Denial and Jeopardy: Deterring Iranian Youth from NBC Weapons" (Washington, D.C.: National Defense University, 1997), pp. 65–66.

9. Genty, "Military Force in an Age of National Cowardice," p. 186.

10. Cited in M. Bowden, *Black Hawk Down* (London: Bantam, 1995), pp. 334–335.

11. Williamson Murray, "Military Culture Does Matter," *Strategic Review* (Spring 1999): 39.

12. See my discussion of Richard Rorty, *Humane Warfare* (London: Routledge, 2001), pp. 133–142.

13. MacIntyre, *After Virtue*, pp. 6–22.

14. Mark Le Fanu, "Arthouse Lives," *Prospect* (November 2000): 31–32.

15. Walter Kaufman, *Tragedy and Philosophy* (Princeton, N.J.: Princeton University Press, 1992), p. 85.

16. Ibid., p. 317.

17. MacIntyre, *After Virtue,* pp. 163–164.

18. *The Observer*, March 5, 2000.

19. Michael D. Ploughman, *Warmaking in American Democracy: A Struggle over Military Strategy, 1700 to the Present* (Kansas City: University Press of Kansas, 1999), p. 397.

20. John Aquilla/Carmel, *Welcome to the Revolution*, pp. 260–261.

21. Robert Keohane and Joseph S. Nye, "Power and Interdependence in the Information Age," *Foreign Affairs* 77, no. 5 (September–October 1998): 91.

22. Ibid., p. 90.

23. Geoffrey Smith, *War and Press Freedom: The Problem of Prerogative Power* (Oxford: Oxford University Press, 1999).

24. Ian Hird, "Legitimacy and Authority in International Politics," *International Organisation* 53, no. 2 (Spring 1999): 381.

25. Martin Libicki, "Rethinking War: The Movies' New Roar," *Foreign Policy* 117 (Winter 1999–2000): 41.

26. Cited in Jonathan Dworkin, "ROE's Lesson from Restore Hope," *Military Review* (September 1994).

27. Peter Euben, *Greek Tragedy and Political Theory* (Los Angeles: University of California Press, 1986), p. 288.

28. E. L. Doctorow, *The City of God* (Boston: Little, Brown, 2000), p. 215.

29. Cited in Walter T. Anderson, ed., *The Fontana Post-Modern Reader* (London: Fontana, 1995), p. 218.

30. Ibid., p. 68.

31. Julia Kristeva, *Strangers to Ourselves* (New York: Columbia University Press, 1991), p. 1.

32. See John Leckte, *Fifty Key Contemporary Thinkers: From Structuralism to Post Modernism* (London: Routledge, 1994), pp. 153–157.

33. Lara L. Miller and Charles Moskos, "Humanitarians or Warriors? Race, Gender and Combat Status in Operation Restore Hope," *Armed Forces and Society* 21, no. 4 (Summer 1995): 626.

34. Bowden, *Black Hawk Down*, p. 76.

35. Friedrich Nietzsche, *On the Genealogy of Morals,* ed. Keith Ansell-Pearson (Cambridge: Cambridge University Press, 1995), essay 1, sections 13–14, pp. 28–31.

36. See Robert L. O'Connell, "The Origins of War," in Robert Cowley and Geoffrey Parker, eds., *The Osprey Companion to Military History* (London: Osprey, 1996), p. 346.

37. Angela Hobbs, *Plato's Heroes: Courage, Manliness, and the Impersonal Good* (Cambridge: Cambridge University Press, 2000), p. 201.

38. Ibid., pp. 215–217.

39. Cited in Wickersham, *Hegemony and the Greek Historians,* p. 65.

40. Dawson, *The Origins of Western Warfare,* p. 35.

41. Ibid., p. 190.

42. Friedrich Nietzsche, *The Gay Science,* trans. Walter Kaufman (New York: Vintage, 1974), book 5, section 344, p. 280.

43. Nietzsche, *On the Genealogy of Morals,* book 1, section 17, p. 36.

44. Fyodor Dostoyevsky, *Crime and Punishment* (London: Penguin, 1951), p. 291.

45. See Aaron Ridley, *Nietzsche's Conscience: Six Character Studies from The Genealogy* (Ithaca: Cornell University Press, 1998), p. 133.

46. Ibid., p. 150.

47. Alvin Toffler and Heidi Toffler, *War and Anti-War: Survival at the Dawn of the Twenty-first Century* (London: Warner Books, 1994), p. 54.

48. Andrew Rutherford, *Literature of War: Five Studies in Heroic Virtue* (London: Macmillan, 1978), p. 105.

49. Michael Shapiro, "Representing World Politics—the Sport-War Intertext," in Michael Shapiro and James Der Derian, eds., *International/ Intertextual Relations—Post-modern Readings of World Politics* (New York: Lexington, 1989), p. 107.

50. Ridley, *Nietzsche's Conscience,* p. 11.

CHAPTER 5

1. Cited in Niall Ferguson, ed., *Virtual History: Alternatives and Counterfactuals* (London: Picador, 1997), pp. 32–33.

2. Herodotus, *Histories,* trans. A. D. Selincourt (London: Penguin, 1986), 8.95.

3. Aeschylus, *The Persians* (London: Penguin, 1979), pp. 413–415.

4. Lawrence Tritle, *From Melos to My Lai: War and Survival* (London: Routledge, 2000), p. 104.

5. Anthony Podlecki, *The Political Background of Aeschylean Tragedy* (Ann Arbor: University of Michigan Press, 1966), p. 12.

6. Christian Meier, *Athens: A Portrait of the City in Its Golden Age* (London: John Murray, 2000), pp. 32–33.

7. Edith Hall, *Inventing the Barbarian: Greek Self-Definition Through Tragedy* (Oxford: Clarendon Press, 1989), p. 85.

8. John Keegan, *War and Our World* (London: Hutchinson, 1998), p. 3.

9. Michael Carrithers, *Why Humans Have Cultures: Explaining Anthropology and Social Diversity* (Oxford: Oxford University Press, 1992), p. 29.

10. Felipe Fernandez-Armesto, *Civilisations* (London: Macmillan, 2000), pp. 113–114.

11. Cited in Robert Asprey, *War in the Shadows: The Classic History of Guerrilla Warfare from Ancient Persia to the Present* (New York: Little, Brown, 1994), p. 3.

12. Ibid.

13. Neil Acherson, *Black Sea* (London: Jonathan Cape, 1995), p. 51.

14. Maria Michela Sassi, *The Science of Man in Ancient Greece* (Chicago: Chicago University Press, 2001), pp. 112–113.

15. Bruce Chatwin, *Anatomy of Restlessness: Uncollected Writings,* ed. Jan Born and Matthew Graves (London: Jonathan Cape, 1996), p. 85.

16. Ibid.

17. Cited in Edward Creasy, *Fifteen Decisive Battles of the World* (London: Everyman, 1969), p. 24.

18. Bernard Sheehan, *Savagery and Civility: Indian and Englishmen in Colonial Virginia* (Cambridge: Cambridge University Press, 1980), p. 145.

19. Ibid., p. 146.

20. Cited in John Hale, *War in Renaissance Europe,* p. 39.

21. Ibid.

22. Ernest Gellner, *Conditions of Liberty: Civil Society and Its Rivals* (London: Penguin, 1994), p. 67.

23. Cited in Lloyd Matthews, ed., *Challenging the United States: Symmetry and Asymmetry—Can the United States Be Defeated?* (Carlisle Barracks, Penn.: U.S. Army War College, Strategic Studies Institute, July 1998), p. 215.

24. Peters, *Fighting for the Future,* p. 90.

25. Colin Gray, *Modern Strategy* (Oxford: Oxford University Press, 2000), p. 279.

26. Scott Gerwehr and Russell Glenn, *The Art of Darkness: Deception and Urban Operations* (Santa Monica: Rand Corporation, 2000), p. 20.

27. Jeremy Black, *War: Past, Present and Future* (Gloucestershire: Glous Sutton, 2000), p. 17.

28. Gray, *Modern Strategy,* p. 279, note 23. "For a century the army fought Indians as if they were British or Mexicans or Confederates. Each Indian war was expected to be the last and so the Generals never developed a doctrine or organisation adapted to the special problems posed by the Indian style of fighting." Robert Uttey, *Cavalier in Buckskin: George Armstrong Custer and the Western Military Frontier* (Norman: University of Oklahoma Press, 1988), p. 206.

29. Barry Lopez, *Crossing Open Ground* (London: Picador, 1989).

30. Douglas Porch, *Wars of Empire* (London: Cassell, 2001), p. 16.

31. Clive Ponting, *World History: A New Perspective* (London: Chatto and Windus, 2000), p. 127.

32. Michael Wood, *Conquistadors* (London: BBC, 2000), p. 37.

33. Ibid., p. 72.

34. Blok, *Honour and Violence,* p. 110.

35. Wood, *Conquistadors,* p. 85.

36. Lopez, *Crossing Open Ground,* p. 147.

37. Carlos Fuentes, *The Buried Mirror: Reflections on Spain and the New World* (Boston: Houghton Mifflin, 1992), p. 107.

38. Ibid.

39. Tzevan Todorov, *Conquest of the Americas: The Question of the Other* (New York: Harper and Row, 1984), pp. 98–123.

40. Wood, *Conquistadors,* p. 16.

41. Ibid.

42. Akhbar Ahmed, *Discovering Islam: Making Sense of Muslim History and Society* (London: Routledge, 1988), p. 112.

43. Harold Bloom, *The Western Canon: The Books and Schools of the Ages* (London: Macmillan, 1994), p. 341.

44. Breyten Breytenbach, "Writing at the Darkening Mirror," in *The Memory of Birds in Time of Revolution* (London: Faber and Faber, 1996), p. 6.

45. Cited in Peter James and Nick Thorpe, *Ancient Inventions* (London: Michael O'Mara Books, 1994), p. xviii.

46. Cited in Michael Howard, "The Military Factor in European Expansionism," in Hedley Bull and Adam Watson, eds., *The Expansion of International Society* (Oxford: Clarendon Press, 1984), p. 39.

47. John Ellis, *The Social History of the Machine Gun* (London: Random House, 1993), pp. 81–82.

48. Thomas Sowell, *Conquerors and Cultures* (New York: Basic Books, 1998), p. 336.

49. Jeremy Black, *Warfare in the Eighteenth Century* (London: Cassell, 1999), pp. 31–32.

50. Edward Gibbon, *The Decline and Fall of the Roman Empire* (London: Pelican, 1963), p. 16.

51. Cited in Black, *Warfare in the Eighteenth Century,* p. 209.

CHAPTER 6

1. See Joseph A. Amato, *Victims and Values: A History and Theory of Suffering* (New York: Praeger, 1990), pp. 32–33.

2. See Philip Windsor, "Cultural Dialogue in Human Rights," in Windsor et al., eds., *The End of the Century: The Future in the Past* (Tokyo: Kodansha International: 1995), p. 419.

3. Michael Gillespie, *Hegel, Heidegger and the Ground of History* (Chicago: Chicago University Press, 1984), p. 3.

4. Cited in Nicholas Humphrey, *Consciousness Regained: Chapters in the Development of Mind* (Oxford: Oxford University Press, 1984), p. 6.

5. Diane Collinson and Robert Wilkinson, *Thirty-Five Oriental Philosophers* (London: Routledge, 1994), p. 138.

6. Blok, *Honour and Violence,* pp. 103–114.

7. Keegan, *History of Warfare,* p. 44.

8. See Rene Dumont, *Essays in Individualism: Modern Ideology and Anthropology in Perspective* (Chicago: University of Chicago Press, 1986), pp. 279–280.

9. The term *revaluation of values* is, of course, associated with Nietzsche. He argued that what made the modern world modern was that every value became conditional. It was Nietzsche's insight to recognize that a society would not long survive if it continued to adhere to values that were no longer creative. Institutions must be replaced or revived. In turn, new institutions create new values. In proposing that every culture should be revalued from time to time, Nietzsche believed he was expressing a demand of modernity: that we cease to take received estimation of things for granted and question all values that we have held, including those we have cherished the most.

10. Dennis C. Washburn, *The Dilemma of the Modern in Japanese Fiction* (New Haven: Yale University Press, 1995), p. 3.

11. Blomberg, *The Heart of the Warrior*, pp. 191–192.

12. Robert Bellah, *Tokugowa Religion: The Values of a Pre-industrial Japan* (Glencoe, Ill.: Free Press, 1957), p. 19.

13. Blomberg, *The Heart of the Warrior,* p. 114.

14. Brian Vittoria, *Zen at War* (New York: Weatherhill, 1997), p. 101.

15. Ibid., p. 106.

16. Ibid., p. 31.

17. Jonathan Lewis and Ben Steele, *Hell in the Pacific* (London: Channel 4 Books, 2001), p. 191.

18. Akira Iriye, *Power and Culture: The Japan-America War 1941–45* (Cambridge, Mass.: Harvard University Press, 1981), pp. 1–35.

19. Cited in John Dower, *Embracing Defeat: Japan in the Aftermath of World War Two* (London: Penguin, 1999), pp. 156–157.

20. Ibid.

21. See Richard Samuels, *Rich Nation, Strong Nation: National Security and the Technological Transformation of Japan* (Ithaca: Cornell University Press, 1994); Patrick Smith, *Japan: A Reinterpretation* (New York: Pantheon, 1996).

22. David Landes, *Wealth and Poverty of Nations* (New York: Norton, 1998), p. 391.

23. Martin Van Creveld, *The Art of War: War and Military Thought* (London: Cassell, 2000), p. 119.

24. David L. Hall, "On Looking Up 'Directives' in a Chinese Encyclopaedia," in William Desmond and Joseph Grange, eds., *Being and Dialectic: Metaphysics as a Cultural Presence* (New York: State University of New York Press, 2000), pp. 203–205.

25. Jack Goody, *The East in the West* (Cambridge: Cambridge University Press, 1996), pp. 234–235.

26. See the entry on Sun Tzu in Richard Holmes, ed., *The Oxford Companion to Military History* (Oxford: Oxford University Press, 2001), p. 887.

27. A. Graham, "The Place of Reason in China's Philosophical Traditions," in R. Dawson, ed., *The Legacy of China* (Oxford: Oxford University Press, 1964), p. 30.

28. Cited in James Marshall Cornwall, *Napoleon as Military Commander* (London: Batsford, 1967), p. 24.

29. Ibid., p. 281.

30. Ralph D. Sawyer, *The Six Secret Teachings in the Way of Strategy* (Boston: Shambala, 1997).

31. Edward L. Dreyer, *China at War, 1901–1949* (London: Longman, 1995), p. 352.

32. Cited in introduction by Thomas Cleary, ed., in Sun Tzu, *The Art of War* (Boston: Shambala, 1988), p. 10.

33. Peter James and Nick Thorpe, *Ancient Inventions* (London: Michael O'Mara Books, 1995), p. 236.

34. R. G. Collingwood, *The Idea of History* (Oxford: Oxford University Press, 1970), pp. 61–63.

35. Winn Schwartov, "Asymmetrical Adversaries," *Orbis* 44, no. 2 (Spring 2000), p. 199.

36. Chen-Ya Tien, *Chinese Military Theory: Ancient and Modern* (Stevenage: Spa Books, 1992), pp. 73–87.

37. Cited in James Adams, *The Next World War: The Warriors and Weapons of the New Battlefields in Cyberspace* (London: Hutchinson, 1998), p. 252.

38. Schwartov, "Asymmetrical Adversaries," p. 199.

39. Ross H. Monro, "Eavesdropping on the Chinese Military: Where It Expects War, Where It Doesn't," *Orbis* 38, no. 3 (Summer 1994).

40. Sawyer, *The Six Secret Teachings,* p. 42.

41. Sun Tzu, *The Art of War* (trans. Thomas Cleary) (Boston: Shambala, 1998), p. 6.

42. Ibid., p. 6.

43. Cleary in Sun Tzu, *The Art of War,* p. 12.

44. John Keay, *India: A History* (London: HarperCollins, 2000), p. 97.

45. Ibid., pp. 80–81.

46. See Kautilya, *Arthashastra,* trans. R. Shamasastry (Mysore: Mysore Printing Company, 1967).

47. George Tanham, "Security and India: Strategic Thought in Practice: An Interpretative Essay," in Kanti Bajpal and Amitah Amattoo, eds., *Securing India* (Delhi: Manohai, 1996), p. 43.

48. Stephen Rosen, *Societies and Military Power: India and Its Armies* (Ithaca: Cornell University Press, 1996), p. 56.

49. Ibid., pp. 75–76.

50. Cited in Eli Kedourie, *Hegel and Marx: Introductory Lectures* (Oxford: Blackwell, 1995), pp. 134–135.

51. Philip Mason, *A Matter of Honour: An Account of the Indian Army, Its Officers and Men* (London: Jonathan Cape, 1974), p. 37.

52. Octavio Paz, *Conjunctions and Disjunctions* (New York: R. K. Publishing, 1982), p. 32.

53. Cited in Eleke Boehmer, *Colonial and Post-Colonial Literature: Migrant Metaphors* (Oxford: Oxford University Press, 1995).

54. Ibid., p. 95.

55. Cited in V. G. Kiernan, *Imperialism and Its Contradictions* (London: Routledge, 1995), p. ix.

56. Tanham, *Securing India,* p. 59.

57. Ibid., p. 73.

58. John Sparrow, *The Sepoy and the Raj: The Indian Army 1860–1940* (London: Macmillan, 1994), pp. 21–25.

59. Harland Orman and James Wade, *Rapid Dominance—a Force for All Seasons: Technologies and Systems for Achieving Shock and Awe: A Real Revolution in Military Affairs.* Whitehall Papers. (London: Royal United Services Institute, Whitehall Papers, 1998), pp. 43–44.

60. Edward Luttwak, "Strategy," in R. Cowley and G. Parker, eds., *The Osprey Companion to Military History* (London: Osprey, 1996), pp. 447–448.

61. Ibid.

62. Cited in Houlgate, *Freedom, Truth and History: An Introduction to Hegel's Philosophy,* p. 67.

63. John Jandora, "War and Culture: A Neglected Relation," *Armed Forces and Society* 25, no. 4 (Summer 1999): 541–556.

64. William O. Staudment, "The Strategic Analysis," in Shirin Thair Khel and Shaheen Ubi, eds., *The Iran-Iraq War: New Weapons, Old Conflicts* (Westport, Conn.: Praeger, 1983), pp. 40–41.

65. Charles Lindholm, *The Islamic Middle East: An Historical Anthropology* (Oxford: Blackwell, 1996), p. 63.

66. Ibn Khaldun, *The Mukaddimah: An Introduction to History,* vol. 1, trans. Franz Rosenthal (Princeton, N.J.: Princeton University Press, 1980).

67. Ibid.

68. Lindholm, *Islamic Middle East,* p. 66.

69. Ernest Gellner, *Muslim Society* (Cambridge: Cambridge University Press, 1981), p. 36.

70. *Washington Post,* February 27, 1991.

71. Bowden, *Black Hawk Down,* p. 336.

72. Cited in Anatol Lieven, "Nasty Little Wars," *The National Interest* 62 (Winter 2000–2001): 69.

73. Cited in Edwards, *Mars Unmasked,* p. 73.

74. Anne Norton, *Reflections on Political Identity* (Baltimore: Johns Hopkins University Press, 1988), p. 6.

75. Joseph Rothschild, "Culture and War," in Stephanie Newman and Robert Harkovy, eds., *The Lessons of Recent Wars in the Third World,* vol. 2 (Lexington, Mass.: Lexington Books, 1985), p. 53.

76. Carl Lowith, "The Historical Background of European Nationalism," in Arnold Levinson, ed., *Nature, History and Existentialism and Other Critical Essays on the Philosophy of History* (Evanston, Ill.: Northwestern University Press, 1966). See also Roland Stromberg, *Redemption by War: The Intellectuals of 1914* (Lawrence: Regents Press of Kansas, 1982); and Eric Leads, *No Man's Land: Combat and Identity in World War One* (Cambridge: Cambridge University Press, 1979).

77. Marguerite Yourcenar, *Fires* (London: Iden Ellis, 1982), p. 11.

78. Friedrich Nietzsche, *Ecce Homo,* trans. R. J. Hollingdale (London: Penguin, 1992), p. 97.

79. Friedrich Nietzsche, *Untimely Meditations,* trans. R. J. Hollingdale (Cambridge: Cambridge University Press, 1995), p. 148.

80. Kristeva, *The Crisis of the European Subject,* p. 135.

81. Lindholm, *Islamic Middle East,* p. 173.

82. Ernest Gellner, *Anthropology and Politics: Revolutions in the Sacred Grove* (Oxford: Blackwell, 1995), p. 179.

CHAPTER 7

1. Cyril Connolly, *Enemies of Promise* (London: Penguin, 1979), p. 202.

2. Cited in Oliver Sacks, *The Man Who Mistook His Wife for a Hat* (London: Picador, 1986), pp. 29–30.

3. Don DeLillo, "Human Moments in World War Three," *Esquire* (July 1982), p. 122.

4. Friedrich Nietzsche, "On the Uses and Disadvantages of History for Life," in *Untimely Meditations,* trans. R. J. Hollingdale (Cambridge: Cambridge University Presss, 1995), p. 60.

5. Clifford Geertz, *The Interpretation of Cultures: Selected Essays* (London: Fontana, 1993), pp. 67–68.

6. Chris Gamble, *Timewalkers: The Pre-history of Global Civilisation* (London: Penguin, 1992), p. 246.

7. See A. C. Grayling, *Wittgenstein* (Oxford: Oxford University Press, 1988), pp. 104–106.

8. Patocka, *Heretical Essays,* pp. 35–41.

9. Brian Fagan, *Floods, Famines and Emperors: El Nino and the Fate of Civilisations* (London: Pimlico, 2000), p. 110.

10. Noel Cowan, *Global History: A Short Overview* (Cambridge: Polity, 2001), p. 36.

11. Cited in Robert Heilbronner, *Visions of the Future* (New York: Oxford University Press, 1995), p. 24.

12. Karl Jaspers, *The Origin and Goal of History* (New Haven: Yale University Press, 1953), pp. 1–21.

13. Eric Voeglin, *Order and History,* volume 2: *The World of the Polis* (Baton Rouge: Louisiana State University, 1957), pp. 168–169.

14. Marcel Gauchet, *The Disenchantment of the World: A Political History of Religion* (Princeton, N.J.: Princeton University Press, 1998), p. 94.

15. See the discussion of the Axial Period in Stefan Rossbach, *Gnostic Wars: The Cold War in the Context of Western Spirituality* (Edinburgh: Edinburgh University Press, 1999), pp. 11–14.

16. Cited in Ehrenreich, *Blood Rites,* p. 148.

17. Ibid., p. 159.

18. Gauchet, *Disenchantment of the World,* p. 56.

19. I. F. Stone, *The Trial of Socrates* (New York: Doubleday, 1989), p. 52.

20. See Virgil, *The Aeneid,* trans. C. Day Lewis (Oxford: Oxford University Press, 1966), pp. 311–313. See also Brooks Otis, *Virgil: A Study in Civilised Poetry* (Oxford: Oxford University Press, 1964).

21. Karl Jaspers, *The Way to Wisdom: An Introduction to Philosophy* (New Haven: Yale University Press, 1954), p. 99.

22. Robert Pepperell, *The Post-Human Condition* (Exeter: Intellect, 1995), p. 1.

23. Martin van Creveld, *Technology and War* (London: Brasseys, 1991), p. 225.

24. Chris Gray, *Post-Modern War: The New Politics of Conflict* (London: Routledge 1997), p. 3.

25. Cited in Christopher Norris, *Uncritical Theory: Postmodernism, Intellectuals and the Gulf War* (London: Lawrence and Wishart, 1992), p. 123.

26. Jurgen Habermas, *The Past as Future* (Cambridge: Polity, 1994), pp. 2–31.

27. James Blinn, *The Aardwark Is Ready for War* (London: Anchor Press, 1997), p. 278.

28. *The Times,* December 20, 1998.

29. Cited in Mark Bowden, *Black Hawk Down*, pp. 345–346.

30. Douglas Kellmer, "Virilio, War and Technology," in John Armitage, ed., *Paul Virilio: From Modernism to Hypermodernism and Beyond* (London: Sage, 2000), p. 114.

31. Cited in Keith Ansell-Pearson, *Viroid Life: Perspectives on Nietzsche and the Trans-human Condition* (London: Routledge, 1997), p. 32.

32. Aldous Huxley, *Brave New World Revisited* (London: Flamingo, 1994), pp. 112–113.

33. David Grossman, *On Killing* (New York: Free Press, 1999), p. 270. According to a U.S. congressional report, by 1971, 50.9 percent of U.S. troops in Vietnam used marijuana. The greater danger came from heroin, which was introduced to U.S. troops in the spring of 1970. By 1971, an estimated 28.5 percent were using it regularly or occasionally. U.S. Army studies show that the heaviest drug use was among the combat infantry units (see Kenneth J. Campbell, "Once Burned, Twice Cautious: Explaining the Weinberger and Powell Doctrines," *Armed Forces and Society* 24, no. 3 [Spring 1998]: 359).

34. Hans Jonas, *Mortality and Morality: A Search for the Good After Auschwitz* (Evanston, Ill.: Northwestern University Press, 1999), p. 102.

35. Ansell-Pearson, *Viroid Life,* p. 34.

36. Robert Pepperell, *The Post-Human Condition,* p. 168.

37. Francis Fukuyama, "Second Thoughts: The Last Man," in *The National Interest* 56 (Summer 1999).

38. Theodor Adorno, *Minima Moralia* (London: Verso, 1993), p. 55.

39. Joachim Ritter, *Hegel and the French Revolution: Essays on the Philosophy of Right* (Cambridge: MIT Press, 1982), p. 43.

40. George Orwell, "The Decline of the English Murder" (1946), in *The Penguin Essays of George Orwell* (London: Penguin, 1994), p. 347.

41. Evelyn Waugh, *Unconditional Surrender* (London: Penguin, 1964), p. 190.

42. Adam Piette, *Imagination at War: British Fiction and Poetry 1939–1945* (London: Macmillan, 1999), pp. 76–77.

43. Keith Douglas, *Alamein to Zem Zem* (London: Faber and Faber, 1992), p. 28.

44. For a discussion of both *We* and *The War of the Worlds,* see Mark Rose, *Alien Encounters: The Anatomy of Science Fiction* (Cambridge, Mass.: Harvard University Press, 1981).

45. See Christopher Coker, *War and the Twentieth Century* (London: Brasseys, 1994), p. 165.

46. Bruce Sterling, "War Is Virtual Hell," *Wired* (March–April 1998): 8.

47. Cited in Tim Jordan, *Cyberpower: The Culture and Politics of Cyberspace and the Internet* (London: Routledge, 1999), pp. 112–113.

48. Vivian Schobchack, "Democratic Franchise and the Electronic Frontier," in Ziauddin Sardar and Jerome Ravetz, eds., *Cyberfutures: Culture and Politics on the Information Superhighway* (London: Pluto Press, 1996), p. 81.

49. Ibid., p. 82.

50. Arturo Escobar, "Welcome to Cyberia: Notes on the Anthropology of Cyber Culture," in Ziauddin Sardar and Jerome Ravetz, eds., *Cyberfutures: Culture and Politics on the Information Superhighway* (London: Pluto Press, 1996), p. 117.

51. Jordan, *Cyberpower,* pp. 187–189.

52. Cited in Margaret Wertheim, *The Pearly Gates of Cyberspace: A History of Space from Dante to the Internet* (London: Virago, 1999), p. 246.

53. Interview with Virilio, in John Armitage, ed., *Paul Virilio: From Modernism to Hypermodernism and Beyond* (London: Sage, 2000), p. 48.

54. Bruce Barnes, *Kaleidoscope Century* (London: Phoenix, 1995).

55. See Stephen Shaker and Alan Wise, *War Without Men: Robots on the Future Battlefield* (London: Pergamon-Brasseys, 1988), pp. 174–175.

56. Manuel de Landa, *War in the Age of Intelligent Machines* (New York: Zone, 1991), p. 157.

57. Cited in Gray, *Post-Modern War,* p. 71.

58. Cited in D. Boucher, *Political Theories of International Relations* (Oxford: Oxford University Press, 1998), p. 342.

Selected Bibliography

Acherson, N. *Black Sea*. London: Jonathan Cape, 1995.

Adams, J. *The Next World War: The Warriors and Weapons of the New Battlefields in Cyberspace*. London: Hutchinson, 1998.

Adorno, T. *The Jargon of Authenticity*. Evanston, Ill.: Northwestern University Press, 1973.

———. *Minima Moralia*. London: Verso, 1993.

Amato, J. *Victims and Values: The History and Theory of Suffering*. New York: Praeger, 1990.

Anderson, W., ed. *The Fontana Post-Modern Reader*. London: Fontana, 1994.

Arnold, T. *The Renaissance at War*. London: Cassell, 2001.

Avineri, S. "The Problem of War in Hegel's Thought." In J. Stewart, ed., *The Hegel Myths and Legends*. Evanston, Ill.: Northwestern University Press, 1996.

Berlin, I. "Science and the Mind." In J. F. Lively, ed., *The Enlightenment*. London: Longman, 1967.

Black, J. *Warfare in the Eighteenth Century*. London: Cassell, 1999.

Blanning, T. *The French Revolutionary Wars 1787–1802*. London: Arnold, 1996.

Blok, A. "The Meaning of 'Senseless' Violence." In A. Blok, ed., *Honour and Violence*. Cambridge: Polity Press, 2001.

Blomberg, C. *The Heart of the Warrior: Origins and Religious Background of the Samurai System in Feudal Japan*. Richmond: Curzon Press, 1994.

Bloom, H. *The Western Canon: The Books and Schools of the Ages*. London: Macmillan, 1994.

Bowden, M. *Black Hawk Down*. London: Bantam, 1995.

Breytenbach, B. "Writing at the Darkening Mirror." In *The Memory of Birds in Time of Revolution*. London: Faber and Faber, 1996.

Calasso, R. *Literature and the Gods*. London: Vintage, 2000.

Carrithers, M. *Why Humans Have Cultures: Explaining Anthropology and Social Diversity*. Oxford: Oxford University Press, 1992.

Chatwin, B. *Anatomy of Restlessness: Uncollected Writings*. Ed. Jan Born and Matthew Graves. London: Jonathan Cape, 1996.

Connolly, C. *Enemies of Promise*. London: Penguin, 1979.

Danto, A. "Some Remarks on *The Genealogy of Morals*." In R. Solomon and Kathleen M. Higgins, eds., *Reading Nietzsche*. Oxford: Oxford University Press, 1988.

Dawson, D. *The Origins of Western Warfare: Militarism and Morality in the Ancient World*. Boulder, Colo.: Westview Press, 1996.

De Landa, M. *War in the Age of Intelligent Machines*. New York: Zone, 1991.

Dower, J. *Embracing Defeat: Japan in the Aftermath of World War Two*. London: Penguin, 1999.

Dreyer, E. *China at War 1901–1949*. London: Longman, 1995.

Dumont, R. *Essays in Individualism: Modern Ideology and Anthropology in Perspective*. Chicago: University of Chicago Press, 1986.

Edwards, S. *Mars Unmasked: The Changing Face of Global Operations*. Santa Monica, Calif.: Rand Corporation, 2000.

Ehrenreich, B. *Blood Rites: Origins and History of the Passions of War*. London: Vintage, 1997.

Ellis, J. *The Social History of the Machine Gun*. London: Random House, 1993.

Escobar, A. "Welcome to Cyberia: Notes on the Anthropology of Cyber Culture." In Z. Sardar and J. Ravetz, eds., *Cyber Futures: Culture and Politics on the Information Superhighway*. London: Pluto Press, 1996.

Euben, P. *Greek Tragedy and Political Theory*. Los Angeles: University of California Press, 1986.

Fanon, F. *The Wretched of the Earth*. London: Penguin, 1967.

Ferguson, A. *Essay on the History of Civil Society*. Cambridge: Cambridge University Press, 1995.

Fernandez-Armesto, F. *Civilisations*. London: Macmillan, 2000.

Finley, I. *Ancient History: Evidence and Morals*. London: Pimlico, 2000.

Foucault, M. "Nietzsche, Genealogy, History." In P. Rabinow, ed., *The Foucault Reader*. London: Penguin, 1991.

Fuentes, C. *The Buried Mirror: Reflections on Spain in the New World*. Boston: Houghton Mifflin, 1992.

Fukuyama, F. "Second Thoughts: The Last Man." *The National Interest* 56 (Summer 1999).

Gatt, A. *A History of Military Thought from the Enlightenment to Clausewitz*. Oxford: Oxford University Press, 1987.

Gauchet, M. *The Disenchantment of the World: A Political History of Religion*. Princeton, N.J.: Princeton University Press, 1998.

Gay, P. *The Enlightenment: An Interpretation*. Volume 2: *The Science of Freedom*. London: Wildwood House, 1973.

Geertz, C. *The Interpretation of Cultures: Selected Essays*. London: Fontana, 1993.

Gellner, E. *Conditions of Liberty: Civil Society and Its Rivals*. London: Penguin, 1994.

———. *Muslim Society*. Cambridge: Cambridge University Press, 1981.

———. *Anthropology and Politics: Revolutions in the Sacred Grove*. Oxford: Blackwell, 1995.

Gentilcore, D, "The Fear of Disease and the Disease of Fear." In W. Naphy and P. Roberts, eds., *Fear in Early Modern Society*. Manchester: Manchester University Press, 1997.

Genty, A. "Military Force in an Age of National Cowardice." *Washington Quarterly* 29, no. 4 (Autumn 1998).

Gerwehr, S. *The Art of Darkness: Deception in Urban Operations*. Santa Monica, Calif.: Rand Corporation, 2000.

Gillespie, M. *Hegel, Heidegger and the Ground of History*. Chicago: Chicago University Press, 1984.

Goldsworthy, A. *The Punic Wars*. London: Cassell, 2000.

Goody, J. *The East in the West*. Cambridge: Cambridge University Press, 1996.

Gray, C. *Modern Strategy*. Oxford: Oxford University Press, 2000.

Griffin, J. *Homer: On Life and Death*. Oxford: Clarendon Press, 1983.

Hale, J. *War and Society in Renaissance Europe*. London: Fontana, 1985.

Hall, E. *Inventing the Barbarian: Greek Self-Definition Through Tragedy*. Oxford: Clarendon Press, 1989.

Hanson, V. "No Glory That Was Greece: The Persians Win at Salamis, 480 BC." In R. Cowley, ed., *What If? Military Historians Imagine What Might Have Been*. London: Macmillan, 1999.

———. *The Wars of the Ancient Greeks and Their Invention of Western Military Culture*. London: Cassell, 1999.

———. *The Western Way of Warfare: Infantry Battles in Classical Greece*. Oxford: Oxford University Press, 1989.

Hassner, P. "The Bourgeois and the Barbarian." In G. Prins and H. Tromp, eds., *The Future of War*. The Hague: Kluwer Law International, 2000.

Heilbroner, R. *Visions of the Future*. New York: Oxford University Press, 1995.

Hird, I. "Legitimacy and Authority in International Politics." *International Organisation* 53, no. 2 (Spring 1999).

Hollingdale, R. *Nietzsche: The Man and His Philosophy*. Cambridge: Cambridge University Press, 1999.

Houlgate, S. *Freedom, Truth and History: An Introduction to Hegel's Philosophy*. London: Routledge, 1991.

Howard, M. "The Military Factor in European Expansionism." In H. Bull and A. Watson, eds., *The Expansion of International Society*. Oxford: Clarendon Press, 1984.

———. *The Invention of Peace: Reflections on War and International Order*. London: Profile, 2000.

Humphrey, N. *Consciousness Regained: Chapters in the Development of Mind*. Oxford: Oxford University Press, 1984.

Ibn Khaldun. *The Mukaddimah: Introduction to History*. Volume 1. Princeton, N.J.: Princeton University Press, 1980.

Ignatieff, M. *The Warrior's Honor: Ethnic War and the Modern Conscience*. New York: Henry Holt, 1997.

Iriye, A. *Power and Culture: The Japan-America War 1941–45*. Cambridge, Mass.: Harvard University Press, 1981.

Jandora, J. "War and Culture: The Neglected Relation." *Armed Forces and Society* 25, no. 4 (Summer 1999).

Jaspers, K. *The Origin and Goal of History*. New Haven: Yale University Press, 1953.

———. *The Way to Wisdom: An Introduction to Philosophy*. New Haven: Yale University Press, 1954.

Jonas, H. *Mortality and Morality: A Search for the Good After Auschwitz*. Evanston, Ill.: Northwestern University Press, 1999.

Kaplan, R. *The Ends of the Earth: A Journey at the Dawn of the Twenty-First Century*. London: Macmillan, 1996.

Kaufman, W. *Tragedy and Philosophy*. Princeton, N.J.: Princeton University Press, 1992.

Kautilya. *Arthashashtra*. Trans. R. Shamasastry. Mysore: Mysore Printing Company, 1967.

Keegan, J. *History of Warfare*. London: Pimlico, 1996.

———. *War and Our World*. London: Hutchinson, 1998.

Kellmer, D. "Virilio, War and Technology." In J. Armitage, ed., *Paul Virilio: From Modernism to Hypermodernism and Beyond*. London: Sage, 2000.

Kristeva, J. *The Crisis of the European Subject*. New York: Other Press, 2000.

———. *Strangers to Ourselves*. New York: Columbia University Press, 1991.

Lewis, J., and B. Steele. *Hell in the Pacific*. London: Channel 4 Books, 2001.

Libicki, M. "Rethinking War: The Movies' New Roar." *Foreign Policy* 117 (Winter 1999–2000).

Lieven, A. "Nasty Little Wars." *The National Interest* 62 (Winter 2000–2001).

Lindholm, C. *The Islamic Middle East: An Historical Anthropology*. Oxford: Blackwell, 1996.

Lloyd, G. E. *Demystifying Mentalities*. Cambridge: Cambridge University Press, 1990.

———. "Democracy, Philosophy and Science in Ancient Greece." In J. Dunn, ed., *Democracy: The Unfinished Journey*. Oxford: Oxford University Press, 1992.

Luttwak, E. "Peace in Our Time." *Times Literary Supplement*, October 6, 2000.

———. "Strategy." In R. Cowley and G. Parker, eds., *The Osprey Companion to Military History*. London: Osprey, 2000.

MacIntyre, A. *After Virtue*. London: Duckworth, 2000.

Maier, H. "Potentials for Violence in the Nineteenth Century: Technology of War, Colonialism and the 'People in Arms.'" *Totalitarian Movements and Political Religions* 2, no. 1 (Summer 2001).

Mason, P. *A Matter of Honour: An Account of the Indian Army, Its Officers and Men*. London: Jonathan Cape, 1974.

Matthews, L., ed. *Challenging the United States: Symmetry and Asymmetry—Can the United States Be Defeated?* Carlisle Barracks, Penn.: U.S. Army War College, Strategic Studies Institute, July 1998.

Meier, C. *The Political Art of Greek Tragedy*. Cambridge: Polity Press, 1993.

———. *Athens: A Portrait of the City in Its Golden Age*. London: John Murray, 2000.

Miller, L., and C. Moskos. "Humanitarians or Warriors? Race, Gender and Combat Status in Operation Restore Hope." *Armed Forces and Society* 21, no. 4 (Summer 1995).

Monro, R. "Eavesdropping on the Chinese Military: Where It Expects War, Where It Doesn't." *Orbis* 38, no. 3 (Summer 1994).

Moorhead, J. *The Roman Empire Divided, 400–700*. London: Longman, 2001.

Murray, W. "Military Culture Does Matter." *Strategic Review* (Spring 1999).

Nietzsche, F. "Homer's Contest." In W. Kaufman, ed., *The Portable Nietzsche*. London: Penguin, 1976.

———. *On the Genealogy of Morals*. Ed. K. Ansell-Pearson. Cambridge: Cambridge University Press, 1995.

———. *Ecce Homo*. Trans. R. J. Hollingdale. London: Penguin, 1992.

———. *Untimely Meditations*. Trans. R. J. Hollingdale. Cambridge: Cambridge University Press, 1995.

Norris, C. *Uncritical Theory: Post-modernism, Intellectuals and the Gulf War*. London: Lawrence and Wishart, 1992.

Ober, J. *The Athenian Revolution: Essays in Ancient Greek Democracy and Political Theory*. Princeton, N.J.: Princeton University Press, 1996.

———. "Hoplites and Obstacles." In D. Hanson, ed., *Hoplites: The Classical Greek Battle Experience*. London: Routledge, 1993.

O'Connell, R. "The Origins of War." In R. Cowley and G. Parker, eds., *The Osprey Companion to Military History*. London: Osprey, 1996.

Patocka, J. *Heretical Essays on the Philosophy of History*. Chicago: Open Court, 1996.

Paz, O. *Conjunctions and Disjunctions*. New York: R. K. Publishing, 1982.

Pepperell, R. *The Post-Human Condition*. Exeter: Intellect, 1995.

Peters, R. *Fighting for the Future: Will America Triumph?* Mechanicsburg, Pa.: Stackpole Books, 1999.

Ploughman, M. *Warmaking in American Democracy: A Struggle over Military Strategy, 1700 to the Present*. Kansas City: University Press of Kansas, 1999.

Podlecki, A. *The Political Background of Aeschylean Tragedy*. Ann Arbor: University of Michigan Press, 1966.

Ponting, C. *World History: A New Perspective*. London: Chatto and Windus, 2000.

Porch, D. *Wars of Empire*. London: Cassell, 2001.

Ridley, A. *Nietzsche's Conscience: Six Character Studies from* The Genealogy. Ithaca: Cornell University Press, 1998.

Rosen, S. *Societies and Military Power: India and Its Armies*. Ithaca: Cornell University Press, 1996.

Rothschild, J. "Culture and War." In S. Newman and R. Harkoby, eds., *The Lessons of Recent Wars in the Third World*. Volume 2. Lexington, Mass.: Lexington Books, 1985.

Rutherford, A. *Literature of War: Five Studies in Heroic Virtue*. London: Macmillan, 1978.

Sardar, Z., and J. Ravetz. *Cyberfutures: Culture and Politics on the Information Superhighway*. London: Pluto Press, 1996.

Sassi, M. *The Science of Man in Ancient Greece*. Chicago: Chicago University Press, 2001.

Sawyer, R. *The Six Secret Teachings in the Way of Strategy*. Boston: Shambala, 1997.

Schiavone, A. *The End of the Past: Ancient Rome and the Modern West*. Cambridge, Mass.: Harvard University Press, 2000.

Shapiro, M. "Representing World Politics—the Sport-War Intertext." In M. Shapiro and J. Der Derian, eds., *International/Intertextual Relations—Postmodern Readings of World Politics*. New York: Lexington, 1989.

Shay, J. *Achilles in Vietnam: Combat Trauma and the Undoing of Character*. New York: Simon and Schuster, 1994.

Sheehan, B. *Savagery and Civility: Indian and Englishmen in Colonial Virginia*. Cambridge: Cambridge University Press, 1980.

Shipley, G., and J. Rich, eds. *War and Society in the Greek World*. London: Routledge, 1993.

Smith, G. *War and Press Freedom: The Problem of Prerogative Power*. Oxford: Oxford University Press, 1999.

Sowell, T. *Conquerors and Cultures*. New York: Basic Books, 1998.

Sterling, B. "War Is Virtual Hell." *Wired* (March–April 1998).

Tanham, J. "Security in India: Strategic Thought in Practice: An Interpretative Essay." In K. Bajpal and A. Amattoo, eds., *Securing India*. Delhi: Manohai, 1996.

Todorov, T. *Conquest of the Americas: The Question of the Other*. New York: Harper and Row, 1984.

Toffler, H., and A. Toffler. *War and Anti-War: Survival at the Dawn of the Twenty-First Century*. London: Warner Books, 1994.

Van Creveld, M. *The Transformation of War*. New York: Free Press, 1991.

———. "War." In R. Cowley and G. Parker, eds., *The Osprey Companion to Military History*. London: Osprey, 2000.

Vernant, J. P., ed. *Problems de le guerre in Grèce ancienne*. Paris: Mouton, 1968.

Veyne, P. *Did the Greeks Believe in their Myths? An Essay on the Constitutive Imagination*. Trans. Paula Wissing. Chicago: University of Chicago Press, 1988.

Vittoria, B. *Zen at War*. New York: Weatherhill, 1997.

Voeglin, E. *Order and History*. Baton Rouge: Louisiana State University Press, 1957.

Weighley, R. *The American Way of Warfare: The History of U.S. Military Strategy and Policy*. Bloomington: Indiana University Press, 1973.

Wickersham, J. *Hegemony and the Greek Historians*. Boston: Rowman and Littlefield, 1994.

Windsor, P. "Cultural Dialogue and Human Rights." In P. Windsor et al., eds., *The End of the Century: The Future in the Past*. Tokyo: Kodansha International, 1995.

Wood, M. *Conquistadors*. London: BBC, 2000.

Woodruff, P. *Thucydides on Justice, Power and Human Nature—Selections from the History of the Peloponnesian War*. Cambridge: Hackett, 1993.

Index

About the Book

In the past, posits Christopher Coker, wars were all-encompassing; they were a test not only of individual bravery but of an entire community's will to survive. In the West today, in contrast, wars are tools of foreign policy, not intrinsic to the values of a society—they are instrumental rather than existential. The clash between these two "cultures of war" can be seen starkly in the recent struggle in Afghanistan.

Coker offers both a history of martial cultures and an analysis of how these are now changing. He locates the origins of the Western way of war in ancient Greece, in the heroic ideals of Homer's *Iliad*. He then traces the development of this warrior spirit, moving from Rome's systemization of violence to encounters with such alternative ways of war as Sun Tzu's, the Islamic tradition, and Japan's kamikaze actions during World War II. This trajectory, he finds, ends in a crucial contemporary fault line: for the first time in history, war is no longer considered humankind's most revealing behavior.

What does this mean for the future? Coker argues that tomorrow's combatants will be technicians and even machines, divorced emotionally from the battlefield. He elegantly explores the significance of an evolving culture of war devoid of the figure of the heroic warrior.

Christopher Coker is reader in international relations at the London School of Economics and Political Science. His many books include *War and the Twentieth Century, War and the Illiberal Conscience, Twilight of the West,* and, most recently, *Humane Warfare.*